PEOPLES AND PR

1. Imagruen, *Banc d'Arguin NP, Mauritania*
2. Bisnoi, *Thar Desert, India*
3. Kanum, Marind, Marori, Yei, *Wasur NP, Irian Jaya, Indonesia*
4. Con Dao Islanders, *Con Dao NP, Vietnam*
5. Cree, *St. James Bay, Quebec, Canada*
6. Sherpa, *Mt. Everest NP, Nepal*
7. Kuna, *Kuna Yala Reserve, San Blas, Panama*
8. Torres Strait Islanders, *Torres Straits, Australia*
9. Melanesians, *Solomon and Fiji Islands, South Pacific*
10. Shona, Batonka, Endele, *CAMPFIRE, Zimbabwe*
11. Maori, Pohueroro, *North Island, New Zealand*
12. Yanomami, *Alto Orinoco Biosphere Reserve, Venezuela and Yanomami Reserve, Brazil*
13. Anangu/Aborigine, *Uluru NP (Ayers Rock), Australia*
14. Aborigine, *Kakadu NP, Northern Australia*
15. Hatam, *Arfak Mountains NP, Irian Jaya, Indonesia*
16. Kogi, Arhuaco, Asario, *Sierra Nevada de Santa Marta NP, Colombia*
17. Shimshali, *Khunjerab NP, Pakistan*
18. Vietnamese Villagers (non-indigenous), *Tram Chim Reserve, Vietnam*
19. Bodo, *Manas NP, India*
20. Karen, *Huay Kha Khaeng NP, Thailand, Burma*
21. Hmong, *Doi Suthep National Park, Chaing Mai, Thailand*
22. Fulani, Fulbe, Bandu Tribes, *Faro, Bouba-Njida and Benoue NP, Cameroon*
23. Tuareg, *Air Ténéré NP, Niger*
24. Miskito, *Miskito Cays Protected Area, Nicaragua*
25. Inuit, *Isabella Bay Whale Sanctuary, Canada*
26. Ewenk, *Lena Delta Nature Reserve, Siberia*
27. Phoka, *Nyika NP, Malawi*
28. Ba Aka Pygmies, *Dzangha-Sangha Dense Forest Special Reserve, Central African Republic*
29. Haitian Villagers (non-indigenous), *Les Arcadins, Haiti*
30. Mijikenda, *Kaya Sacred Groves, Kenya*

NP = National Parks

The Law of the Mother

PARKS CONGRESS

A World Congress on National Parks and Protected Areas has been held each decade since 1962. The objective of the Congress process is to promote the development and most effective management of the world's natural habitats so that they can make their optimal contribution to sustaining human society. The IVth Congress, held in Caracas, Venezuela, from February 10–21 1992, aimed to reach out to and to influence numerous other sectors—beyond those professionals directly concerned with protected areas: management agencies, nongovernmental conservation organizations, traditional peoples' groups, relevant industries, and resources managers were brought together and involved to enhance the role of protected areas in sustaining society—under the theme "Parks for Life."

The Law of the Mother

Protecting Indigenous Peoples in Protected Areas

Edited by Elizabeth Kemf

- Foreword by Sir Edmund Hillary

- Introduction by Dr. Claude Martin, Director General,
  WWF-International

- Afterword by Jeffrey McNeeley, Secretary-General,
  IV World Congress on Parks and Protected Areas

SIERRA CLUB BOOKS • *San Francisco*

The Sierra Club, founded in 1892 by John Muir, has devoted itself to the study and protection of the earth's scenic and ecological resources—mountains, wetlands, woodlands, wild shores and rivers, deserts and plains. The publishing program of the Sierra Club offers books to the public as a nonprofit educational service in the hope that they may enlarge the public's understanding of the Club's basic concerns. The point of view expressed in each book, however, does not necessarily represent that of the Club. The Sierra Club has some sixty chapters coast to coast, in Canada, Hawaii, and Alaska. For information about how you may participate in its programs to preserve wilderness and the quality of life, please address inquiries to Sierra Club, 730 Polk Street, San Francisco, CA 94109.

Production of this work has been made possible in part by a grant from the Commission of the European Communities.

LIBRARY OF CONGRESS CATALOGING IN PUBLICATION DATA
The Law of the mother : protecting indigenous peoples in protected areas /
edited by Elizabeth Kemf ; foreword by Sir Edmund Hillary.
    p. cm.
Includes bibliographical references and index.
ISBN 0-87156-451-3 : $25.00
    1. Indigenous peoples—Cross-cultural studies. 2. Human ecology—Cross-cultural studies. 3. Conservation of natural resources—Cross-cultural studies.
4. Natural areas—Management—Cross-cultural studies. I. Kemf, Elizabeth.
GN380.L39 1993
306'.08—dc20   93-21848
                                                    CIP

Production by Susan Ristow · Jacket & book design by Amy Evans · Composition by Wilsted & Taylor
Editorial Assistant: Marleen David · Photo Research: Michèle Dépraz · Research Assistant: Nick Bird
Text printed in the United States of America on acid-free paper containing a minimum of 50% recovered waste paper, of which at least 10% of the fiber content is post-consumer waste
Inserts printed in Hong Kong. Inserts produced by Global Interprint, Inc.

10 9 8 7 6 5 4 3 2 1

For the world's indigenous people
in the hope that their cultures,
their languages, their homelands,
their beliefs and their dreams
will survive forever
and
for the Kogi *mamas,*
the Elder Brothers of Humanity,
who believe, like most indigenous peoples,
that their unwavering observance of
"The Law of the Mother"
keeps our world in balance.

CONTENTS

FOREWORD

Over the centuries, indigenous peoples in remote areas developed wise procedures to protect their natural resources—they could be called the original environmentalists. Sacred forests were established, regular times for planting and harvesting were carefully observed, and a close liaison was established with nature in all its forms. Of course, survival was made easier by a limited population, a simple life, and, frequently, an abundance of natural food.

The escalating growth in world population has produced the most important changes to our global environment. There has been a vastly greater need for good arable land. Forests have been attacked with fervor to clear land and to cut timber for housing and firewood. Traders from the developing industrialized nations have searched the world for valuable products to be shipped back to their home countries, usually with little benefit to the people whose resources were being harvested.

Changes can happen in a relatively short period. In forty years, I have seen the transformation of the remote Khumbu area on the southern slopes of Mount Everest. In 1951, the Khumbu was a place of great beauty, with 3,000 tough and hardy Sherpas living a remarkably full and cooperative life despite their rigorous environment. Now it has become largely a tourist area, with 12,000 foreigners streaming in each year, leaving their litter and tempting the Sherpas to break their traditional forestry customs and sell hundreds of loads of firewood for luxury fires.

I must take some of the blame myself. I built the Lukla Mountain airfield, which made access to the Khumbu so much easier both for the foreigners and for the administrators from the capital, Kathmandu. In the central village of Namche Bazar, there are now sixty soldiers, forty civil servants, and many policemen. I remember seeing none of them when I first arrived there in 1951, but life was very peaceful, and the hospitality was amazing.

The influx of visitors has produced some good from it all. The standard of living of the Sherpas has undoubtedly improved. In response to requests by the Sherpas, we have built schools and a hospital, bridges and safer tracks on the steep mountainsides. Reafforestation has been undertaken, and foreign technology and money are producing a hydroelectric scheme, with a depressing line of power poles crossing the beautiful Namche hill, outlined against the great icy summit of Mount Tamserku.

Sagarmatha National Park is a World Heritage site and remains very dramatic and beautiful. The Sherpa people have always been regarded as an important and unique part of the area. Their main villages within the park's boundary are legally excluded from the park—which I believe is a sensible move. Thankfully, the Sherpas still retain a strong belief in their culture and religion, and they are to be admired greatly.

The remote areas of our world, with their unique flora and fauna and their often remarkable indigenous peoples, must be protected. We cannot allow the voracious appetites of the increased world population to absorb and destroy them. Modern technology and finance can certainly be useful, but not at the expense of crushing a traditional culture or an exceptional natural environment. Often, over the centuries, these indigenous peoples have learned to handle their remote areas in a very efficient and inimitable fashion.

ACKNOWLEDGMENTS

The collaborative effort between WWF and IUCN owes its greatest debt to the indigenous and rural peoples of the world, particularly those who contributed toward creation of this book. Marleen David, Editorial Assistant, was tireless and patient in bringing this book to completion; Michele Depraz, photo researcher, pursued with unflagging determination vivid images to illustrate the book's message; Ivan Hattingh of WWF-UK intervened at a critical moment to steer the manuscript into production; Jeffrey McNeely reviewed the manuscript and ensured that it reflected the voices and views of indigenous and rural peoples; Georgia Valaoras introduced WWF and IUCN to the rich cultural but threatened heritage of the Sarakatsani people in northern Greece; Juan Mayr and Vo Quy guided the editor into treacherous but visionary terrain in Colombia and Vietnam; Hilary de Boerr coauthored and assisted in the editorial process during several critical junctures, as did Alison Wilson; John Cordell faxed one of his chapters from a Queensland hospital where he was recovering from an acute illness; Sylvie Mazardis, Nick Bird, and Tracy Charaf offered their capable assistance during needy moments. Sierra Club Books' copy editor, Pat Harris, kept the text moving along under the skilful editorial guidance of David Spinner, who managed, across all continents and time zones, the elements of contracts, design, illustration, and production. WWF's Wildlands and Human Needs Program, pioneered by Mike Wright of WWF-US, was an important source of information and inspiration for several authors whose efforts forged new partnerships between indigenous people and protected areas.

DR. CLAUDE MARTIN
WWF International

INTRODUCTION

The rocks remain.
The Earth remains.
I die and put my bones in the cave or the Earth.
Soon, my bones will become the Earth.
Then will my spirit return to my land, my Mother.

GAGUDJU PEOPLE OF AUSTRALIA

The Huichol Indians of Mexico are praying, making offerings of animals to their gods. Their incantations are "keeping the world in balance."[1] In West Africa, the Sefwi people of Ghana are celebrating a three-day yam festival and visiting specially chosen sites in the rain forest. A group of men are led to the forest by the tribal chief and a medicine man. They are carrying small stools, or sacred chairs, cut from a single block of wood. The chairs—symbols of the Sefwi's ancestral past—are placed in magical gardens, where the little people, the mythical keepers of the forest, live. Palm wine and spirits are poured onto the ground, and food is offered to the invisible keepers of the forest and to the souls of the dead Sefwi ancestors.[2] In Australia, an aboriginal woman is painting on a strip of bark; she sometimes paints on rocks or in caves as her ancestors did 40,000 years ago in the Dreamtime, when, according to aboriginal belief, life began. Before written language was developed 5,000 years ago, the aboriginal people passed from generation to generation the story of how "Warramurrungudji came from the sea and created land. A female in human form, she gave birth to people and gave them their languages. Other creator beings were also given life: Ginga, the giant ancestral crocodile; Marrawuiti, the sea eagle. The act of creation over these ancestors put themselves into the landscape."[3] High in the Himalayas, on the earth's tallest mountain, the snow of Sagarmatha (Mount Everest) is melting. The snows from the Mother of the Ocean, the literal translation of the Sanskrit word *sagarmatha,* move slowly down the mountainside to feed the streams until they rush forward to reach Gangamatha, or Mother Ganges, the sacred river of India. The holy waters flow toward the great ocean. Far away, on another continent, the *Mamas,* or Kogi high priests, are singing and dancing on their snowfields, praying that when they die they will return to the source of all life—the highest snow peak in the Sierra Nevada of northern Colombia, known to them as the Land of the Mother.

Like most indigenous people, the Kogi live by what they call "the Law of the Mother," a complex code of behavior developed by the Tayrona people in pre-Columbian times that regulates human behavior in harmony with plant and animal cycles, astral movements, climatic phenomena, and the sacred geography of the mountains.

Indigenous peoples, who number around 300 million today, are the traditional guardians of the Law of Mother Earth, a code of conservation inspired by a universally held belief that the source of all life is the earth, the mother of all creation. In Greek mythology, the ancient poets wrote of Gaia, the Earth Goddess, and of *thalassa,* the sea, the source of all life. Long before the Greeks, the ancient Egyptians revered the Mother Heavens, who symbolizes the whole heavenly sphere.[4] Like the Kogi, the aborigines, and the early Greeks, the Egyptians also believed that the world was created out of the dark waters of chaos. Their legends are etched into stone in the great tombs and temples in the Valley of the Nile.

As Julian Burger, author of the *Gaia Atlas of First Peoples* and secretary for 1993 of the United Nations' International Year for the World's Indigenous People, says: "For the First Peoples the land is the source of life—a gift from the creator that nourishes, supports, and teaches. Although indigenous people vary widely in their customs, culture, and impact on the land, all consider the Earth a Parent and revere it accordingly. 'Mother Earth' is the center of the universe, the core of their culture, the origin of their identity as a people. She connects them with their past (as the home of the ancestors), with the present (as a provider of their material needs), and with the future (as the legacy they hold in trust for their children and grandchildren). In this way, indigenousness carries with it a sense of belonging to a place."[5]

Indigenous or ethnic peoples inhabit nearly 20 percent of the planet, mainly on land where they have lived for thousands of years. Compared with protected area managers, who control about 5 percent of the world's land mass, indigenous peoples are the most important stewards of the earth. Often, the territories of indigenous peoples overlap protected areas, and the traditional inhabitants find themselves sharing their land with newcomers.

Having lived and worked in India and in West Africa, both in and around protected areas, I recognized early on that protected areas and local people need each other for their survival. Without the full backing of local communities, protected areas, and the human life they sustain, cannot survive.

In order to acknowledge this critically important relationship between local communities and protected areas and to explore and better understand this link, WWF hosted a six-day workshop at the Fourth World Congress on National Parks and Protected Areas in Caracas, Venezuela, in 1992. When I opened the workshop as its chairman, I found that almost 300 people had tried to jam into the room reserved for our meeting. We had to move to a larger room to accommodate discussions on the most topical issues at the congress: the dramatically changing relationship between people and protected areas and the need for a new understanding and definition of protected areas, which involves multiple and harmonious use of these habitats by people as well as wildlife.

In the past, it was generally believed that protected areas were places where boundaries of protection were established and people were either kept out or removed. Today, as population pressure increases and the rights of indigenous people and local communities gain recognition and respect, an expanded approach to protected areas is emerging. Wilderness areas are shrinking, and human activity is spreading. For example, in Latin America, 86 percent of the national parks and protected areas are inhabited or affected by people. Gerhard Heiss, a consultant to the Council of Europe and to the European Economic Community, estimates that in western and northern Europe, 80 to 90 percent of the national parks and protected areas are used seasonally, mainly by pastoral people grazing their flocks.[6] According to Heiss, 30 percent are probably permanently inhabited. In some cases, this is having devastating effects. Yet in many areas, the presence of local people upholding traditions, including the Law of the Mother, has had a positive effect on the environment.

In order to illustrate the benefits and disadvantages of people living in or near or using protected areas, and to offer examples of how to involve resident people in planning, creating, and managing protected areas, WWF and IUCN have compiled this book, based mainly on presentations made during the Workshop on People and Protected Areas in Caracas in 1992. It also draws on presentations made in other congress workshops that relate to this crosscutting theme. The chapters are divided into four thematic sections: people living in or near protected areas; land tenure or ownership of protected areas; conflict resolution and protected areas; and communities creating protected areas.

The underlying message of the contributions is that unless property rights (land tenure) of long-term residential people are respected and economic benefits from the creation of protected areas accrue in part directly to the communities living in and near them, it is unlikely that the nature reserves will endure. Local communities must also be involved in the planning and boundary marking of reserves. Most important, their traditions must be respected. In the case of the Kogi of Colombia or the Anangu people of Kakadu in Australia, that means our staying away from their sacred sites, no matter how fascinating or attractive they might be. According to the Law of the Mother, uninvited visitors are not welcome in these very special places, the Land of the Dead, the sacred groves of the *Kayas*—described in part four, "Creative Communities"—and the *dusun*s, or gardens of the forest, in Irian Jaya, or holy places of ancient ritual and human burial.

Traditions and rituals upheld by tribal chiefs and village elders mystified early explorers, captured the imagination and interest of anthropologists, and angered colonial governments that were trying to centralize forest management and, later, to create protected areas. Original forest inhabitants and pastoralists had never heard of conservation. But the survival of their culture and way of life depended on it, embodied it. Their life meant conservation.[7] In earlier times, and even today, governments create forest reserves, timber concessions, and even protected areas, frequently with the best of intentions but with little or no regard for the local residents. Many of these residents are asking that their land be returned—and they may forever resent the fact that they were dispossessed and that their indigenous rights were withdrawn.

At the time of publication of this book, Mungo National Park in New South Wales, Australia, was on the verge of being returned to its original inhabitants, the Mutti Mutti tribal group of aborigines, whose indigenous occupation dates back over 40,000 years. The government offered to lease the parkland from them for one Australian dollar a year.[8] But the Mutti Mutti rejected this symbolic gesture and are demanding compensation similar to that agreed on between the federal government and the aboriginal inhabitants of Kakadu and Uluru, described by John Cordell in part two, "Boundaries and Bloodlines." According to Cordell, these terms still are not fully satisfactory, especially when it comes to tourism. Aboriginal people in

Australia are open to benefiting from tourist visits to their areas but not to allowing pilfering and desecration of their rock engravings. In 1984, a group of aborigines blockaded access to a section of Mootwingee National Park after discovering that tourists were removing pieces of rock engravings from their sacred caves. To the tourists, the engravings were souvenirs, but to the aborigines, their taking was a theft from the Dreamtime, an act akin to chipping off bits of statues from Notre Dame or hacking away mementos from the Taj Majal.

As the contributions to this book show, traditional and modern park management methods are at a crossroads. If they can meet on the same road, they have great potential for creating protected areas that conserve and enrich cultural and biological diversity. It was evident from the large number of participants at the People and Protected Areas workshop, particularly in the group dealing with indigenous views, chaired by Chief Bill Erasmus of the Dene Nation of Canada, that the voices of indigenous peoples are being heard. Yet listening to their voices and paying lip service to their needs and rights is not enough. Action must be taken now, during the United Nations' International Year for the World's Indigenous People, to ensure their survival and their long-term involvement in caring for the earth.

The Great Spirit is our father, but the earth is our mother. She nourishes us; that which we put into the ground she returns to us, and healing plants she gives us likewise. If we are wounded, we go to our mother and seek to lay the wounded part against her, to be healed. Animals too, do thus, they lay their wounds to the earth. When we go hunting, it is not our arrow that kills the moose however powerful be the bow; it is nature that kills him. The arrow sticks in his hide; and, like all living things, the moose goes to our mother to be healed. He seeks to lay his wound against the earth. . . .

BIG THUNDER OF THE WABANAKIS NATION, *circa 1900*

PART ONE

In Search of a Home

ELIZABETH KEMF

In Search of a Home
People Living in or near Protected Areas

Our roots are deep in the lands where we live. We have a great love for our country, for our birthplace is here. The soil is rich from the bones of thousands of our generations. Each of us was created in these lands and it is our duty to take great care of them, because from these lands will spring the future generations of our peoples. We walk about with great respect, for the Earth is a very Sacred Place.

SIOUX, NAVAJO, AND IROQUOIS DECLARATION, 1978

In the summer of 1992, the forests of Greece were burning, perhaps more quickly and furiously than ever before. In August, during the height of the heat—with temperatures averaging 40 degrees centigrade—some forty-six fires were raging simultaneously, many of them started deliberately to make way for agricultural land. In the northeastern part of the country, one community was keeping a twenty-four-hour vigil over its last tract of virgin deciduous woodland, the Dadia-Soufli Forest Reserve.

One of the two reserve wardens, Kostas Pistolas, who has lived next to the forest and who cared for it even before it was declared a protected area in 1980, said, "Fire trucks don't protect this forest from burning down; people do." Pistolas also explained to a group of ecologists visiting the reserve—which harbors twenty-six birds of prey, including several rare species—that it was in his tradition to safeguard the land over which his ancestors, the Sarakatsani people, had herded their sheep and goats from their summer grounds in Bosnia to their winter homes on the shores of the Black Sea.[1] In the small Greek village of Dadia near the northern border of Bulgaria, Pistolas's eighty-five-year-old grandmother recalled how Sarakatsani caravans traveled with their flocks for a month at a time to reach seasonal grazing grounds. There, as far away as Constantinople or Montenegro, they erected beehive-shaped houses and crescent-shaped enclosures for their animals, which they constructed from wicker and rush. Today, near the Dadia-Soufli Forest Reserve and throughout much of the Rhodope Mountains in northern Greece, the dome-shaped houses still nestle in small circular clearings in the forest. From the air, they resemble Yanomami settlements in the Amazon or Bagandan villages in East Africa.

Most of the traditional houses in Greece are falling into ruin, but some are being reconstructed as symbolic reminders to the Sarakatsani of their rich cultural heritage. Like many ethnic or indigenous peoples, the Sarakatsani represent just one of the world's 6,000 cultural groups, speaking one of 6,000 languages. Unfortunately, half of these languages are moribund, that is, spoken only by middle-aged or elderly people, such as Pistolas's parents and grandmother. According to David Harmon, who presented a paper titled "Indicators of the World's Cultural Diversity" at the People and Protected Areas Workshop at IUCN's Fourth World Congress on National Parks and Protected Areas: "Most moribund languages are indigenous tongues, locally distributed. In the USA and Canada, 80% of the native languages are moribund, as are 90% of Australia's Aboriginal languages." In the coming century, he predicts, it is likely that we will witness the devastation of linguistic diversity.[2] As a language dies, so does the culture.

The number of indigenous people surviving today is a matter of definition. The United Nations estimates that of the 5.5 billion people who live on the earth, 300 million are indigenous people living in more than seventy countries, in habitats ranging from the Arctic to the Amazon.[3] The Worldwatch Institute says that roughly 200 to 600 million people are indigenous, taking into account a wide range of varying ethnic groups.[4] Over the past 150 years, some 30 to 50 million indigenous people have died, including eighty-seven entire indigenous groups in Brazil alone.[5] In part two of this book, concerning land tenure, several authors (Centeno and Elliott; Ramos) describe the plight of the Yanomami people of Brazil and Venezuela and their ongoing struggle for survival. Despite the creation of two adjoining Yanomami Reserves—equal in size to the country of Uruguay—on each side of the Brazilian-Venezuelan border, gold mining, malaria, influenza, and mercury (introduced into their rivers by miners, who have also brought in the diseases) are killing the people and poisoning the land.

It is universally recognized that indigenous, that is, "tribal, native, ethnic, aboriginal or remote-dwelling," people occupy as much as 19 percent of the world's surface and are, as such, stewards of a significant portion of the earth's fragile ecosystems.[6] Five percent of the world's surface is legally protected by 130 countries in nearly 7,000 officially declared protected areas.[7]

Many of these protected areas overlap the homelands of indigenous people. Regrettably, many were also created without consultation with the communities that lived in or near them, whether they were by definition indigenous or other long-term residents. Ironically, it was these people who were for millennia the custodians of the earth, not always, but usually, caring for it so well that it had maintained its natural ecosystems in an unspoiled state. Frequently, when protected areas were established, indigenous and local residents were moved out, often to the detriment of the land itself.

Initially, protected areas were generally modeled after the world's first national park, Yellowstone, established on Crow, Blackfeet, and Shoshone-Bannock territory in 1872. A subtribe of the Shoshone lived year-round within the present bounds of the park, while the other tribes used the area for hunting and fishing on a seasonal basis. Burial grounds accidentally uncovered in 1941 revealed that Native Americans had been resident—at least 800 years earlier—at Fishing Bridge, now one of Yellowstone's most popular campgrounds.[8] When the park was created in the 1870s, the Native Americans, some of whom were referred to as "buffalo eaters," "sheep eaters," "deer eaters," "salmon eaters," and "root diggers," according to their dietary preferences, did not leave the park "willingly," as Aubrey Haines suggests in his book, *Yellowstone National Park: Its Exploration and Establishment.*

Haines, whose detailed record is sympathetic to the plight of the Shoshone, acknowledges that the "very real danger for the Shoshone-Bannock 'sheep eaters' who were living in the Yellowstone region in the old way of pre-horse days" was from gold prospectors and other explorers. Haines reports that the Shoshone were referred to as "sneaking red devils . . . a body of savages" but that this "was not true in any respect." He says that they "willingly accepted Chief Washakies's invitation to join his Shoshones on the Wind River Reservation in 1871, and abandoned their Yellowstone home forever." Haines also concludes in his detailed historical account that the body of knowledge available at the time was extensive but fragmentary and "often contradictory" and that it "did not constitute a comprehensive view of the Yellowstone region and its wonders." A later book on Yellowstone bears this out, noting that in the summer of 1877, 300 people were killed in a series of pitched battles between tribal groups and civilian superintendents. "In 1886, administration of the park was turned over to the US Army," says Robert Scharff, editor of the handbook *Yellowstone and Grand Teton National Parks*. Writing in 1966, and reflecting the thinking of park managers at the time, Scharff says of Grand Teton National Park, created in 1929 and enlarged in 1950 by the addition of a 13,468-hectare area of Jackson Hole National Monument: "Until shortly after 1800, Jackson Hole truly belonged to the Indians. Nothing was particularly outstanding about their history. . . ."[9]

In conformity with the "Yellowstone model," many national parks around the globe were developed as wilderness preserves for public recreation, without permanent human habitation or extractive use. Yellowstone's outstanding beauty and natural features—the largest mountain lake in North America, its geysers, breathtaking waterfalls, snow-covered peaks, and an abundance of wildlife—spawned the birth of thousands of parks around the world. For years, park managers strove to create parks based on the Yellowstone model and moved people, sometimes forcibly, from the land where they had lived for centuries. According to Harmon, "The consequences [of adopting this model] can be terrible."[10] Recognizing the limitations of a global application of the Yellowstone model, which at the time was adopted in good faith and with the best intentions, park managers today are developing new approaches, methods, and guidelines for establishing protected areas, with the assistance of IUCN's Commission on National Parks and Protected Areas (CNPPA). These guidelines, which have been under serious review by the CNPPA since 1984, were the subject of an intensive workshop at the 1992 Parks Congress in Caracas, and by the time of publication of this book a new set of guidelines should be published. These guidelines will reflect the need for more flexible interpretations to meet the varying conditions around the world.

Meanwhile, the rights and demands of indigenous and local peoples to continue living in parks and reserves and to use them on a sustainable basis is gaining acceptance. Commenting on the evolution of Australia's national park system, David Foster of the Phillip Institute of Technology, who is also an IUCN consultant, says: "Park managers have had to come to terms with a whole new set of issues, concepts and ideas as well as to learn to communicate with a group of people with a different language, culture and world view. Of particular concern to many has been the challenge to their fundamental beliefs about the very nature of national parks themselves."[11] It was evident during the WWF-chaired Workshop on People and Protected Areas at the Caracas Congress that conservationists are divided into several schools of thought: those who think resident people should be able to fish, hunt, and forage in national parks; those who do not; and those who think there should be a compromise between the camps. But it was also apparent that the human factor in creating and managing national parks and protected areas had long been overlooked and misunderstood.

Many of the participants were amazed to find that 86 percent of the protected areas in Latin America were inhabited, either permanently or temporarily.[12] The IUCN-sponsored project, carried out by Drs. Stephen and Thora Amend with the assistance of the German Agency for Technical Cooperation, that revealed these surprising figures also showed that the greatest problems facing park managers in Latin America were extraction of natural resources, including timber and gold; agricultural encroachment by landless peasants as well as ranchers; illegal grazing; occupation; mining and oil exploration; fires; drug trafficking; and terrorist activities. The second biggest problem after extraction of natural resources was the lack of qualified staff to deal with these threats. Invasion of the 184 surveyed national parks was not by indigenous peoples, most of whom "live in remote areas, almost unnoticed and unseen within their own country," but by newcomers.[13] According to the Amends and a number of workshop participants, including contributors to part one of this book, indigenous people are reclaiming their lands, sometimes calling for the creation of nature reserves and national parks in order to ensure that both they and their land are protected.

In the first chapter of part one, the authors explain why the government of Mauritania ensured the rights of the Imraguen people to continue living within the boundaries of the Banc d'Arguin National Park right from the time of its creation in 1976. The government recognized the integral relationship between the people and the natural environment that has endured for centuries, to the mutual benefit of both. Also in part one, Mingma Norbu Sherpa, one of the first Sherpa park wardens in Nepal, describes the serious concerns that the Sherpas, an ethnic group originating in Tibet, expressed when they thought they would be moved off their land outside of the proposed boundaries of Sagarmatha (Mount Everest) National Park. Around 3,000 Sherpas have remained in the park under what Sherpa calls "a novel concept" that allows for varying use zones, including traditional use areas as well as two strict nature protection areas that are free from human interference.

Although a modicum of recognition has been given to the rights of indigenous peoples over their homelands, as described in part two, which examines issues of land tenure and ownership, much more needs to be done. The Amends say that the situation is more difficult for other types of settlers, who inhabit newly declared national park or reserve land and who have over several generations developed close links, traditions, and customs with that land.[14] In Vietnam's Con Dao National Park, nonindigenous long-term residents living adjacent to the park are exploiting its natural resources on a sustainable basis. Similarly, people living adjacent to or in Wasur National Park in the Indonesian province of Irian Jaya are permitted to hunt and forage on land that they own inside the park. Rights to ownership inside the park have been recognized not only for indigenous peoples but also for long-term residents who have lived there for several generations and who have maintained close links to their land. In contrast, new settlers and cattle ranchers have been asked to move out of the park. In part one, Ian Craven, who worked with indigenous peoples in developing management plans and setting up boundaries for Irian Jaya's Arfak Mountain Strict Nature Reserve and for Wasur National Park, describes how the presence of long-term residents in the park could enhance biodiversity (through their growing support of the rules of the park) rather than diminish its conservation goals. Craven, who has lived in Irian Jaya for seven years, describes the park residents' "forest gardens," or *dusun*s, the "traditional sacred sites [used by the areas' tribes] . . . for hunting, gardening, and spiritual events." Says one tribal elder who assisted in delineating the boundaries of Wasur National Park, "To restrict our access to these sites would be the same as barring the door of your church, mosque, or shop." People outside the park are now asking that their land be brought inside park boundaries.

In other countries, from the polar regions to the tropics, people are beginning to call for the setting up and management of their own protected areas that they can continue to live in or use. The chapter by Diane Jukofsky on the Miskito Indians of Nicaragua in part four and the chapter by Guillermo Archibold and Sheila Davey on the Kuna Indians of Central America in part one illustrate the giant steps that have been taken toward integrating people into the development and management of protected areas. For centuries, most indigenous societies did this unofficially and even, at times, officially. For example, the Aztec emperor Montezuma "maintained parks and protected areas, including a zoological park and a botanical garden," while the Mayan people managed extractive and untouchable reserves.[15] Even earlier, Emperor Aśoka of India passed an edict protecting fishes, forests, and animals.[16] Here in part one, Bryan Alexander tells how the Cree Indians have tried to manage their land, combining modern and traditional methods, better than most trained park managers have managed officially declared nature reserves or national parks. Like the Cree, the Bisnoi people of Rajasthan, who have inhabited the Great Indian Desert, known as the Thar, have conserved the land as it was for centuries—

covered by trees and bushes and inhabited by wildlife that lives unafraid of and in close proximity to one of the most remarkable communities in the world. Kailash Sankhala, a renowned Indian environmentalist whose firm hand held India's Project Tiger in place for the first five of its now twenty years, sketches the 500-year history of the Bisnois and how their presence in the Thar has ensured its survival. He also reveals the threats that this culture and the land are facing today and explains his recommendation for establishing the Thar Desert as an international biosphere reserve.

A biosphere reserve, probably the most appropriate or globally acceptable category for a protected area, is an internationally designated site that includes the presence and involvement of local people in research, education, and training. It integrates resident peoples, employs their traditional knowledge, and conserves natural areas through the establishment of various use or nonuse zones.[17] These zones include a strict protection zone in the core area, where all disturbance is prohibited; buffer areas surrounding the strictly protected interior, where limited human activity is permitted or even encouraged; and multiuse zones, where traditional human activities are permitted. A biosphere reserve usually encompasses national parks or other types of protected areas. The Man and Biosphere Program was initiated in 1971 under the auspices of UNESCO, the United Nations Educational, Scientific, and Cultural Organization. Together with World Heritage sites and Ramsar sites (wetlands of international importance), the biosphere reserve concept complements or embraces one of eight official international systems of categories classified (by IUCN's CNPPA) according to management objectives. The most well known of these categories, presented in Glossary One, is the widely used term "national park," in category II. This is the most commonly used definition—and the most commonly misused, according to the strict definition of the CNPPA. The first three categories include category I, strict nature reserve/scientific reserve; category II, national park; and category III, natural monument/natural landmark, established with the objective of maintaining biological diversity and natural formations. These categories prohibit human activity or extractive use and "protect nature in an undisturbed state."[18] The other categories that allow some degree of regulated human use and activity are category IV, managed nature reserve/wildlife sanctuary; category V, protected landscape or seascape; category VI, resource reserve; category VII, anthropological reserve/natural biotic area; and category VIII, multiple use management area/managed resource area.[19]

Although this system is widely used, particularly in accordance with national legislation, it does not always reflect the locally used terms. For example, in Britain, 250,000 people live in what the British call national parks. According to the CNPPA's classification, these areas fall under category V, protected landscape or seascape, an area where "traditional land uses are maintained." Similarly, Indonesia has declared the Arfak Mountains as a strict nature reserve, which would by definition fall under category I, but villagers are allowed to live in the reserve. According to the CNPPA category, it would thus be a protected landscape, but Indonesia, like many other countries, exercises the right to call its protected areas what it deems most appropriate. The CNPPA has, however, adopted a universal definition for all protected areas: "an area of land and/or sea especially dedicated to the protection and maintenance of biological diversity, and of natural and associated cultural resources, and managed through legal or other effective means."

The definitions of the eight CNPPA categories (as of the time of publication of this book) and the various international sites are presented here as a road map, or a trail guide, to the protected areas described throughout this book. The type of protected area that is probably the most faithful to definition is the World Heritage site. Since the World Heritage Convention came into force in 1975, 127 countries have become state parties to the convention, but fewer than 100 natural areas have become inscribed.[20] World Heritage sites, including Mount Everest (Sagarmatha) in Nepal, the Banc d'Arguin in Mauritania, Kakadu and Uluru in Australia, and Manas National Park in India, described in the following chapters, were inscribed in the convention in order "to protect the natural features for which the area is considered to be of universal outstanding significance."[21]

Inscription of a World Heritage site under the convention is usually a source of great pride for the host country. But as Sanjoy Deb Roy and Peter Jackson's chapter on Manas in part three points out, this national park is under serious threat from civil unrest spearheaded by the Bodo tribal people. In December 1992, it was placed on the World Heritage in Danger list, together with five other new sites, including the Aïr-Ténéré Nature Reserve in Niger, where in 1992 several park staff members were kidnapped by rebel groups operating in the protected area. "Rather than being considered a 'blacklist,' the danger list serves as an early warning signal, and corrective actions are being taken in all six sites on the danger list," says Jim Thorsell, senior advisor, Natural Heritage.

The chapters on Manas and the Aïr-Ténéré, like all contributions to this book, underline the importance of recognizing and involving local communities in creating and managing protected areas. When necessary, protected areas should be established to safeguard both cultural and biological diversity. Conservationists, including some park managers, are finally learning what indigenous and ethnic people like Kostas Pistolas of Greece have known for a long time: categories, electric fences, fire trucks, and armed guards do not protect parks and the diversity of nature; people do.

HADYA AMADOU KANE, LUC HOFFMANN, & PIERRE CAMPREDON

Fishermen of the Desert

When Portuguese settlers first explored the shallow waters of the Banc d'Arguin more than 500 years ago, they found hundreds of fishermen herding shoals of mullet—with the help of coastal dolphins—into large hand-woven nets. They also discovered thousands of monk seals frolicking along the shore.

Thanks to the vigilance of the Mauritanian government, fishermen still cooperate with the dolphins to hunt for food, and the seals constitute the largest remaining group of monk seals in the world. Although the number of seals has dropped radically, the animals enjoy protection in a special, rigidly guarded area of Banc d'Arguin National Park on Mauritania's coast in West Africa. The largest concentration of waders and shorebirds in the world also winters in the area, often traveling as far as 10,000 kilometers to reach their destination. It is a rare haven, where man still lives in harmony with nature. Millions of migratory birds create a living, peaceful link between nations; sand dune landscapes slope down to the water's edge; and fishermen's boats sail the shallows, escorted by dolphins.[1]

The fishermen, known as the Imraguen, are almost totally dependent on the migratory fish for their livelihood. About 800 people live in seven villages inside the national park, harvesting fish on a sustainable basis.[2] They use traditional hand-woven nets and handmade wooden boats propelled by rectangular sails.

The Imraguen, whose name in its singular form, Amrigin, literally means "the one who gathers life," have managed to conserve their ancient fishing methods in the face of growing pressure for development. The most spectacular of these methods is the way they capture grey mullet with the help of bottle-nosed dolphins, several hundred of which are resident in the Bay of Timiris in the southern part of the park.

When the shoals of mullet arrive, the dolphins appear—numbering at times over 100—and, swimming parallel to the beach only 20 to 30 meters from the shore, prevent the mullet from swimming back out to sea. The Imraguen men then get into the water, their nets on their shoulders, and block the fishes' path. The disrupted mullet jump in all directions, throwing out brilliant flashes of silver. Many of them are caught, while others try to stampede to safety. The dolphins take advantage of the chaos and capture their prey much more easily than in normal conditions.[3]

This collaboration between the fishermen and the dolphins, which seems so natural to the Imraguen, illustrates clearly the level of integration these people have with their natural environment. To overlook this interaction when Mauritania was creating the national park would have proved to be negative for both the dolphins and man.

Banc d'Arguin National Park was established by the Mauritanian government in 1976 along 180 kilometers of the country's coast. Its 12,000-square-kilometer area is split equally between inhospitable, arid land and water; it is where the sea meets the desert, stretching out to shallow water to a maximum of 60 kilometers and inland into the Sahara to a maximum of 35 kilometers.

Its sizable area makes it one of the five largest parks in Africa, greater in size than the Gambia. Its situation at the junction of two biogeographic realms—the Palearctic and the Ethiopian—means that it contains species of flora and fauna on the edge of their distribution range. The park is, for example, the northern limit for such species as the long-tailed cormorant, the bridled tern, and the western-reef heron and is the southern limit for the spoonbill and the yellow wagtail.

The park protects one of the few remaining large, virtually intact ecosystems in the world, composed of mud flats, mangrove swamps, marshes, islands, sand dunes, and expansive desert. It is one of the world's most important marine habitats, protected historically from destruction by seafarers because of its dangerous, shallow waters and the belief that—even if sailors did not get stranded—the sea was unlikely to contain significant resources. So special is the Banc d'Arguin that in 1982 its wetland area was designated a Ramsar site, meaning that it is protected under the Ramsar Convention on Wetlands of International Importance. In 1989, the park was listed as a World Heritage site.

The abundance and reliability of food sources in the park, such as fish and crustaceans, attract millions of birds. The Banc d'Arguin is host to the largest breeding colonies of waterfowl in West Africa, including flamingoes, spoonbills, terns, and 3,000 pairs of pelicans. During the winter, more than 3 million waders and shorebirds flock to the park's vast expanse of mud flats. The mild climate of the area and the absence of human disturbance, which reduces the amount of time spent in flight, allow the birds to live very economically in terms of energy expenditure. The resources can therefore be shared even more widely.[4]

The Banc d'Arguin's importance to conservation is matched by its importance to the economy of the country. It represents the main spawning and nursery ground of the Mauritanian coast, and its fish and seafood provide 60 percent of Mauritania's revenue. Its thousands of kilometers of shallow water are carpeted with aquatic grasses that are an ideal nursery ground for crustaceans and mollusks. In addition to their value as a habitat for other species and their nutritive potential, the seagrass beds also modify the general hydrological conditions. In deflecting the current and slowing the flow rate, they create a sheltered environment in which the water remains clear. Their roots also help to consolidate mud flats and hold their sediments in place.[5]

The Imraguen live sustainably in the park, meeting almost all of their needs through fishing. They do not hunt birds and do not as a rule hunt the park's animal species, such as gazelles and jackals. There is little opportunity to utilize a desert area that has been suffering from persistent drought for more than a decade. Their traditional wells have dried out, so fresh water has to be imported by truck from 50 kilometers away or by boat from a distance of 160 kilometers. Since practically nothing can be cultivated, the Imraguen depend on people traveling into the park, who buy their fish, to supply them with tea, sugar, and dried fruit and vegetables.

The Imraguen are traditionally a nomadic people, following the migrating shoals of fish along the coast. The introduction of sailboats late in the nineteenth century by fishermen from the Canary Islands enhanced their traditional techniques, allowing the Imraguen men to follow by sea the migrations of mullet and meagre, their staple fish species. Imraguen society is divided according to work—the domain of men is the sea and the domain of women, the village. The women are traditionally responsible for processing and drying the fish, either for sale or for village consumption.

Since the 1980s, the Imraguen's land and livelihood have been increasingly threatened by the pressures of development in Mauritania. Industrial trawlers have been operating increasingly closer to the park's water because of dwindling offshore fish stocks. There is a growth in illegal small-scale fishing by outsiders, especially Senegalese fishermen who move up from the south in their motorized pirogues, or fishing boats. Temporary settlements have even been discovered on the park's coast. Also, seafood dealers circulate in Imraguen villages to buy fresh fish. The Imraguen, suffering from poverty and drought, are thus encouraged to increase their fishing and to reduce their production of dried fish, a vital source of protein and emergency food during shortages.

On land, poachers in Jeeps chase animals and further worsen the physical effects of the drought. Poaching has already wiped out Dama gazelles, oryxes, and ostriches from the area. Now, the survival of dorcas gazelles and bustards is threatened by unchecked hunting.

Meanwhile, the monk seals in the area have reduced in number to only about 150—representing about a quarter of the world population. As early as the fifteenth century, the seals were being slaughtered in large numbers for their skins and oil. In 1982, an important breeding cave collapsed, further threatening survival. The monk seal is a priority in the conservation efforts of the park, and the seals' specially protected area is allowed only limited human activity, thus restricting disruptive fishing.[6]

The struggle to maximize short-term profits from fishing—along with the growing feeling that the park was solely for the benefit of the birds and was not aiding economic development—has endangered the protected area. The per capita product of Mauritania is low, at $440 in 1987, and severe droughts have diverted government resources to emergency relief efforts. Some development proposals have recommended that the Imraguen be provided with motorized boats to increase their fishing resources from the park and that outsiders be allowed to fish inside the area. Park authorities have therefore had to develop economically viable arguments for protecting the Banc d'Arguin.

One way of convincing government authorities of the importance to the country's economy of maintaining the park in its present state is by increasing and altering scientific research on the area, which first began in the 1980s and highlighted the wealth of natural resources there. The focus of recent research has been the park's role in the country's fishing economy as well as the ways in which fisheries resources, fishermen, and birds interact and what their interactions imply for the management and sustainable use of the whole system.

Institutional measures have also been adopted to help save the Banc d'Arguin, including the formation in 1986 of the Fondation Internationale du Banc d'Arguin (FIBA), a group of foreign and international organizations with the aim of attracting international attention to the park and providing it with financial, technical, and moral support. FIBA has been very active in helping to develop a conservation and management strategy for the park, and in its first five years it raised $800,000 to invest in the park. External funding has proved vital—strict austerity policies imposed on the Mauritanian government mean that the park budget is minimal and cannot be increased. World Heritage site status and Ramsar site status have further underlined the importance of the area, both nationally and internationally.

However, all this action to protect the biological wealth of the park probably would not succeed without measures to improve the economic and social positions of the Imraguen. They live in the park and have traditionally managed its resources responsibly and sustainably. Park authorities had therefore to initiate projects that concentrated on conservation *and* development in a fashion that respected the local people's livelihoods. Alternative sources of income or improved returns from existing activities were seen as a means of reducing pressure on the park.

A great concern for the Imraguen has been the deterioration of their sailboats, called *lanches;* they still fish with the very same boats left to them about fifty years ago by the Canary Island fishermen. The *lanches,* which are about 8 meters long, look like simple Mediterranean sailboats. Replacing them with motorized boats could cause untold problems, such as wildlife disturbance, pollution, and noise, and could create difficulties in distinguishing legitimate Imraguen fishermen from illegal outsiders. The low-technology, inexpensive *lanches* not only are economically viable but also maintain the people's cultural identity and even offer some opportunities for tourism.

Sailboat programs have focused on boat repair and the construction of new vessels, and training of marine carpenters has been assisted by IUCN (the World Conservation Union) and the Ramsar Convention. A craftsman from Brittany in France who is training local fishermen in boat building and helping the Imraguen to repair their *lanches* estimates that thirty of the forty-five existing boats could last another ten to twenty years with repairs costing an average of $6,000 per boat. New *lanches* have been designed, similar to the existing ones but with easier construction techniques, in a project assisted by the Netherland's Den Helder Foundation and the Netherlands government. The new versions require less wood and are faster, lighter, and easier to maintain. Workshops in Indonesia have produced some boat kits for assembly in the park's villages.[7]

The contribution to Imraguen society is to be matched by the Imraguen's contribution to the welfare of the park. Imraguen fishermen benefiting from the boat project will be asked to help with park surveillance and to participate in tourist or research activities. Great emphasis is placed on patrolling the park to prevent illegal fishing and disturbance to nesting waterfowl. In 1989, the government temporarily released from service several Méharistes—members of the country's camel corps—to act as park wardens in the terrestrial part of the park.

Another project, initiated by FIBA, aims to enhance the people's living conditions by improving the quality of fish production techniques, thus raising incomes. Drying methods and preservation and packaging techniques will focus on quality rather than quantity, and more effective commercial outlets will be provided. Resource management techniques will encourage Imraguen participation and the development of new skills. The project has gained the support of Imraguen women, whose traditional role as fish processors is being guarded by the rebuilding of their old drying pens. Other activities are planned to improve village living conditions through education, health, and water supply programs.

Conservation and management plans for the park involving FIBA and WWF have provided operating expenses and staff training for the park as well as transportation equipment and spare parts, including a truck to transport fresh water. There are also moves to establish fishing cooperatives in the villages and to produce an educational pamphlet on the monk seal for schoolchildren and the general public.

Tourism is seen as another opportunity for contributing to the local economy, although all such efforts are to be carefully controlled. Intelligent development of tourist activities would give selective access to a diversity and abundance of unique flora and fauna, the dramatic meeting of sea and desert, and the preserved culture of the local people.

Giving the Imraguen exclusive rights of exploitation in the park when it was created has encouraged a sense of property and responsibility. Had this not been the case, the park probably would have been invaded long ago by other fisheries that were less compatible with conservation ideals.

As FIBA told the People and Protected Areas Workshop at IUCN's parks congress in February 1992: "To preserve Mauritania's fishing economy, one must save the Banc d'Arguin, and to save the Banc d'Arguin, the Imraguen's way of life must be maintained." The Banc d'Arguin National Park experience is an example of a development model in which both people and nature are having their needs fulfilled.[8]

Prospering from the Desert

Drive westward from Delhi. The land becomes drier and sandier and the vegetation sparser until you arrive in the heart of Rajasthan, the Great Indian Desert, known as the Thar. Through vast distances the landscape is barren. Suddenly, the scene is transformed. There are many trees and bushes. Antelopes and gazelles wander in herds, and coveys of partridges abound. Even more surprising is to see men, women, and children going about their business in close proximity to the wild animals, which show no fear. You are in the land of the Bisnois, one of the most remarkable peoples in the world. Members of this community are renowned for their religious principles, which for centuries have taught them to conserve trees and wild animals for their own welfare. Although this vast, unspoiled area is not yet officially protected, the people themselves have safeguarded its natural treasures since the fifteenth century.

A tall, handsome man with a fine, parted beard under a large white turban is unmistakably a Bisnoi. His wife, too, is conspicuous among other desert women, with her colorful dress and equally colorful veil. Her rich ornaments of silver and gold—almost like a mobile safe-deposit box—make her stand out as a prosperous person. Sharp featured and well proportioned, she is a true rustic beauty, surpassing her husband in informality and casual innocence. It appears that their way of life—disciplined by the principle of living in harmony with the harsh environment of the desert—has evolved the Bisnois.

The Thar, home of the Bisnois, covers more than 1.3 million square kilometers, 15 percent in Pakistan and 85 percent in India, at the eastern end of the great desert belt extending from the Atlantic through the Sahara and Arabia. It has been nominated as, but not yet declared, a biosphere reserve.

Some 500 years ago, the Thar was overrun by invaders from the West. Looting, plundering, forced conversion, and killing were the order of the day. In reaction,

Hindu society became a closed culture with innumerable social parasites and exploiters. Need gave way to greed. The cutting of trees, and the killing of animals for sport and trade became a destructive way of life. Drought, famine, migration, death, and poverty prevailed.

Moved by the hopeless lot of the people, the heir apparent of the village of Pipasar meditated and prayed for a solution to the problem. He came to realize that the real problem was the ecological devastation of the desert. He laid down certain principles that could help overcome the people's misery and later came to be known as Guru Jameshwarji, who taught the significance of conserving trees and wild animals. He considered the *khejri* (*Prosopis cinerarea*) among trees and the blackbuck (*Antilope cervicapra*) to be indices of environmental quality. Because the guru's principles numbered twenty-nine, his followers became known as Bisnois ("twenty-niners" in Rajasthani). The principles spread like wildfire among the semipastoral and marginal agriculturists of some five centuries ago, when ecology in its present form was unknown.

Using the fragile and scanty resources of fodder, food, and water judiciously, the Bisnoi has emerged as a distinct character in the desert. The Bisnois live in homesteads; their houses, simple thatched huts, have mud-plastered walls with separate chambers for cooking and sleeping. They do not believe in maintaining large herds of cattle. Only a few buffaloes and cows form their dairy cattle. Rearing of goats is taboo. Their agricultural holdings are small, and they raise only one crop during the monsoon season—largely millet, with intercropping of pulses, watermelons, and cucumbers. Their use of a simple wooden plow and bullock power leaves a lot of bushy growths of zizyphus, a fodder species. The Bisnois' agriculture is a chancy affair that depends on the uncertain rains. In the event of crop failure, the zizyphus bushes provide alternate fodder to tide the cattle over the bad years of famine.

The strategy for a successful life-style in the desert is based on alternatives and opportunism. For this reason, the Bisnois keep the maximum number of *khejri* trees on their farms. The species is tended from the day of its appearance as a seedling or a root sucker and is cared for over a hundred years until it ages, dies, and dries. No one fells a *khejri* tree, even in times of direst need. A deciduous species, *khejri* has a tremendous capacity to withstand severe lopping and throws out vigorous coppice shoots every spring. The tiny leaves provide excellent fodder, the branches make good fencing material and firewood for cooking, and the pods are nutritive for cattle as well as humans. Normally, shade from a tree in cropland hampers production. But in the desert, soils are light and sandy, needing cover for conservation of soil moisture. Fallen leaves under the *khejri* trees improve soil texture, and the roots of this leguminous species help to fix free nitrogen and enrich the soil. Crops under the shade of the *khejri* therefore fare better than they would in the open. *Khejri* roots go deep, more than 100 meters, in search of water, so droughts of a year or two's duration do not affect the tree's growth and forage production, nor do the roots compete with crops. *Khejri* is therefore beneficial to the farmer in every way. It is protected at all costs and is almost worshiped.

In their passion to preserve the *khejri* tree, the Bisnois have no parallel in human history. Legend has it that some 250 years ago, when the 400-year-old Mehrangarh fort at Jodhpur needed repairs, Maharaja Ajit Singh's men could find no sizable trees to fire the lime kilns except in the Bisnoi village of Khejarli. But the Bisnois protested the cutting of their trees, even at the cost of their lives. The first victim was a woman named Amrita. Then her daughters were slain. Thereafter, the sacrificial ceremony was simple. One by one, the Bisnois came, bathed, and had their heads chopped off by their own relatives in protest against the cutting of the trees. The story goes that 363 trees were cut but only after 363 men, women, and children had been beheaded. The maharaja was shocked, and since then no tree has been felled and no animal killed in Bisnoi villages. The incident can easily be passed off as fiction, but the rich environment, density of trees, and large number of birds and antelopes visible today in Bisnoi country, in stark contrast to the adjoining overfelled and wasted land, give substance to the story. The Bisnois, who, like most Hindus, are vegetarians, eating only nuts, fruit, and grains, continue to be the custodians of the flora and fauna of the desert in the name of their guru.

The Bisnois' agricultural fields are marked by their open character. Damage done to their crops by wild animals and birds is considered as the latter's share in their agricultural system. In fact, when the first furrow is made and the first handful of seeds is sown, it is done in the name of the birds; the second, for the wild animals—the blackbuck and the gazelle (*Gazella gazella*)—and the third, for guests and charity. Only then is it the family's turn. Since crop failure is the rule rather than the exception, the farmers hope that someone's luck will work for better rains and ensure immunity from rust disease and pests. Thus the agricultural gamble is played in everyone's name. Naturally, everyone has a stake and a share in the product. Wild animals and birds are therefore an integral part of the Bisnoi agrarian culture.

Since no animal or bird may be killed for any reason within Bisnoi territory, any stray movement of a stranger is watched by whole villages; at the slightest doubt, all the men, women, and children come out to scatter the animals and chase the intruder away. Anyone defying their customs is severely dealt with; sometimes casualties occur on both sides.

Centuries of Bisnoi protection of wildlife have led to mutual understanding, and the wild animals repose utmost confidence in the Bisnois and their settlements. This protection is not limited to antelopes; not even the predators—jackals (*Canis aureas*), foxes, and snakes—may be killed. The wolf (*Canis lupus*), a disaster incarnate for ranchers and shepherds, is protected here. The howl of the jackal is considered a good omen and a sign of a good environment in the village; its absence is believed to spell disaster. Truly, long before biologists discovered it, the Bisnois knew the role of predators in maintaining a natural balance.

Antelopes, gazelles, foxes, partridges, quails, and many species of birds, including the demoiselle crane (*Arthropides virgo*), which migrates to the region in the thousands during the winter and can devastate crops, are all part of the Bisnoi environment. The greenery of the *khejri* trees, good crops, prosperous houses, and healthy and well-to-do people are the hallmarks of the Bisnoi ethos, in contrast with that of other people living in the same environment with similar resources. The difference is in the former's understanding of desert ecology and care of the environment. Bisnoi settlements are an example of a perfectly functional (though undeclared) biosphere reserve, a place where ecology and economy have been balanced well.

The Bisnois worship fire. In their temples, a small lamp is always burning. On special days, they light a large fire in the temple, pour ghee (purified butter from the sacred cow) over the fire, fold their hands in prayer, and recite the teachings of their guru. They follow reformed Hinduism, in which there are neither elaborate ceremonies nor rigid customs and the presence of the legendary Brahman priest has been ruled out. Marriage is a simple affair, and divorce is rare. Since many hands are needed on the farm, family planning, as in much of rural India, is not popular. However, the Bisnoi people are beginning to realize that they may have to control the size of their population. Their commitment to environmental care is so deeply rooted that unlike most other Hindus, whose remains are cremated, they prefer to be ceremonially buried directly in the soil of the farm in order to enrich the soil.

Bisnoi festivities and get-togethers include assemblies of thousands at the tomb at Mukam in Bikaner on the night of total darkness in February. They pay homage to their guru, who showed them the path to prosperity, and rededicate themselves to the twenty-nine principles of desert discipline after night-long prayers and an early morning bath. The two days are also days of brisk business, with camels and carts selling like hotcakes.

The twenty-fifth day after the full moon in September is a day of remembrance, when Bisnois gather at Khejarli and pay their respects to Amrita and her daughters and all of the 363 men, women, and children who sacrificed their lives to protest the cutting of the trees. Activities start with fire worship in the morning and continue all day. Everyone brings ghee as an offering.

There has been no second guru in the past 500 years to rejuvenate the twenty-nine principles, yet the flame burns undimmed and the spirit of sacrifice is still alive. No other example exists of a conservation culture with such levels of commitment, continued over such a long period of time, and practiced, moreover, on such an extensive stretch of what is mainly desert terrain. But one must not carry the false impression that the Bisnois are a backward people or that the preservation of their environment is an animist tribal custom. The Bisnois are an educated people, part of the mainstream of India; they are equipped with mechanized farms and are advanced in every walk of life, including politics.

Unfortunately, there are saddening new trends. The introduction of tractors and mechanized farming has led to the uprooting of all of the zizyphus bushes from the fields, reducing an alternative forage resource. The Bisnois have also brought grazing lands under the plow. But the worst development is an increasing emphasis on conflicting politics at the expense of environmental awareness. The Bisnois have a partially elected and appointed governing body of five to six people who decide all matters, including such details as marriage dates and invitations to weddings, and the rededication days are increasingly being used as political platforms for election campaigns rather than as opportunities to renew awareness of the guru's twenty-nine principles. It is to be hoped that the wise people of the community will rule out politics from these days of thanksgiving and try to keep alive the spirit of zealous preservation of the desert environment for continued prosperity.

Gardens in the Forest

In Indonesia's savannah forest, on its many lakes and rivers and out on its open grasslands, the Kanum, Marind, Marori, and Yei tribes of Wasur National Park arduously pursue a livelihood similar to that of their ancestors. On foot, with bow and steel-tipped arrows, men stalk wallaby, pig, and deer; women chatter as they glide through the forest on their way to fish the streams. Sometimes they disappear for several days or weeks, uprooting their children from the village schools to help at the traditional sago grounds, which are often far from the villages, deep in the national park. Traditional rites and festivals, visits to sacred grounds, and dwellings on the sacred places continue to forge unbreakable cultural links between the people and the land, a pattern similar in some ways to that of the Australian aborigines found only a few hundred kilometers south across the Arafura Sea. Over thousands of years, such activities have helped mold the landscape of today.

About 2,550 people inhabit thirteen villages inside Wasur National Park, which lies in Irian Jaya, a province in the far eastern part of Indonesia, near its border with Papua New Guinea. Most of them live in a delicate balance with nature and manage its resources well. Each clan and family has traditional sacred sites called *dusuns*—predefined by past generations—for hunting, gardening, and spiritual events. WWF, together with a local nongovernmental organization, YAPSEL, and local landowners, has mapped and catalogued hundreds of *dusun* sites and discovered that they spread over the entire 413,810 hectares of the park. There is no unclaimed land at all.

"To restrict our access to these sites would be the same as barring the door of your church, mosque, or shop," says one tribal elder. Another adds, "We wish to support the ideas laid before us concerning this national park, but we cannot if our *dusun*s are affected." The ideas the elder refers to are contained in management plans for the park—in the PHPA/WWF Management and Implementation of Wasur National Park Project, run by WWF and Indonesia's Directorate General of Forest Protection and Nature Conservation (PHPA). The project, started in March 1991, aims to find sustainable ways of utilizing the resources of the park, considered to be the most threatened of any protected area in Irian Jaya.

Until recently, the PHPA's understanding of the tribal peoples of Wasur was very limited, but the situation is changing. The PHPA's director general, Mr. Sutisno, who is the highest authority over protected areas in Indonesia, now believes: "The cultural aspects of Wasur National Park must be considered and supported during planning and management; the people must continue to use their *dusun*s in a traditional manner."

Wasur National Park is a transfrontier park adjacent to the Tonda Wildlife Reserve in Papua New Guinea. Its wildlife and ten habitat types are exceptionally rich, including many habitats found only in the region. Estimates of at least 400 bird species in the park include many migrants that visit its extensive mud flats and wetlands. Hundreds of cranes pirouette through mating rituals on the expansive grasslands; birds of paradise inhabit the grassy forest; and pelicans, ducks, storks, herons, and ibises gather on the glistening lakes and sea. Alongside the cranes grazes the agile wallaby, the largest marsupial in New Guinea. Other than introduced species such as rats and deer, there are about eighty mammals, many nocturnal and all marsupial. The entire area lies within the monsoon climate zone, so savannah forest, grasslands, permanent wetlands, and monsoon forest predominate. There are two main seasons: a cool dry season, from around June to November or December, and a wet season, which accounts for about three-quarters of the region's annual rainfall. Flooding is common in much of the park during the wet season, and extensive grass fires occur often during the dry season. The park provides Merauke, a town 18 kilometers from its border, with its only year-round source of fresh water. Local people's lives are dominated by the fluctuating abundance and absence of water.

When the Wasur National Park Project opened its headquarters in Merauke, the park faced numerous infringements on its resources. Illegal sand quarrying, road building, settling, logging, small plantation development, and motorized hunting with rifles and machetes took place on an unprecedented scale, in some cases even backed by local government. Some infringements had the backing of security forces, the only people legally permitted to carry firearms in Indonesia. About 65,000 people live in urban areas on the park's fringes, some with designs on the protected area's "empty" land. Further complications came from the isolated nature of Merauke, a town of 43,000 people accessible only by a two-day, triweekly flight from

Jakarta and a boat once every two weeks. Communications of all kinds are difficult, and the isolation makes enforcement of central government conservation policy extremely problematic. The PHPA asked WWF to assist the local Natural Resources Conservation Office (KSDA), which was severely understaffed and underfunded, to deal with the problems by designing a management system for the park.

Yet the biggest threat to Wasur National Park is economic poverty. People hunt, log, and sell animals and land to increase family security—to get cash to buy such items as salt, rice, cooking oil, clothing, education, improved housing, and medication. The Wasur project acknowledges this. As Mr. Sutisno says, "Economic development is a priority for park residents, and park resources may be used in a well-managed and sustainable manner as a basis and stimulus for this."

Indonesia's regulations for land and resource use in national parks allow room for creating traditional people-centered economic development. The challenge is to match national park objectives with the needs of park residents and the demands of modern economics and resulting land pressures. Through planning, consultation, and implementation, the Wasur project aims to establish guidelines and norms acceptable to both government and local communities, to develop culturally compatible economic incentives based on use of park resources. Such incentives could encourage communities to help protect the park, eventually providing a diverse range of economic activities fostering village development.

The first step in carrying out this plan was to secure priority access for park residents to the park's resources in order to raise morale and confidence and empower the traditional owners. In mid-1991, the government agreed that residents should remain in the park and be integrated into the park's planning and management. Mr. Sutisno said, "We acknowledge the importance of bottom-up planning and wish the local communities to be involved in designing the zoning system for Wasur National Park."

The project then began seeking community support by developing economic incentives in cooperation with the government and local nongovernmental organizations (NGOs). A sound management plan required community participation, which in turn required the government to gain community trust by providing concrete evidence that the national park could be of benefit to its residents. Too many unkept promises and unfinished projects had fostered skepticism among rural park communities. The project chose to focus on developing potentially sustainable economic incentives, such as deer hunting for meat and hide, extraction of aromatic oils, traditional crafts, tourism, and village-based activities.

Deer hunting has been particularly successful in transferring power and profits to the park residents. One of the main reasons for WWF's involvement in Wasur National Park was to help combat intensive deer hunting within the park's boundaries by townspeople with motorbikes, jeeps, and guns. The deer (*Cervus timorensis*), which are exotic to the park, once represented 80 percent of the townspeople's meat source. At its peak, the deer industry generated an estimated $200,000 per year, but almost no money went to the economically stressed park residents, who had no access to motorized vehicles. On a dry-season night, the park grasslands would sound like a war zone, with rifle fire originating from three or four different directions. People with Jeeps could take between twenty-five and forty deer at each hunt; motorbike riders, five each on a good night. The disturbance and rapidly diminishing deer numbers threatened traditional hunting practices. "The population had crashed below a sustainable threshold. Around 7,500 animals remain in the park, with a past kill rate of 5,000 animals a year," said Dr. Albert Franzman, a WWF consultant and member of the IUCN (World Conservation Union) Deer Specialist Group. Park residents saw others exploiting a resource they believed to be their own, but they felt powerless to deal with the problem. They were skeptical of the project's ability to control hunting by outsiders or to transfer deer resource benefits back to them.

An initial step was to assess deer numbers and establish monitoring methods. An agreement was then reached with the director general of the PHPA allowing park residents to hunt deer with traditional weapons to generate an economy and keep deer numbers down—the first such agreement for a national park in Indonesia. Police and community assistance helped the KSDA control motorized hunting— no easy task in a park that is flat and has many access points. Park residents now hunt on foot, using bows and arrows, and receive $50 per animal through a marketing scheme being developed by two local NGOs, YAPSEL and Kamaryey (an acronym combining three tribal names), and WWF, and supported by local government and the KSDA. Success has fostered strong support for the park from nearby communities and a willingness among community members not only to try new incentives but also to follow regulations and organize themselves. Reporting of trespassers by park communities has increased, providing the KSDA with accurate daily information and enabling efficient treatment of offenders.

A landowner from the village of Kuler says that he is less skeptical of the project now: "We did not believe WWF and KSDA when they said it was possible to stop the poachers, but they have begun to stop most of them. And now, three months later, the deer and kangaroo are tame again and easier for us to catch with bow and arrow." Four villages earned $3,750 over three months from traditional hunting. Some park residents have even become involved in catching trespassers by waiting at park exit routes with KSDA staff members and halting suspect motorbikes returning from nocturnal hunts.

The success of deer hunting has led to written agreements with the director general of the PHPA for the establishment of a traditional-use zone, the first of its kind in Indonesia. This development will provide the policy and regulations allowing deer utilization by traditional methods as well as access to *dusun*s for traditional residents.

In workshops and meetings, zoning and other aspects of management are discussed with influential village representatives, including those who are breaking the law, such as illegal settlers and cattle ranchers. Workshops involving ninety or more people have led to decisions requiring the settlers and cattle ranchers to leave the park, in spite of the fact that they provided work for some park residents and that agreements between tribal people and the new settlers would have to be broken. Park residents have proved readily able to understand park management and zoning; it is similar to their own tribal resource management, whereby people and certain activities are sometimes restricted to specific areas. Community support is strengthened by the fact that zoning would help protect sacred sites.

Local NGOs play a decisive role in the policy of Wasur National Park by helping to set guidelines and acting as go-betweens to promote dialogue between the community and WWF. They are neutral mediators at community meetings. WWF has been working with one of the NGOs, Kamaryey, to enable it to take over the community organization and development aspects of the park.

Another benefit is increased local government support as suspicion of the park project decreases. Over a period of eighteen months, community and government support have successfully tackled the main threats to the park. The needs of villagers in buffer zones adjacent to the park are also being addressed, and programs to promote sustainable agriculture are being planned.

Not long ago, Irian Jaya community members were asking why their land should be included in protected areas. Now the queries come from people outside the park: "Why are our village and land outside the park boundary?" asked a landowner from Nasem, a village on the edge of Wasur National Park, at a park communities workshop on park management. The landowners said that land belonging to Nasem was being eaten away by sand quarrying that was being carried out to provide building materials for the town of Merauke. Some landowners were selling land for fast cash, turning Nasem into a moonscape of pits and gullies. Dissenting villagers felt powerless to halt the destruction.

Today, it is becoming more and more advantageous to live or have land within national park boundaries in Irian Jaya. The community-centered management approach is receiving increased support from all sectors and government levels in Indonesia. Most encouraging is the growing enthusiasm of the local people themselves—the Kanum, Marind, Marori, and Yei, whose ancestral homes and sacred garden sites are now safeguarded inside Wasur National Park.

Vietnam's Guardians of the Islands

The scars on Ho Hoang Son's legs have faded in the eighteen years since he was held prisoner on an island in the South China Sea. They are most visible in the mornings, when he rolls up his pant legs and patrols Con Son Island's coral reef or monitors newly made turtle nests. Ho, whose livelihood depends on the health of the reef, is on the lookout daily for turtle-egg poachers or fishermen trying to dynamite the reef in order to stun the fish, in the hope of making an easy catch.

Ho, a former inmate on Con Son Island before it became part of the Con Dao marine reserve, was held for seven years in a range of detention centers, including a "tiger cage," a narrow, rectangular cell about 2¾ meters long and 1⅓ meters wide. The tiger cage gets its name from its ceiling of bars, through which shafts of light enter the crowded chamber, which holds an average of six people. Both the North Vietnamese and South Vietnamese (ARVN) armies used such cages to hold captive enemy soldiers.

Today, Ho is a guardian of the archipelago, which was declared a nature reserve in 1984 and proposed as a national park in 1990. He was taken to the islands following his capture as a Vietcong prisoner of war. After surrendering to U.S. and South Vietnamese troops in the Mekong Delta on the mainland of Vietnam, he was transported with thousands of other soldiers to the Con Dao, or Con Son, Islands, 179 kilometers southeast of the coastal town of Vung Tau. He considers himself very lucky to have survived the inhospitable conditions of the prison complex, where 20,000 people died after it began operation under the French in 1862, then the South Vietnamese in 1954. Former prime minister Pham Van Dong and Le Duc Tho, counterpart to Henry Kissinger during the Paris peace talks between the United States and Vietnam, were among the prisoners who survived their French jailers.

Ho is one of fifteen former prisoners who decided to make a life on the archipelago's main island of Con Son after the prison was officially shut down in 1975. Most of the people left Con Dao, but approximately 200 families stayed behind. Half of these work for the government in administering the island; the other half are farmers and fishermen. In the early days of his capture, Ho spent most of his time shackled at the ankle in a huge room with hundreds of other inmates. His bed was a concrete slab; his bathroom, a wooden bucket. On good days, he was marched down to a spectacular sandy beach fringed by a massive coral reef. At low tide, he waded out with thousands of others across the back of the spiky coral in shallow water. His feet were lacerated, but not as badly as his hands, as he ripped up the coral bed, breaking it with his bleeding fingers and piling it into hand-woven baskets. He carried the coral back to shore to a pyramid-shaped smelter, where it was melted down to make lime to build more prison cells and the grand houses where the wardens lived. On the main island, a monument has been erected near the "914 Bridge," in honor of the 914 people who died during its construction. In 1990, Ho and many of the islanders were still living in some of the prison buildings, most of which were in need of repair. Geckos, including the tokay, the largest gecko in the world, and fruit bats have also taken refuge in the ruins. The government hopes to restore the buildings as a tourist attraction, particularly for the Vietnamese families whose relatives died on the islands.

"The smelter used to make limestone was shut down in 1987," Ho told me in 1989, during my first visit to the archipelago, where he had just been made a reserve warden. In 1992, thanks to a $20,000 grant to the reserve from the Vietnamese government, the staff of the reserve had grown to forty-nine. But with a salary of around $20 per month, it was hard to keep reserve staff for long periods. Thus, some reserve staff members choose a different arrangement, which allows them to exploit the islands' resources on a sustainable basis while enforcing park regulations and engaging in scientific research. In 1992, like a number of other people on the main and only inhabited island of Con Son, Ho opted to work on a contract, or consulting, basis.

The archipelago's sixteen islands, measuring 7,642 hectares (of which 6,043 hectares are a nature reserve), are an attractive habitat for birds, including an emerald dove and a white pigeon that are endemic to Con Dao; the Javan duck, which lives on a freshwater lake on the large island; white-bellied sea eagles, of which there are ten pairs; and the edible-nest swiftlet.[1] The swiftlets make their nests—entirely of saliva—in caves wedged into the islands' steep limestone cliffs. Twice a year, approximately 4,500 nests (about 30 kilograms) are harvested for sale, mainly to Hong Kong and Taiwan, for use in making a high-priced bird's-nest soup. Surveys conducted by the park staff show that the swift population is stable and may even be increasing, indicating to park officials that they have struck the right balance between conservation and sustainable exploitation of the birds.

Considered the best diver in the islands, Ho still leads groups of visiting scientists and prospective investors on tours of both recovering and unspoiled coral beds. "The reef off the main island is coming back to life after decades of destruction," he says happily, his hands turning toward the young coral growing on the old calcium skeleton. Sea urchins, several species of crabs, prawns, lobsters, and iridescent green anemones are slowly returning. Shimmering shoals of brightly colored fish feed at the deeper, less spoiled reaches of the reef, while in the untouched areas, some of the rarest species of mollusks still abound. Three species of giant clam thrive in the reserve, glittering like multicolored jewels beneath the surface of the crystal-clear waters.

Except at the port off the main village on the biggest island, fishing is prohibited in the coastal waters. A 4-kilometer protected sea zone has been established, but enforcement is difficult because of lack of boats. The reserve bought one new boat in 1992 and hopes to buy another. Despite the paucity of equipment, the fishing grounds are still rich because the islands are difficult to reach from the mainland. Today, island residents can get to the mainland once a month at most during the monsoon season and weekly if the seas are calm. There are no regularly scheduled flights to Con Dao and no telephone lines. Contact between the main island and the mainland is by radio. The bountiful seas surrounding the Con Dao Islands provide more than enough seafood for its 2,500 inhabitants, 800 of whom are soldiers. But the local market for fish products is limited to sale on the island or the occasional foreign ship that ventures into the waters, as Marco Polo did in 1224 while en route from China to Italy. Around the unprotected island of Phu Quoc, which is served by biweekly flights from Ho Chi Minh City (formerly Saigon), off the coast of southwestern Vietnam, the giant clams, along with the sea turtle population, have virtually disappeared because of overhunting for sale to fishing boats from Taiwan and Hong Kong and to tourist shops on the mainland.

The Con Son Islands have maintained a military presence because they have always been vulnerable to attack from foreign powers attracted by their beauty and their strategic location between Vietnam and China. Coins left behind by the Spanish in the sixteenth century indicate that they may have occupied the archipelago briefly; the British declared it a colony in 1702 and built a catheral on the main island but were soon ousted by the Vietnamese. The French successfully colonized the Con Son Islands, known to them as the Poulo Condore, in 1861 and established a prison there in 1862. Few, if any, of their descendants remain on the island.

Conditions on the island were especially difficult in 1975, according to Ky Van Thuan, an administrator of the islands, who was posted in Con Dao for sixteen years. He moved to the mainland with his family in 1992 so that he could undergo treatment for cerebral malaria, from which he recovered in early 1993. "We were lucky to get a newspaper once a month," he told me in Vung Tau shortly after resuming work.

"Even though it was hard living there, most of the people who had lived there for years wanted to stay. They were given the choice of returning to the mainland, but they had developed ties to the islands." In 1990, Con Dao opened its first bakery, and its owner, a woman, is running a healthy business. Heineken and 333, or "Ba-Ba-Ba beer," is also shipped in about once a week, along with other food supplies, from the mainland.

The prison was started originally by a Vietnamese emperor, who incarcerated his wife, Hoang Phi Yen, and his son because they objected to the presence of French colonialists in the ancient imperial capital of Hue. The prison was later expanded to hold Vietnamese prisoners during French colonial times and Vietcong prisoners during the Vietnam War. Of the sixteen islands, only the largest, Con Son, is inhabited and cultivated. The others are largely covered by tropical forest, which is rich in wildlife, including crab-eating macaques, wild boars, flying squirrels, foam-nesting frogs, and fruit bats. Three species of marine turtle and a variety of dolphins and sharks also inhabit the waters surrounding the islands. One isolated island, jutting out of the sea like a bare lump of white rock, is called Egg Island or Bird Island. It is the habitat for thousands of seabirds, which breed on the ledges, and the seas below swarm with sea cucumbers and other marine life that feed on the birds' droppings. Seen from a helicopter, the island looks like a giant egg set completely alone in a vast, blue sea.

Although a number of conservation inroads have been made on the islands, their fragile ecosystems could be threatened by the growing trade in sharks' fins, tropical fish, swifts' nests, giant clams, and turtle carapaces. The clams are supposedly harvested on a sustainable basis, but the demand of the Japanese, Taiwanese, Hong Kong, and Thai markets for the islands' riches could soon begin to have an impact on the islands' natural resources if strict controls are not upheld.

Following visits in 1987, 1988, 1990, and 1991 by Professor Vo Quy of the University of Hanoi, together with scientists from his Center for Natural Resources Management and Environmental Studies, hunting bans have been declared on turtle eggs, turtles, coral, and island-based species. The former chairman of the island, Ba Giao, told me in 1991 that every time the professor surveys the reserve, he persuades the islanders to forfeit the right to exploit something: "The first time, he recommended we stop hunting the turtles; the second time, he asked us to stop collecting coral and to outlaw dynamiting; and the third time, he said we should stop eating the giant clams. We wonder what will be next," he said with a good-natured smile. According to Ky Van Thuan, it was the visit by Vo Quy's team in 1987 that moved the islands' authorities to shut down the smelter for good and prohibit the collection of coral for building materials.

Professor Vo, who interviewed some islanders and park staff members by radio in January 1993, says that he would like to see the hunting of sharks for their fins stopped and asked the resident fishermen of Vung Tau and the islands to prevent the accidental drowning of dolphins and sea turtles in their fishing nets. He encouraged the local authorities of the Peoples Committee of the Con Dao and of the newly created province of Ba Ria–Vung Tau (formerly the Vung Tau–Con Dao Special Economic Zone) to revive their tradition of respecting marine mammals and revering them as the helpers of the sea.

In Vietnam, there is an expression: "He cried as if his father had died." There can be no greater loss or grief. The fisherman who finds a marine mammal washed ashore or who accidentally kills it honors the mandarin, or prince of the sea, with a funeral as if it were his own son.[2] In Vung Tau, the local fishermen maintain a Temple of the Whale, where the bones of dolphins, whales, and other marine mammals are taken if they are drowned accidentally in nets or are found dead on the shore. In 1991, together with WWF-Italy and Canale 5 television, Professor Vo Quy and I recorded the human burial of five dolphins at the Temple of the Whale in Vung Tau. Two years earlier, in 1989, the villagers of Con Dao had told me of their finding a small whale stranded on one of their beaches. After unsuccessful attempts to return it to the sea, they gave it a human burial.

Out of curiosity and loneliness, the Con Dao islanders inevitably descend on the guest house whenever Vo Quy and his team arrive. After informal talks during his early visits, Ba Giao usually called the villagers together to hear Vo Quy explain the need to conserve the islands' precious natural resources. Soldiers, former prisoners, and scientists gathered at the modest community center or at the guest house itself to listen to suggestions of how they could carry out the proposed management plan for the area's national park, presented to the Ministry of Forestry in 1990. Under the management plan, fishermen are permitted to moor in one harbor off the main island. The only patrol boat, used by the newly appointed park director, Le Xuan Ai, to enforce this ruling, is not sufficient. During routine patrols, Le and his conservation team often reprimand the captains of boats fishing illegally in off-limit areas. Le has also asked a number of fishermen to return dozens of baby giant clams back to the sea and has confiscated scores of shark fins, which are increasingly found drying on the decks of boats illegally anchored in one of the best coral bays.

"Fishermen come to Con Dao from different provinces, so it is difficult to educate them. These families who fish in the Con Dao live on their boats, not on the island. They are selling their fish to people on foreign ships that travel to the waters of the Con Dao," says Professor Vo.

Every day, Ho and staff guards patrol the island by foot; they are hoping for extra boats to help them make their sea rounds more thoroughly. Ho often walks before sunrise from one end of the island to the other, sometimes with his friend Bay, a former schoolteacher who was also a prisoner in Con Dao. Bay, who is now vice president of the nature reserve, looks after the forest, and Ho looks after the sea. Together with the local people, they have set up a number of innovative conservation projects. Under the guidance of Bay, the Con Dao Womens Group is planting trees, and under the guidance of Vo Cong Hau, the first director of the park, they have built a holding pen for nesting female turtles. Wild female turtles, green, hawksbill, and loggerhead, are caught in the wild and placed in the enclosure. The Vietnamese reserve officials know that the holding pen is unsatisfactory, as the frightened turtles lay their eggs in the water rather than on the tiny shelf of beach built for them inside the pen. Isolated on the remote islands, the reserve managers are learning by trial and error. In 1992, the local conservationists tagged 300 green turtles on three different beaches. On a shoestring budget of $20,000 per year and with the help of the park wardens, the majority of the islanders are trying to sustain and manage the nature reserve, which is their backyard and, for many residents, has been a home place for several generations. When the management plan is approved by the Ministry of Forestry, various zones, including a tourist zone, a buffer zone, an exploitation zone, and a strictly protected core area, will be better enforced. Hunting is already prohibited on the islands, as is the cutting of trees outside the residential borders adjacent to the park. The main challenge facing the reserve managers is the need to establish economic incentives (such as carefully controlled tourism and improved marketing of fish) for protecting the reserve and to increase the islanders' understanding of how the park will maintain their valuable watershed and their main source of food, the surrounding seas.

Sometimes, while making their rounds of the islands, Ho and Bay are joined by Phuoc, a former officer in the South Vietnamese Army who was held in a reeducation camp for years after the war ended in 1975. Phuoc, who speaks with an Oklahoma accent, is teaching the former prisoners English. And they are showing him, as the head of the future tourist office, where to find the beauty spots of the islands and how to enjoy them without destroying them. The guardians of the islands, representing an odd mixture of backgrounds, are people who, like Ho and Bay, overlook both the mental and the physical scars on both sides. In their search for something positive, they have found a way of putting their years of suffering behind them. Ever since the B-52 bombers were sold as scrap and removed from the old U.S.-built runway, into which only Soviet-built helicopters flew until 1990, they rarely talk about the war. They speak instead, during the long, lazy evenings with spectacular sunsets splashing across the big stretch of sky, of the way the sea eagles call and how they mate when they fly . . . and how the sea turtles are nesting safely on Queen's Beach again.

BRYAN ALEXANDER

Gifts from the North Wind

I was at a Cree Indian bush camp in northern Quebec one autumn when a local representative of the Cree Trappers Association gave out the latest fur prices over the radio. For the hunters, the news was not good. The average price of a lynx skin had dropped from $500 to $200; mink was down, from $30 to $20; and beaver had fallen from $50 to $40. Only the price of marten, at $100, had stayed the same.

The reaction of the Cree hunters to the radio announcement was mixed. There were anger, dismay, bewilderment, and, above all, confusion. "Why?" they asked. "Why have the prices gone down?" Some offered possible explanations: "It must be the white men's fur farms . . . the animal rights groups . . . that are causing it!" The only conclusion agreed on was that there would be less cash for basic necessities during the coming winter.

The Cree describe themselves as a "hunting people," for they have lived by hunting, fishing, and trapping for several thousand years. Up until the 1950s, almost the entire Cree population was fully engaged in this traditional life-style. Many Cree now live a more sedentary existence as wage earners within their communities, but they still have close links with the land. They have been living on the eastern shores of James Bay since their ancestors first settled there, soon after the end of the last ice age. Their forebears lived as nomads, roaming in relatively fixed areas on a seasonal basis and eeking out a living from the taiga's resources. Then, with the arrival of the Hudson's Bay Company and the fur traders in the late seventeenth century, small settlements, mainly on the coast of James Bay, gradually developed and over the past few decades have become their permanent homes. Their livelihood, however, remained in the "bush," where they hunted and trapped far into the interior. Although not officially declared a nature reserve or natural park, the territory on which the Cree live is by their definition a protected area because they have cared for it and looked after it for centuries.

This land of approximately 176,000 square kilometers was part of the unilateral grant by Charles II to the Hudson's Bay Company in 1670. It was transferred to the Dominion of Canada after confederation and was later claimed by the government of the province of Quebec. The Cree, however, saw history differently; as far as they were concerned, they had never relinquished the aboriginal rights to their ancestral lands. Plans for an extensive hydroelectric power complex in their territory brought the matter to a head. Described in 1971 as the "project of the century" by Quebec's prime minister, Robert Bourassa, this vast hydroelectric complex was eventually to flood 15,519 square kilometers of northern Quebec's boreal forests and tundra, yet the Cree were not even asked whether they wanted such a scheme on their land. In 1973, they took legal action to stop the project. After a six-month trial, they won an injunction blocking construction. However, their legal success was short-lived; only a week later, the Quebec Court of Appeal overturned the decision. The Cree had no real option but negotiation, which culminated in the signing of the James Bay and Northern Quebec Agreement in 1975.[1]

Under the terms of the agreement, the Cree and some Inuit people relinquished their claims to Quebec's northern territories in return for $225 million in Canadian dollars, to be paid out over twenty years, and 14,000 square kilometers of native land reserves, with exclusive hunting rights over an additional 156,000 square kilometers.[2]

The 1975 James Bay Agreement and the subsequent 1984 Cree-Naskapi (of Quebec) Act enabled the Cree to break away from the administrative supervision of the federal government that they had been under for so long. It gave each of the Cree bands the power of self-government within the territory of its own reserve, generating optimism and initiative within the Cree communities. For the first time, many Cree felt that they had some control over their own destiny.

The Cree have also set up a number of organizations to meet their communities' needs, such as a construction company, a housing corporation, an arts and crafts association, and even an airline—Air Creebec—which now employs 300 people and brings in $30 million per year in revenues. The Cree also operate an outfitting and tourism association.

Most tourists who travel into the remote areas of northern Quebec are sport hunters and fishermen. I found that the Cree's attitude toward them varied. At one goose-hunting camp north of Chisasibi, where in the past wealthy southerners paid handsomely for the privilege of shooting migrating geese each spring and fall, I was told, "Only the Cree can hunt here now, and that is the way we want it to stay!" However, other communities took a different line. The chief of the Waswanipi

Band told me that his community welcomed white hunters. "We figure that they will probably come up here anyway. We provide a guiding and outfitting service that brings money into our community, and at the same time we are also able to keep an eye on the hunters. And believe me, some of those white hunters need watching!"

I found a similar attitude at Mistassini, the largest of the James Bay Cree communities. Each summer, the Cree operate three fly-in fishing camps for sport fishermen from the south. In Mistassini, which has a population of 2,800, it is estimated that 60 percent of the Cree families still depend primarily on hunting, trapping, and fishing for a livelihood, while a significant proportion of the wage earners hunt part-time.

Twenty-five years ago, Mistassini consisted of only two houses, a Hudson's Bay Company store, and a church. The Cree lived there only during the summer months, in tents along the lakeside, leaving each fall for their winter hunting grounds. But in the past few years, the Cree have adopted a more sedentary existence, mainly because they have found it increasingly harder to live off the land— particularly with the loss of market outlets for hunted and trapped furs. Today, Mistassini is a fast-growing community, with a new, well-equipped secondary school, an ice hockey arena, and extensive housing. A number of fledgling businesses have also been started by the Cree, including their own small airline, Waasheshkun (Clear Skies) Airways, which serves the Cree hunting camps and flies sport fishermen around in the summer.

In Mistassini and some of the other eight smaller Cree communities, both full-time and part-time hunters follow the annual cycle determined by the movements of the animals and the seasons, but it is only the full-time hunters who leave their villages each fall for the winter hunting and trapping season, which can last for six to nine months.

During this winter hunting period, the Cree are dispersed over 170,000 square kilometers of the James Bay territory. The region is divided into areas that are used by each of the Cree bands and then subdivided into individual or family hunting areas, known as traplines. These traplines vary in size from about 26,000 to 389,000 hectares.

Life at the camps on these traplines is a mixture of traditional and modern. Nowadays many Cree fly from their villages to their camps in chartered bush aircraft (not Air Creebec, which mostly operates larger aircraft)—not that there is anything very modern about the planes. They are mainly forty-year-old De Havilland Otter and Beaver models, often flown in classic seat-of-the-pants style by Cree bush pilots. For transportation on their traplines, the Cree use modern canoes until the lakes and rivers freeze over; then they use snowmobiles.

The Cree have built log cabins at some camps, but many spend the entire winter in canvas tents heated with small wood-burning stoves. They prepare and tan their own moose and caribou hides, using flensing tools and other traditional equipment that they make themselves. They also make some of their own hunting clothes, such as moccasins and mittens, as well as snowshoes and sleds, but they buy their parkas, earflap hats, rifles, and fishnets at local stores.

The Cree usually have little difficulty in providing enough "bush food" for their family's needs while they are out at their camps. Even if moose and caribou prove elusive, there is always an abundance of fish in the lakes to fall back on.

The trapping season begins in October, when the animal furs have reached peak winter condition, and continues until March. November is usually the best month. By then the lakes are frozen, and new snow on the land makes it easier for the Cree to observe the animals' movements. A hunter will usually set traps from a winter camp by following the hunting trails of predatory fur-bearing animals from one stream or lake to another, in a circuit that eventually leads back to the camp. Of the animals trapped for their fur, beaver is the most common, representing 65 percent of the average trapper's income from fur sales, but marten, lynx, mink, otter, muskrat, squirrel, and fox are also taken.

It was the arrival of the fur traders in the seventeenth century that made the trapping of fur-bearing animals important to the Cree. At that time, fine northern furs like marten, mink, otter, and fox were in great demand. Furs were a renewable resource that was easily transportable, and the traders saw the potential for making vast profits by selling the furs on the European and Far Eastern markets. The early fur traders saw the Cree and other North American Indians as a useful means of collecting fur. The Indians' knowledge of the land and their skill at catching animals far exceeded those of most white trappers. However, the fur traders viewed the Cree as both unpredictable and unreliable: they disappeared into the bush for months on end, roaming the boreal forests of northern Quebec and hunting in what appeared to whites to be a haphazard manner. In fact, it was anything but that.

These early traders lost little time in selling the Cree "white men's" goods, and the Cree regularly visited the trading posts with furs to sell. Some of the less scrupulous fur traders gave the Indians alcohol as an incentive to bring furs to trade.

Since these times, income from fur sales has played an important role in the

Cree's "bush economy," for it is one of the few sources of cash to buy necessary equipment and supplies and to pay for the general everyday expenses of hunting and trapping. In a good year, the average Cree family's income from furs may be around $6,000, but the value of the food they harvest from hunting, trapping, and fishing far exceeds that of the furs. Thus, the Cree hunt and trap today not only out of nostalgia but also out of need. Employment is hard to come by, making fur trapping one of the few options available to many Cree families who do not want to be dependent on government handouts.

Those who wish to pursue a traditional life of hunting and trapping are helped by the Income Security Program, a scheme whereby hunters can claim an income guarantee, other benefits, and material help. The income guarantee is calculated on the basis of the number of family dependents and the number of days that the hunter spends in the bush. For most Cree, it works out to less than $40 per day. This provides enough to get by on and supplements money earned from the sale of furs.

For the Cree, whose traplines are in remote parts of the interior, two-way radios are the only link with the outside world for months on end. The radios are used to communicate all kinds of information between the camps and the villages: the latest hunting stories, weather reports, even what has been happening in recent episodes of popular television soap operas. Listening in on bush radio can be very entertaining. On one occasion, a hunter excitedly announced, "A whole pile of geese have just landed right by our camp; I will let you know how many we get." A short while later, the same, but very subdued, voice said, "None."

By the end of May, most of the Cree hunters will have left their winter traplines and returned to the villages. Many take jobs during the summer months, often taking employment that utilizes their bush skills, such as guiding white sport hunters and fishermen or line cutting.

The days when the Hudson's Bay Company had a virtual monopoly on fur trading in James Bay are over. Today, most of the Cree market their fur through the Cree Trappers Association, which has an office in each of the villages in order to maintain contact with all of the bush camps. The association is also responsible for monitoring the trappers' catches so that if there is a decline in a particular species, they can take appropriate action. For example, although lynx are plentiful in some other areas of James Bay, their population in the Mistassini district has declined in recent years. The local branch of the Cree Trappers Association reduced the trapping season for lynx to two weeks in December to allow their numbers to increase again.

Nobody could dispute the fact that over the thousands of years that the Cree have occupied the vast northern areas of Quebec, they have looked after their environment. Their annual harvest of animals, birds, and fish has on the whole been less than the productivity of the species. This is borne out by consistent catches. I spent some time with a Cree trapper on his trapline approximately 320 kilometers north of Mistassini. He told me that he catches an average of thirty beaver per year and that the annual figure has remained constant for the past thirty years. Like most Cree, he uses his land rotationally, concentrating his hunting and trapping activities on half of the area one year and then resting it the next, to allow the animal populations to build up again. A respected hunter among the Cree is not one who goes in for big numbers but one who regularly produces consistent catches.

There would seem to be a natural incentive in any hunting culture to conserve game for future generations, but the real reason for the Cree's success in wildlife management may lie deeply rooted in their traditional beliefs. The Cree perceive animals as being like humans. They believe that animals have intelligence and character and that most have souls and spirits just as people do. The hunters believe that the animals they catch are a gift from Chuetenshu, the North Wind and lord of the animals, and from the animals themselves. Most animals, they believe, willingly give themselves to the hunter. These "gifts" place the hunter under an obligation to cause the animal no unnecessary suffering; to observe set procedures for retrieving, butchering, and disposing of the animal; and to utilize completely the flesh and other useful parts. With certain species that the Cree hunt, like bear, beaver, otter, and porcupine, there are restrictions on the eating of the meat; certain parts of the animal must be eaten only by men and other parts only by women. Failure to observe these procedures, the hunters believe, will result in punishment by either the North Wind, who can freeze them, or by the animals, who will no longer allow themselves to be caught.

From the Cree viewpoint, the animal's body feeds the hunter and the hunter's family, but the animal's spirit returns to be reborn. By sacrificing themselves, animals enable humans to live. Humans, in turn, by careful hunting, provide the conditions for the animal populations to survive; thus, when humans and animals are in balance, animals are killed but their numbers are not diminished, and in this way both humans and animals survive. The Cree see this process as not completely one-sided, for when humans die, their bodies also become food for other living things.

Many Cree have been converted to Christianity, but for them this is a surface religion that has become intertwined with their own long-held beliefs. Once when I was staying with a Cree family who were devout born-again Christians, the hunter's wife apologized to me for preparing a meal of otter for the third day running. Otter is not considered as good to eat as beaver or caribou. "We have to eat it all," she explained. "Otters are clever; they would know if we threw it out, and then we wouldn't catch any more. We have to show respect to the animals."

Many Cree still feel that their hunting culture is in jeopardy. They fear that campaigns by extreme animal rights groups could eventually bring a total collapse of fur prices, possibly causing some countries to impose import bans. Their fears would seem to be justified; 1992 saw fur prices tumble even further, with an average beaver skin at auction fetching only $13; marten, $40; lynx, $50; and fox, $7.[3]

One of the most ironic aspects of the fur-trapping controversy is that the Cree and the animal rights groups have something in common: they both share a deep love of animals.

"Even if furs were worth nothing, the Cree would continue to hunt and trap," Rick Cuciurean of the Cree Trappers Association told me. "They will just use the skins to make tents and sleeping mats. The main reason we hunt fur-bearing animals like the beaver, lynx, and otter is for food."

Anything that in any way harms or reduces the habitat of the animals they depend on is viewed by the Cree as a threat to their culture. Recently their traditional way of life has come under increasing pressure from a variety of sources, including industrial mining, clear-cutting of forests, and hydroelectric schemes that have gradually encroached on their land.

For example, the first phase of a hydroelectric development plan begun in 1973, the La Grande Project, involved the diversion of three great rivers—the Eastmain, the Caniapiscau, and the Opinaca—into La Grande Rivière. Reservoirs for the project's three power stations flooded nearly 10,000 square kilometers of forested land.

The second phase of hydroelectric development, known as James Bay II, was due to begin in 1990. It involves the damming of the Great Whale River and three smaller rivers, the Nottaway, the Broadback, and the Rupert. It is designed to produce more than 11,000 megawatts from reservoirs covering an area of 9,895 square kilometers, at a cost estimated to be in excess of $100 billion in Canadian dollars.[4]

A woman prepares dried fish caught by traditional methods and sold by a
fishing cooperative, Banc d'Arguin National Park, Mauritania.
Courtesy WWF/Meg Gawler.

Imraguen fishermen haul in the morning catch in Mauritania's Banc d'Arguin National Park. Courtesy Jacques Trotignon.

A temple painting commemorating Bisnoi women in India who were slaughtered while defending trees against cutting. The action of these women gave rise to the Chipko or "tree hugger" movement. Courtesy Peter Jackson.

A Bisnoi woman in India. She is part of a group of people whose strict
code of conservation does not permit them to cut trees or kill animals.
Courtesy Kailash Sankhala.

A shepherd on a camel in Rajasthan, India. Courtesy Peter Jackson.

Collecting melaleuca leaves in the buffer zone of Wasur National Park in Irian Jaya. The leaves are distilled into aromatic oil in the local village. Collection of melaleuca leaves is still a family activity, and all pitch in to help. Courtesy Michèle Bowe.

Vietnam's Con Dao Islands, one of the country's national parks. The islands are located off Vietnam's southeastern coast, in the South China Sea.
Courtesy WWF/Elizabeth Kemf.

A dolphin funeral in Vung Tau, gateway to Con Dao National Park. In South Vietnam, marine mammals are given human burials at some special temples dedicated to cetaceans. Courtesy WWF/Elizabeth Kemf.

Ho Hoang Son, a former inmate of the prison at Con Dao and former chief marine warden of the national park, shows how the reef off the main island is coming back to life. Courtesy Elizabeth Kemf.

Coral reefs were destroyed and smelted into lime to build "tiger cages" in Con Dao's prison. Courtesy Elizabeth Kemf.

The coral in Con Dao National Park is coming back to life after decades of
overexploitation mainly for prison construction. A ban on coral collection has
been in place for several years, but it is difficult to enforce.
Courtesy Elizabeth Kemf.

A Cree woman displays the skin of a beaver, the animal most commonly
trapped by the Cree for fur. The Cree Trappers Association monitors
the catches closely. Courtesy Bryan and Cherry Alexander.

A Cree Indian uses his boat to break his way through the ice.
Courtesy Bryan and Cherry Alexander.

A spillway and dam on the James Bay II hydroelectric
project, built by Hydro-Quebec on Cree territory.
Courtesy Bryan and Cherry Alexander.

A Kuna family making a necklace out of monkey's teeth; the man is drilling the teeth. Courtesy Victor Englebert.

The Khuldighar forest nursery project in the Annapurna Sanctuary was created to regreen Nepal. Courtesy Galen Rowell.

Mingma Norbu Sherpa, the first Sherpa park warden of Sagarmatha (Mount Everest) National Park in Nepal. Courtesy Hum B. Gurung.

A woman preparing traditional carpets (sold to tourists under ACAP patronage), Chandruk, Nepal. Courtesy WWF/Marco Pagliani.

New road to Bhotecdar, Marsyangdi River. Annapurna Conservation Area Project, Nepal. Courtesy WWF/Galen Rowell.

Braga village, Manang village, Annapurna Conservation Area Project, Nepal.
Courtesy WWF/Galen Rowell.

At a meeting held at Great Whale in March 1989, chiefs representing the region's nine Cree communities unanimously decided to oppose further hydroelectric development in the area. The Cree claimed that the government and Hydro-Quebec already were in breach of the James Bay Agreement and that James Bay II would be an "environmental catastrophe." An environmental and social impact assessment of the Great Whale River segment of the James Bay II project—sponsored by Hydro-Quebec and provincial and federal officials—was expected to be completed in early 1993.[5]

The first damaging environmental effects of hydroelectric development in the region began to emerge in the early 1980s. During the filling of La Grande Reservoir, scientists discovered that mercury levels in the region's freshwater fish were rising. Between 1982 and 1986, physicians found a twofold increase in mercury levels in the bodies of natives who ate fish caught in the region encompassed by the project. Now, two-thirds of the total Cree population, approximately 9,800 individuals, have mercury levels that exceed the World Health Organization's safe limits. The increase in mercury levels is due to the vast volume of rotting vegetation that lies submerged in the project's man-made reservoirs.[6]

Some environmental groups, especially the National Audubon Society in the United States, have publicized their belief that this huge hydroelectric project threatens the existence of millions of geese, ducks, and other migratory birds that arrive on the shores of James Bay each spring to breed. Naturalists have also expressed alarm that such a major alteration to the landscape could have a devastating effect on a whole range of animals, both land and marine based, from mice to moose. Since the flow of fresh water into James Bay during the winter months is likely to be ten times the normal amount, some biologists believe that James Bay's fish stocks, as well as sea mammals such as beluga whales, polar bears, and seals, will also be affected because they all depend largely on a saltwater habitat.

So far, the Cree's opposition to the project has been very successful in the courts. The Cree have hired consultants to perform energy analyses and lawyers to fight their legal battles. In May 1992, in neighboring New York State, Governor Mario Cuomo decided against signing a contract under which the state would have purchased $19.5 billion worth of electricity from Hydro-Quebec over a period of twenty years. Governor Cuomo concluded that the power was too expensive and that energy conservation measures and alternative energy sources within the state were sufficient to meet New York's needs in the near future. Utilities in Connecticut and Massachusetts made similar decisions.

"Advances were also made on other fronts," says environmental policy analyst Mercédès Lee of the National Audubon Society. "The state of New York has introduced legislation that would mandate a full environmental review of impacts of proposed hydroelectric facilities before renewing existing [contracts] or proceeding on any new contracts with Hydro-Quebec. Although the bill was unsuccessful in the first round, it sparked a wave of interest among legislators outside New York to propose similar legislation in other New England states.

"But the Cree and environmentalists have not been completely successful at stopping power imports to the U.S. from Quebec's James Bay. Despite public protest and court action in Vermont, the state decided in favor of signing a contract with Hydro-Quebec," adds Lee.[7]

The main question, "whether Hydro-Quebec has the right to develop without Cree consent," may not be resolved until the end of 1993 at the earliest. In the meantime, the Cree people will continue to try to manage their land—combining modern and traditional methods—as they have done for centuries, in a harmonious and sustainable way.

Grass Roots in a Himalayan Kingdom[1]

I remember seeing my first *shingi nawa*, or local forest guard, when I was a young boy. It was in my home village of Khunde, a small mountain settlement at an elevation of 3,810 meters on the south side of Mount Everest (called Sagarmatha in Nepali). One of my relatives in the village was caught cutting live branches from a tree in a nearby sacred forest. The local guard made him return the wood and confiscated his bamboo basket and *khukuri,* a knife that is used to cut wood. He was also assessed a fine in money and *chang,* a local beer, during a village meeting held three months later. Before my village and the ones nearby had ever heard about national parks or protected areas, they possessed a highly developed, locally regulated forest management system.

In the traditional system, a new *shingi nawa* was appointed each year on a rotating basis. In my hometown, there were four guards, selected by the community, with the power to enforce communal rules. Their duties included not only controlling the use of forest resources but also supervising grazing in specified pastures and moving cattle from summer grazing areas to villages and back (transhumance). The guards, who were farmers themselves, took their jobs very seriously and were highly respected. They had the right to fine people who committed serious offenses, such as the felling of many trees. These fines, collected at community meetings, consisted of both local beer and cash. The money and any confiscated items, such as my relative's *khukuri,* were used for community development, such as trail improvement or repair work on a *lha khang,* or communal chapel. The system was very effective for forest management in protected areas and controlled grazing areas. Regulations applied to everybody in the community and were successfully enforced.

During community meetings, the village elders and guards supplied details about the boundaries of protected forest areas and wood collection zones and dates for agricultural activities such as harvesting, hay making, leaf litter collection, and moving of livestock. All communities were expected to conform to these rules, which were of vital importance to all users of the common resources. All forests and grazing land belonged to the federal government, except for a few acres of cultivated land owned by individual households. In Nepal, land that is cultivated is privately owned. Everyone in my village and elsewhere depended on the forest for fuel, timber, fodder, hay, and leaf litter. Traditionally, the Sherpas (an ethnic group) in Khumbu herded yaks and cultivated seasonal crops such as potatoes, barley, and buckwheat. Supplementary income and food were obtained through exchange of goods with Tibet, using the Nangpa-la, a pass situated across the border from Nepal at an elevation of 5,486 meters.

The isolated and once-forgotten valleys of Mount Everest became known to the central government in Kathmandu and to the outside world through various mountaineering expeditions. In 1953, the late Tenzing Norgay and Sir Edmund Hillary, a New Zealander, were the first to climb Mount Everest—the world's highest mountain—and to open its gates to the mountaineering community. Since then, increasing tourism has seriously affected the forest cover and local economy. Important mountaineering expeditions need many local porters to carry their supplies from the lower valleys to the base of the mountains and higher up, requiring large quantities of firewood for cooking and heating. The problem of forest depletion due to increased tourism was further aggravated in 1974, when it became known that the government intended to establish Sagarmatha National Park. At the time, Sherpa guides had traveled with Western tourists in Royal Chitwan and Rara national parks, both of which were established in early 1973. Management rules in these parks were strictly enforced, and local people had been moved out by force and relocated elsewhere. The Sherpas became very worried and cut as many trees as they could for future use before Sagarmatha National Park was officially established in 1976, fearing that firewood cutting would not be allowed after that date. In the rush to cut and store as much firewood as possible, the authority of the *shingi nawas* was undermined. When the government of Nepal nationalized its forests in 1957, the traditional role of the *shingi nawas* was replaced and centralized by the federal government. Appointment of government forest guards overshadowed, and in most places eliminated, the *shingi nawas*.

Konch Chumbi, a well-known local leader, once told Sir Edmund Hillary: "You first opened our children's eyes [with education], but now you are blinding us with salt [taking away our land]." He was questioning Sir Edmund Hillary about the way in which Sagarmatha National Park had been established. Hillary listened to Chumbi's complaints, heeded his suggestions, and for years has been a special friend to the people of Nepal. His organization, the Himalayan Trust, has helped the Sherpas in building schools and hospitals and maintaining monasteries. I myself am a product of Hillary School in Khumjung; later, I became a Hillary Scholar, with the Himalayan Trust funding my secondary education. Over the years, Hillary, along with others, has become deeply concerned about negative environmental changes taking place in the Khumbu Valley, particularly deforestation, overgrazing, and uncontrolled tourism.

In 1974, I accompanied a feasibility study team to the Everest region led by P. H. C. Lucas (now chairman of IUCN's Commission on National Parks and Protected Areas). The team consisted of a forester, a Nepali ecologist, and a planner; I acted as translator. The mission organized a number of village meetings in the most populated areas to introduce the concept of national parks and to assess local concerns. These meetings were well attended, but most Sherpas expressed serious concern as to the continuance of their traditional rights. They were worried that they would be relocated outside the park, as had been done in Rara and Chitwan. The Sherpas particularly feared that they would lose access to local forests and grazing land, on which they depended for their livelihood. These fears were not alleviated during the initial survey meetings, and they were again expressed during later meetings with park administrators. I remember an elderly person who said: "They [the survey team] don't have to come and teach us to protect wildlife. They are here simply to tax us and take away our grazing lands."

The mission recommended a novel concept for establishment of protected areas in Nepal. The team suggested that the main villages in Sagarmatha National Park be legally excluded from the park, since national parks, by definition, could not have people living in them. This approach would establish the Sherpas' rights to remain in their homelands and would ensure their retaining control over their settlement areas, including fields and pastures. It was felt at the time that this would enable the Sherpas to remain in control of their future and choose their own paths of development rather than become museum specimens. Some parts of the park were recommended for strictly controlled wildlife zones; others were to be protected from excessive tourism and other negative influences. It was also recommended that the Sherpas be involved in the park's management by creation of a local advisory committee, which would participate in policy discussions.

Several local Sherpas were sent to New Zealand to be trained in park management. Three of us, who completed this course, were appointed as wardens and assistant wardens of Sagarmatha National Park by the Department of National Parks. We were in charge of the park's day-to-day administration through much of the 1980s. I thus became one of the first Sherpa park wardens in 1980.

In spite of these measures, the Sherpas did not trust the park authorities and continued to disapprove of the park's establishment, which came officially into effect in 1976. The government of New Zealand has had a long-standing commitment to the Himalayas ever since its most well known national, Sir Edmund Hillary, climbed Mount Everest forty years ago. Thus, the New Zealand government provided support, including infrastructure development, during the park's early stages. An excellent management plan was also drawn up by the New Zealand–trained park managers, taking into consideration local issues and tourism, but to date the plan has not been implemented. One reason why this has not yet occurred is that the local people were not involved as much as they would have liked in developing the management plan. Consequently, it is awaiting their endorsement.

The highest park on the "roof of the world" later became a World Heritage site in 1989 because of its unique scenery. It contains three of the ten highest peaks in the world, as well as many other mountains, and provides habitat for numerous plant and animal species, such as snow leopards, musk deer, Himalayan tahrs, and many birds. The area is also home to 3,000 Sherpas, whose subsistence traditionally depends on agriculture, cattle farming, and harvesting of forest resources, activities that are now being supplemented with income from tourism. Although the main settlement areas are not included in the park's jurisdiction, all traditional pastures and forests are administered by the park.

Because local people felt that the concept of the park had been imposed on them and that it had never been fully explained to them, they resented its creation. Thus, to enforce park regulations, the government brought in an armed contingent of sixty-five people, as well as thirty-five civil staff members. The regulations included a total ban on tree cutting and a requirement for official authorization to collect dead wood. This meant that the Sherpas could no longer cut down trees, as they were accustomed to doing, for fuel and timber. The regulation concerning collection of dead wood caused considerable friction between local people and the park staff. Construction materials, such as timber, had to be purchased from outside the park and carried up into the valleys by porters, at considerable cost. Tensions grew as other restrictive land use regulations were introduced.

After a considerable number of complaints from the Sherpas, the park's administration discarded the dead wood regulation and allowed some timber to be cut locally. This was limited, however, to three trees for construction and/or repair purposes, as most local houses require three roof beams. Royalties had to be paid to the park for each cut tree, which had to be marked by the park staff. The Sherpas resented these restrictions on their access to forests that they had used and managed for centuries. In some cases, the new park rules even undermined older and stricter local customs. Some villages, for example, had traditionally prohibited all tree cutting within their sacred forests, where even live branches were protected. These villagers discovered that park officials had authorized residents from other villages to cut down trees within their protected areas. The strong sense of communal forest ownership, with its traditional *shingi nawa,* became powerless in the face of armed guards and government regulations. Local elders in Khumjung Village estimated forest depletion to be twice as high in the first four years of the park's existence as it had been over the previous two decades. This was largely due to local resentment of park rules, as people cut down more firewood and timber than they needed in places where park regulations could not easily be enforced.

When I returned from New Zealand in June 1980 to become a warden in Sagarmatha National Park, I found relations extremely strained between local people and park managers. I also found myself in an uncomfortable position: I was supposed to uphold park rules, yet, being a local myself, I felt sympathetic toward local tradition. In no time at all, I managed to make many enemies among my relatives and friends. I also discovered that the advisory committee that had been formed several years before no longer existed. No other mechanism had been developed to involve local people in the park's management.

The first thing I did—being a Sherpa—was consult the head lamas of the two most prominent monasteries in the area, the *rimpoches* (reincarnated lamas) of Tengboche and Thami. They are regarded by the Sherpas as their spiritual and religious leaders. With the help of the two *rimpoches* and local village leaders, a new Park Advisory Committee was set up, which met twice a year to discuss local issues and concerns. I was able to contribute a small grant from the UNESCO World Heritage Fund to help repair monastery roofs and provide model forest nurseries. Funds from the Himalayan Trust were also used to plant trees in a fenced area, where they could not be damaged by cattle. For the first time, local people were involved in park activities and employed in its tree nurseries. The *rimpoches* were often called on to initiate plantation projects, since fences had been cut or removed by villagers to show their resentment of the park.

Restoring the *shingi nawa* system was my next step. I lived in my old home in Khunde, from which I would walk to my office in Namche Bazar, about 457 meters lower down. Living in Khunde enabled me to develop better relations with my neighbors. With support from local leaders and relatives, I initiated an unofficial *shingi nawa* system in my hometown in August 1980. Four guards were appointed and were authorized to confiscate axes and exact fines for illegal wood collection in protected forests. They were also to inform the park staff if a significant number of trees had been cut down. The *shingi nawas* received a monthly honorarium of 100 rupees (now equivalent to $2.00, but at the time worth considerably more) to compensate them for their time and as an incentive. At the end of the year, the money collected from fines was used for community work, such as repair of the village chapel and trail maintenance. In later years, the honoraria were increased, and the system spread to other villages.

This experimental, ad hoc approach to park management gave me an excellent opportunity to develop effective, locally based conservation initiatives in the Annapurna area (which has become a world model for integrated conservation and development projects under the auspices of ACAP, the Annapurna Conservation Area Project). When I left to continue my studies in Canada, my colleague Lhakpa Sherpa from Thami Village replaced me. He reinforced the local forest management system and used the advisory committee to inform the general public about park policy.

At present, the *shingi nawa* system is operative in every village in the park, and its importance has been recognized by the park administrators. It is being used in the park's daily management but has not yet been given legal standing.

Although the *shingi nawa* system seemed to be an appropriate park management tool, it must be recognized that the new system is not identical to the traditional one. The new system depends on the government officials who administer the park. However, the government does not take village management seriously and intervenes whenever possible. Until it adds a clause to the park act granting legal authority to village forest management and allowing the *shingi nawas* to function independently, local people will continue to regard the new institution as an outside agency and refuse to cooperate. As long as the *shingi nawas* depend on park officials, their function will remain nominal. This experience illustrates that integrating traditional land use practices into park management is a complex process and is not necessarily always successful.

However, significant changes in attitude have taken place in both government officials and local residents. The Sherpas feel that the forests are again their own, at least to a certain extent. This has increased their concern with the protection of forests and pastures. It is obvious that once again they consider the forests to be their own resources and responsibility. In many instances, poaching and illegal tree cutting had first been reported by local people to the park's nearest army post. At present, there is more cooperation and coordination among the villagers and the park. Reafforestation and education programs have been initiated in and around the park. Formerly, park wardens were recruited from Kathmandu, approximately 805 kilometers away, to administer the park. Today, local training programs are starting up, and more local residents are being hired as park guards and managers.

In July 1991, I returned to Namche Bazar to introduce another program, which addressed the park's trash problem. With a small grant from WWF, a revolving fund was set up to pay for operating costs. The Sherpas themselves formed the Khumbu Pollution Control Committee and launched cleanup campaigns throughout the trekking area, a development that would have been unthinkable only a decade before. To my surprise, a Sagarmatha park warden, Surya Pandey, not only supported the activities of the local committee but also cooperated with it to develop a coordinated regional plan for improving waste disposal and sanitation.

The Sagarmatha National Park experience demonstrates that local support is critical to the success of any enduring conservation achievement, especially in inhabited protected areas. Cooperation between park managers and local people is essential for overall ecosystem management. Winning the hearts and minds of local people in the early stages of protected area establishment is equally vital. The problems caused in the past by local resentment of Sagarmatha National Park prove how much is at stake if local support and confidence cannot be gained. In contrast, recently developed local enthusiasm and environmental initiatives serve to illustrate how greater accord and trust between protected area administrators and local residents can make all the difference in terms of conservation achievements.

GUILLERMO ARCHIBOLD & SHEILA DAVEY

Kuna Yala[1]
Protecting the San Blas of Panama

Earth is the great Mother, who offers nature everything she may need and maintains biological and cultural diversity from generation to generation.

GUILLERMO ARCHIBOLD, KUNA SPOKESMAN, 1992

The Kuna Indians of Central America believe that the spirits hang their clothes from the tops of the tallest trees. If they cut down those trees, the spirits will punish them. Disease—even death—could follow.

But the Kuna's respect for nature is founded on more than collective myth. They do not need scientists to tell them what happens when a tropical forest is cut down. They have seen it firsthand in their rain forest reserve on the northeastern coast of Panama.

The 321,159-hectare Indian reserve, known as Kuna Yala, was recognized by the Panamanian government in 1953 as an autonomous, self-governing region. Twenty years ago, Kuna Yala, located in Panama's San Blas District, was accessible only by light plane or boat. But in 1970 work began on El Llano-Carti Road, a new road from the Chepo Plain linking the Pan-American Highway to the coast at Carti. And with it came the cattle ranchers and the landless poor. Areas of the forest were cut and burned and replaced by crops. When the land became exhausted, it was sold or turned into pasture for cattle grazing. Before long, the once-lush tropical forests along the mountain ridge bordering the Kuna reserve had been decimated. The result was a surge in poaching and increasing plunder of forest products from the Kuna lands on the Atlantic side of the mountain ridge.

The climate along the top of the San Blas mountain range (Cordillera de San Blas) is cold and humid, while the coast and lowland areas are humid and warm. As a result, the vegetation is dense and varied and there is a wealth of fauna, both in the sea and on land. The forests shelter a wide variety of bird life, including toucans, hummingbirds, hawks, eagles, curassows, and parakeets. Coral snakes, rattlesnakes, the fer-de-lance, iguanas, and chameleons live in the foliage. Howler monkeys and sloths swing through the trees, while jaguars, pumas, and ocelots lurk in the shadows. Elsewhere, the waters of six rivers are inhabited by caimans, turtles, frogs, and toads. There are also some fifteen species of freshwater fish, which are an important source of protein for the Kuna. Offshore in the crystal-clear waters abound sea turtles, lobsters, shrimp, and sea cucumbers.

The Kuna farm in plots along the narrow coastal strip and live offshore on a network of tiny coral islands, from which they fish in the rich offshore waters along the coral reef. The islands of the Archipiélago de San Blas stretch from Punta de San Blas (east of the Panama Canal) to the northern coast of Colombia. Although many of the Kuna people still live in traditional villages, others now have plumbing, electricity, health centers, and even government offices at hand. On their mainland garden plots they grow bananas, sweet manioc, yams, corn, and other crops.

The Kuna people knew only too well what would happen if deforestation were allowed to continue beyond the ridge of the San Blas Mountains and encroach on their lands. Drinking water supplies would dry up, and soil would be washed down the coastal slopes once there was no vegetation to hold it in place. Kuna farming plots along the shoreline would be the first to suffer. But increasing siltation in coastal waters would eventually bury the offshore coral reefs and destroy the fishery on which the Kuna depend. Not only their way of life but also their survival would be at risk.

Fully aware that their government was actively encouraging colonization of "unused" tracts of rain forest, the Kuna set up an agricultural project in 1975 along the threatened boundary of their territory to demonstrate that their land was not up for grabs. The agricultural experiment was established at Udirbi, the place where the new road entered the region. It was run by a group of volunteers from the Association of Kuna Employees (AKE). The earliest crops were cassava, corn, bananas, and sweet potatoes. When these proved unsuccessful, they tried perennials such as coffee, cacao, cashew, and peach palm. But all succumbed to the rain and cold that are characteristic of the area.

After efforts to raise pigs, chickens, and cattle also failed, the AKE consulted international forestry experts on more effective ways of securing a permanent presence along the mountain range in order to maintain the integrity of their lands. The outcome was PEMASKY, the Management Project for the Forested Areas of Kuna Yala. Mapped out by a joint team of Kuna experts, representative Kuna leaders, international scientists, and technicians, the project is headed by the AKE. Its key aim is to protect natural resources and tropical ecosystems while ensuring that the resources are used sustainably for the benefit of the Kuna people. The project also aims to encourage the development of ecotourism, traditional Kuna crafts, environmental education, and scientific research. Underpinning all of this is a desire to maintain the cultural values of the indigenous Kuna people.

PEMASKY was launched in 1983 with technical assistance from the Tropical Agronomic Center for Research and Education (CATIE) and financial backing from the United States Agency for International Development (USAID). Since then, funding and technical assistance have been provided by a variety of international organizations and institutes, including the Inter-American Foundation (IAF), WWF-US, the Smithsonian Tropical Research Institute, the Tropical Scientific Center, and the John D. and Catherine T. MacArthur Foundation, as well as by governments.

When the project first got under way, a group of Kuna technical experts undertook a program of research and management planning for the forested areas of Kuna Yala. On their recommendation, the area is now managed as a biosphere reserve and divided into a number of management zones on the basis of shared ecological features. Although Kuna Yala is not officially recognized as a biosphere reserve, it is managed along these lines.

The management plan for Kuna Yala defines five separate management zones. There is a Nature Zone (Neg Serret), where only the gathering of medicinal plants is permitted, and a Recovery Zone (Zona de Recuperación), where degraded natural areas are being left to regenerate. The Kuna live, fish, and grow their crops inside the Land and Marine Cultivation Zone (Zona Cultural); a separate area, the Special Zone (Zona Especial), has been set aside for public use, administration of the biosphere reserve, and the sustainable use of natural resources. Meanwhile, a Buffer Zone (Zona de Amortiguamiento) has been established outside the boundaries of the reserve in an area that is under the administration of the state government.

An early priority was the demarcation of a 120-kilometer boundary along the ridge of the San Blas Mountains. The boundary of the Kuna reserve had never been precisely marked because the area had always been densely forested. The work, which took several years to complete, involved cutting a trail along the mountain ridge.

From the outset, the Kuna professionals and technicians were determined to participate as equal partners in the scientific research program and in the planning of resource management. A standard feature of the project is the participation of a Kuna coresearcher in all areas of research. The result has been a genuine two-way exchange of knowledge between two very different cultures.

The Kuna learned this at an early stage, when the opening of the rough track of El Llano-Carti Road in 1972 brought to the area not only would-be settlers but also botanists. Among the region's rich flora, the botanists "discovered" about twenty new species and two new classifications of plants (*Sanblasia* and *Reldia*). But they shared none of these discoveries with the Kuna people. Had they bothered to consult the Kuna, they would have found that many of these species not only were well known but also had been in use as herbal medicines for hundreds of years. The plants include a spiky vine that the botanists called *Randia pepformis*. The Kuna call this plant *akepandup* and use it to cure a wide variety of illnesses. Meanwhile, until 1985 botanists believed that the plant known to the Kuna as *sapi garda*—which they believe can help improve intelligence—was not to be found outside Brazil.

In 1977, scientists "discovered" a tree, which they called *Tachigalia versicolor*. This tree, known to the Kuna as *irasgui,* flowers and fruits only once and then dies. The Kuna will not use the tree, believing that either the person who takes it or his or her offspring will meet with an early death.

The Kuna have extensive knowledge of an entire range of plants that they use for medicinal purposes. These include the *mutu wala* tree, whose bark is used to heal skin infections and prevent diarrhea, and the *guinor* tree, whose bark is cooked in water and used to increase hemoglobin in the blood.

Within the Nature Zone (Neg Serret) of the biosphere reserve, the Kuna recognize a number of sanctuaries—sacred sites (*kalu*) where they believe that the forest spirits are at peace with the environment. They refuse to cultivate these areas for fear of retribution from angry spirits, but they do allow the gathering of plants for medicinal purposes.

Kuna Yala sounds like paradise—and in many ways, it is: a land of lush tropical rain forest, fertile soil, fish-rich coral reefs, and palm-fringed islands, under the guardianship of a resourceful and determined community with a deep spiritual respect for nature. But how long can it last? Western influences and socioeconomic pressure from within already threaten the Kuna way of life.

Population growth is placing increasing strains on once-abundant natural resources. Traditional farming methods and sustainable use of forest resources can support only a small population. With more than 30,000 mouths to feed today, that resource base is no longer sufficient to meet growing demands. The general management plan for Kuna Yala addresses this problem, but action is currently restricted by a shortage of both funds and personnel. Steve Cornelius of WWF-US says that there is now some concern about current land use and fishery practices in Kuna Yala. "Over the past decade, there has been disturbing evidence of a deterioration in the quality and quantity of terrestrial and marine resources in Kuna Yala," he said. "Poor agricultural and fishery practices have replaced traditional techniques and customs."

Although the Kuna people have so far largely succeeded in maintaining their cultural identity, these ties are steadily being eroded as more and more young people drift away in search of better opportunities in Panama City. Some become professionals and return to Kuna Yala; others are lost forever to the city. The Kuna believe that Western-style education is partly to blame. Most Kuna communities have primary schools, and there are high schools in the six principal communities. The Kuna recognize the importance of Western education, but they see it as a mixed blessing. It prepares them well to face the outside world, but they are taught Spanish and the culture of white people at the expense of their own traditions. They begin to lose their Kuna identity. Cornelius maintains that this is a further threat to the Kuna's symbiotic relationship with the environment. "There has been a marked cultural memory loss," he says, "caused by the migration of Kuna to urban centers and the school curricula's failure to address cultural links to environmental conservation."

Uncontrolled tourism is another problem. Thousands of tourists visit Kuna Yala each year, drawn to its beautiful beaches and coral islands. They buy local crafts and services and help the Kuna economy, but at the same time they place increasing pressure on resources and create new sources of pollution. The original management plan included the development of ecotourism—carefully controlled so that it would not damage the fragile ecosystem. But this project, like many others, has been delayed through lack of funds.

The new cash economy is today based less on traditional group work and cooperation and increasingly on the individual pursuit of money to buy food and consumer goods. And it has inevitably brought a drop in standards in certain areas. The Kuna women established a cooperative that sells traditional embroidery (*molas*) for the tourist and export markets. As the volume of production increased to meet growing demand, the craft standards of the *molas* fell. Craft courses have now been organized to help the women maintain the quality of their products and with it their respect for local traditions and culture. Elsewhere, courses and workshops are held on nature tourism, wildlands management, and training of forest rangers. The aim is to ensure that the PEMASKY project always remains in the hands of well-trained Kuna people.

A major problem for PEMASKY is the need to secure external funding. During the initial phase of the project, there was no shortage of funds from international organizations and private foundations to develop infrastructure and to get the project under way. Now, almost ten years later, there is a lack of funds for specific programs such as agroforestry and ecotourism development. And there is no money to carry out much-needed socioeconomic research to find out to what extent the needs of the Kuna people have changed over the past decade.

But the largest threat to the PEMASKY experiment remains the many Panamanian economists and politicians who want to rescind the protected status of Kuna Yala and throw it open to the landless poor. The problem is that by opening the door to paradise and throwing away the key, they will guarantee its destruction and the end of the Kuna way of life. Leonidas Valdez, second general chief of Kuna Yala, has no illusions about what that would mean for his people. "If we were to lose these lands," he says, "there would be no culture, and there would be no people."

PART TWO

Boundaries and Bloodlines

Boundaries and Bloodlines
Tenure of Indigenous Homelands and Protected Areas

"Possession is nine-tenths of the law."

The pub in the Grand Hotel on Thursday Island usually does a brisk trade. But on the evening of June 2, 1992, things were quiet. Torres Strait Islanders were recuperating between big events—their annual Cultural Festival and the upcoming Island of Origin rugby matches. No one was prepared for the next day's headlines: "Island Wins Land Rights"; "*Mabo* Victory Means Treaty Now"; "*Terra Nullius* Is Dead."

What happened is that *terra nullius* ("land belonging to no one"), cryptic legalese for the fiction that pre-European Australia had been an empty, unoccupied continent, was thrown out by Australia's High Court. The unprecedented ruling, dubbed the *Mabo* case, or just *Mabo* (for one of the original Torres Strait Islander plaintiffs, Eddie Koiki Mabo, who died shortly before the decision was handed down), is clearing the way for national land rights across Australia. The *Mabo* decision is the culmination of a ten-year battle by members of the Meriam community, who claim that their rights to 9 square kilometers of islands in Torres Strait—a narrow body of water separating Papua New Guinea and Australia—had never been extinguished when the area was annexed by Queensland in the late 1870s.

In ruling that the Meriam people were entitled "as against the whole world, to possession, occupation, use and enjoyment of the lands of the Murray Island [part of the Torres Strait]," the High Court found that a form of communal title, or "native title," was recognizable under Australian common law and constituted a burden on the radical title of the Crown. Murray Island, 200 kilometers northeast of Thursday Island, is the administrative hub of Torres Strait.

As one of the lawyers in the case put it, the *Mabo* decision helps pull Australia out of the Dark Ages and into the company of progressive countries, including Amazonian nations as well as the United States, Canada, and New Zealand, where similar legislative and judicial processes to restore native title have been put into place. For example, in 1989, the government of Colombia returned nearly 25 percent of the country to its indigenous people (see "Aluna: The Place Where the Mother Was Born" in part three), and in neighboring Venezuela and Brazil, the Yanomami and other Amerindians have regained—after 500 years—partial rights over 17.6 million hectares of the Amazon. In 1991, Venezuela created the Alto Orinoco Biosphere Reserve in order to protect a vast tract of virgin rain forest and to safeguard the survival of the Yanomami and Yekuna people who have lived there for millennia. Land rights for the indigenous people on the Venezuelan side of the border are more advantageous for the Yanomami than on the Brazilian side, where the government retains control over mineral exploitation. Thousands of gold miners still invade the Yanomami reserve despite a presidential decree announced in November 1992. Brazilian anthropologist Alcida Rita Ramos, who has struggled alongside the Yanomami for more than twenty years to create the park (see "Paradise Gained or Lost?"), describes the "long and winding" road from 1968 to the present—and the treacherous path that lies ahead unless the Yanomami gain full control over their land.

"In the past ten years, the theory and practice of protected areas have undergone a remarkable change," says James Morrison, a Canadian legal and historical researcher. Some of the most innovative changes have been in Alaska, in the Gates of the Arctic National Park and Preserve, and in Australia, the latter of which are broadly similar to changes made in Canada.

In Canada's far north, for example, the federal government has been negotiating for the past twenty years with various native organizations over land claims. In 1984, a settlement was reached with the Inuit of the western Arctic, or the Inuvialuit. The terms of this agreement included establishment of the Inuvialuit Game Council (IGC) and the Inuvialuit Regional Corporation (IRC). In July 1992, the IGC, the IRC, the Northwest Territories government, and Canada reached an agreement to establish a national park on Banks Island. Under the terms of this agreement, the Inuvialuit obtain exclusive rights to harvest wildlife in the park, their fishing is given priority over sport angling, and they will have the power to screen archaeological research. In addition, the Inuvialuit will be involved in the drafting of the park's guidelines and management plan, and their traditional knowledge will be drawn upon for both planning and research. The agreement also provides guarantees for employment and training and other economic advantages, such as priority in contracts and business licenses.[1]

In November 1992, the Inuit of the eastern Arctic and subarctic region ratified the largest land claim agreement in Canadian history, covering one-fifth of the country. The landmark agreement will resolve land claims and lead to the establishment of a Nunavut territory, encompassing a huge chunk of the Arctic. The Territory of Nunavut (which means "our land" in the Inuit language, Inukitut) gives the Inuit direct control over 90.7 million hectares of land, including subsurface mineral rights on 9.3 million hectares.[2] The agreement also provides for the creation of three national parks, at Auyuittuq, North Baffin, and Ellsmere. According to Morrison, it was the Inuit themselves who pushed for the creation of these protected areas. Like the Inuvialuit settlement, this agreement also contains specific provisions for native employment and preferential hiring and training ($14 million in Canadian dollars) as well as schemes for management of adjacent areas, so as to reinforce park and Inuit values. The agreement contains one unique clause, however, which stipulates that an Inuit impact-benefit agreement will have to be negotiated prior to the establishment of any national park. This ensures that Inuit rights will be respected in both park planning and park management.[3]

These land claim agreements, from the Amazon to the Arctic—many of which call for creation of protected areas for both people and nature—have occurred on the eve of the United Nations' International Year for the World's Indigenous People, 1993. In Australia, the impact of *Mabo* is taking a while to sink in. It may not be the watershed in black-white relations longed for by many. It may be a bit premature to say that the event is the equivalent of replacing the Union Jack on the Australian flag with the aboriginal sun symbol. Many Islanders, as well as government officials, had simply forgotten about the case—it dragged on for ten years.

Crown solicitors and aboriginal legal services are debating how the justices' findings and qualifications about native title may apply to current permits for mining and pastoral leases and to the ownership status of tidal lands and fisheries. A host of intricate riders were attached to the decision, prompting accusations that the Court gave an inch but took another mile. There are many loose ends that may require more High Court tests for clarification. *Mabo* has rich and powerful detractors. Indeed, the federal opposition's aboriginal policy refuses to countenance any special status or rights for indigenous communities.

In the end, *Mabo* is not a trial of sovereignty, which would have gone to the heart of Australia's legal status as a settled colony, but is about property, especially land; the scope of government power to define what does and does not extinguish native title by law; and which rights are valid and which are not. Meanwhile, the chairman of the Northern Land Council, Galarrwuy Yunupingu, insists that a treaty is now a "must-do" situation. He contends that the federal government must move quickly to negotiate a treaty and implement comprehensive national land rights or it will face a barrage of costly litigation from indigenous groups all over Australia.

The *Mabo* case has fairly straightforward implications for protected area management in Australia. The High Court suggests that the mere circumscribing of land as a national park does not exclude native title. Therefore, many areas in Queensland, in northeastern Australia, for example, set aside for national parks may be available for claims by indigenous communities, providing that continuity of their traditional ownership can be proven. Previously, Murray Islanders had no voice in managing their home reefs, fisheries, and other resources, which are encapsulated in the Torres Strait Protected Zone. From now on, they will be more in control of development of their land, their destiny. Eventually, the terms of the Torres Strait Treaty and management of the protected zone may have to be renegotiated. Under the treaty, which established the Torres Strait Protected Zone between Australia's Cape York Peninsula and Papua New Guinea, local fishing rights were protected. It is a treaty that is supposed to favor the traditional inhabitants.

At a glance, the chain of events affecting a tiny, distant island between Australia and Papua New Guinea might seem to have little relevance to an international anthology concerning people and protected areas. Yet the aftermath of *Mabo* foreshadows the shape of things to come in the changing relationship between indigenous people and protected areas internationally.

The point is that *Mabo* is about social justice, about reforming the social order of things. Above all, it is concerned with clarifying tenure, sorting out who owns resources and who has the right to control what goes on inside a vast territory of reefs, seas, and islands. Tenure considerations such as these are not about nature conservation per se, but increasingly they overflow into it. Conservationists have come to accept the importance to Western science of traditional environmental knowledge. Protected area policymakers and managers, however, must become more aware of the underlying tenure systems that connect indigenous peoples to their resource bases, helping to sustain subsistence and reproduce social relations. The native title recognized in the *Mabo* case affirms indigenous peoples' special relationship to the land, something that tends to be qualitatively different from the Western tradition of private or state ownership.

Significantly, the High Court took pains to clarify native title as a "community title." Ownership rights were not vested in individuals. The whole of the Murray Island community together enjoys this title. Native title arises out of ancient traditions and customs. It does not come from introduced British law. *Mabo* says, Go to your own customs and your own traditions, and that is where you will find the rules. Native title carries great flexibility in allowing a community to define itself and to control what it does with its land.

Increasingly, the type of communal tenure systems that native title acknowledges on Murray Island are regarded as conservation assets. Certain forms of communal tenure have pronounced self-management and self-regulating features that are adaptive to local environments.

The *Mabo* case may also transform indigenous peoples' relationship to the state. A key element in setting tenure policies for the management of resources used in common is the appropriate balance of local community control and state or public control. Development agencies often dismiss customary tenure as something that gets in the way of national priorities, something that holds back investors and progress. Many analysts attribute overuse and degradation of rangelands, forests, and fisheries to a breakdown of systems of local control, caused in part by usurpation of local rights and management by state agencies. They advocate the return of management authority to local people and institutions.

Mabo sends a strong signal to both governments and conservationists who desire closer cooperation with indigenous groups in managing resource commons, which frequently coincide with ancestral lands: the premise on which future partnerships must be founded is support for land rights.

In many cases, future negotiations over the establishment and operation of protected areas of all kinds, where indigenous homelands are affected, will have to take place in the context of campaigns for self-determination and self-government. It is unlikely that vague appeals for greater community participation or community-based management will succeed if they gloss over basic tenure issues. By the same token, indigenous groups are less and less inclined to entrust regulation of their ancestral domains to outside experts and management agencies. They see themselves as increasingly capable of setting policy, managing resources, and policing the environment.

The *Mabo* case illustrates another point about the nature and extent of indigenous tenure systems. The Meriam people also claimed extensive sea rights. For reasons too convoluted to elaborate here, this part of their case was ultimately unsuccessful. However, the Meriam have long practiced sea tenure, as do other Torres Strait Islanders and most of their Melanesian neighbors. In fact, in a great many Pacific island societies, land above water and land covered by fresh water or seawater are one and undivided, linked by an act of creation—albeit with some form of seaward limit, often the outer edge of the outermost coral reef or a point on the horizon where sky and sea meet. Similarly, boundaries of aboriginal ancestral estates do not abruptly end at the water line. They often include vast intertidal zones, inshore marine areas, and offshore islands.

The adequacy of official tenure arrangements and policies for protected areas, and the status of customary tenure within them, was a central theme at the People and Protected Areas Workshop at the IUCN's Fourth World Congress on National Parks and Protected Areas in Caracas, Venezuela, in 1992. Indigenous peoples are at a crossroads in relation to conservation initiatives. Clearly, efforts like *Mabo* to secure tenure and to control ancestral resources and territory will continue as a paramount issue for many indigenous groups well into the 1990s and beyond, taking precedence over strictly conservation needs.

On the one hand, there are grounds for optimism that new links and partnerships can be created—new opportunities for dialogue and cooperation to help sustain biodiversity. Some conservation programs embrace indigenous land rights in principle (the Australian Conservation Foundation, for example). But on this point, there is a wide gap between ideals and practice. Vast confusion and conflict still exist over state versus local customs, laws, and jurisdictions in controlling protected areas. In some places, conservation activities threaten to trigger a new wave of colonialism that would deny indigenous rights in the name of nature conservation, wilderness values, and universal patrimony.

On the other hand, if better working relationships between environmental and indigenous groups and between states and their indigenous communities are to develop, conservation policies need to be in tune with the shifting politics and expanded aspirations of indigenous peoples.

A better grasp of the essentials of customary tenure systems, when they occur, how they evolve, and how they work is provided in part two of this book, comparing indigenous tenure issues in different regions. The narratives focus on salient themes emerging from the Caracas Congress: some of the conservation area management and legal implications of indigenous tenure; problems created by insufficient recognition of customary tenure when protected areas are sited, zoned, and implemented in indigenous homelands; and suggestions to improve cooperation among indigenous groups, conservationists, and governments in environmental management. In this connection, Annette Lees' chapter examines opportunities and problems for increased landowner involvement in sustainable forestry, while John Cordell's chapter analyzes the political economy of two of Australia's best-known protected areas, Uluru and Kakadu, deconstructing some of the dynamics of indigenous involvement that are not well known outside Australia. Some further repercussions of the *Mabo* case are also taken up.

Native title is an uphill battle today, in part because of belated recognition of the value of traditional tenure customs but also because historically Western courts have doubted whether property rights can evolve at all in indigenous hunting, gathering, and fishing societies. It has been taken as virtually axiomatic that common property could not be owned and managed by anyone except the state or the Crown. Hunters and fishermen and people living in horticultural societies could not produce those magic pieces of paper that Western courts like to see verifying title, boundaries, transactions, improvements, and exclusion of outsiders, that is, proof of possession.

Among the principal recommendations put to the Caracas Congress is a series of proposals concerning the pivotal role that indigenous and customary tenure may play in sustaining protected areas. The People and Protected Areas Workshop endorsed the principle that IUCN should support indigenous peoples' and other traditional communities' own tenure-based resource management strategies and, further, that the Commission on National Parks and Protected Areas (CNPPA) should create a task force to explore the key relationship between property rights and protected areas, focusing particularly on ways to strengthen communal tenure, as applied to both land and marine areas.

Second, protected area authorities interested in translating the Caracas recommendations into practice must be equipped to deal with complex issues of indigenous cultural representation and control of cultural resource information. Who can speak for customs and traditions? Who are the experts and the authorities on tenure in indigenous societies? Much writing and work in this area still defers to governments or nonlocal specialists to define what is the norm and what is and is not "traditional." But this is rapidly changing. In the 1990s, indigenous groups themselves are determining and negotiating their bloodlines and boundaries and representing themselves and their cultures in their own voices and meanings. They are less and less inclined to surrender natural resource information, or to entrust regulation of ancestral areas and resources, to outside experts and agencies. Communities have little desire to engage in perfunctory consultation, but they welcome projects that empower and build local capacity and transfer culture and scientific knowledge back home.

My final concern might be termed the "perils of romanticism." Has there ever been a society in harmony with the land? Indigenous societies probably were and are neither significantly better nor worse than European societies at preserving their environments. Many species of plants and animals suffered extinction at the hands of Pacific island cultures, for example, before colonists ever sailed over the horizon. So the traditional tenure systems at issue here, which have come down through the ages, are not panaceas for environmental degradation; they are not formulas for maintaining communities in some ideal state of isolation and equilibrium with their lands. They are not the ancient customs that once existed. Indigenous tenure systems operate today in vastly different economic and political settings than in the past. The growth and movement of population are major factors. Land inheritance principles differ markedly in terms of their effect between a population that is static and stationary and one that is rapidly growing and moving.

Passages from the chapters that follow suggest that protected area managers and indigenous peoples are on the threshold of a new era as far as achieving better communication and coordinating their respective aims. The challenge for all those involved in the various ends of this intriguing business is to blend a sensitivity to social justice concerns with a critical perspective on the environmental management potentials of indigenous tenure and other living customs today.

Melanesia's Sacred Inheritance

At the top of Nggatokae Island we stand in clouds, knee-deep in moss, among the special tree species that find their home in the damp, cool forests of the mountain-tops of the Solomon Islands. Nggatokae is an old volcano, and from its broken peak, through gaps in the clouds, we can see down to the sea, to the island-studded Marovo Lagoon. The Melanesians from the coastal village of Penjuku who lead us up Nggatokae point out the boundaries of their land. "From that ridge to the river and then to the sea," they tell us, "that's our forest." These boundaries are marked by stones hidden by their ancestors, by totem trees planted several generations previously, and by the villagers' legends of the dispersal of their people following the emergence of the first couple from the rocks of the volcano peaks, an event misted over by distance in time and mythology. This land is its people's sacred inheritance, as are its resources of timber, animals, plants, and soil. It has been fought for through interclan warfare; generations of its owners are buried in its soil or have their bones hidden in hollow trees in the forest. Land here is the cornerstone of culture and survival.

After a snack of cold cooked taro and sweet potato, we begin the four-hour walk back to the village. As we descend to the warm lower flanks of the volcano, we leave behind the moss-encased cloud forest and enter a tall tropical lowland forest with its profusion of vines and epiphytes. Our village-scientist guides pause frequently to point out useful plants—a vine shoot good for a fish lure, a sapling that can be used as a spear, a nut that glues shell to wood, a palm that burns like a candle, leaves that yield potent painkillers.

We approach the village and pass through clearings made in the forest for food gardens. Some areas, gardened for several years, have been abandoned and are returning to forest, although fruits and nuts will still be harvested here. Women are working in the gardens, slashing growth with heavy bush knives and gathering taro and greens for the evening meal. Penjuku is sited just above a white sand beach on the lagoon, and when we emerge from the gardened land behind the village, we can see men and women returning from fishing in their small dugout canoes.

After dark, the main meal of the day arrives in our leaf-thatched guest house. On a mat of fresh banana leaves, women lay down food from their gardens and the sea: fish baked in coconut milk; leafy native greens; small, sweet reef fish cooked with mangrove fruit; and a baked wild nut dish. We wash it down with fresh lime juice and stream water. It is an evening meal that many families will be sharing across the country, in a land where 70 percent of the population are subsistence gardeners and fishermen.

After we have eaten, the small community begins to assemble in our guest house for a meeting. The meeting will discuss forest issues, development, conservation, health, education, religion, and economics. We settle in for a long night. Light from the kerosene lanterns flickers over the faces of the assembling families, and beyond the thatch wall of the house I can hear the sound of a tropical Pacific night—waves on the shore, a breeze shuffling in palms, squeaking bats.

In the course of a three-month forest survey in the Solomon Islands, our team of biologists and indigenous community leaders had participated in many meetings in villages like this all over the country. We were investigating potential sites for protected forest areas in the Solomon Islands. Despite the global importance of the Solomons for their unique and diverse biology, none of their forests is in an effective protected area.

The Solomon Islands are a double chain of islands that extend eastward from Papua New Guinea into the South Pacific. There are six main islands, each roughly 5,000 square kilometers in size, and many hundreds of smaller islands, including live volcanoes and tiny atolls. The bulk of land on the larger islands is still forested. In these forests, isolated across the islands of the archipelago, a fauna has evolved that is remarkable for its degree of speciation. There are 163 native forest birds in the Solomons, ranging in size from the world's smallest parrot to the magnificent giant-winged Solomon's sea eagle. Close to half of the land birds that breed in the Solomons are unique to the country. Similarly, the mammal fauna, which includes both the largest and the smallest flying foxes in the world, is one of the most diverse and endemic to be found in any oceanic island biome.

The Solomon Islands have been occupied for more than 5,000 years by Melanesians, who still rely greatly on gardening and fishing for their subsistence life-style. Most people live in scattered villages of fewer than fifty people on islands where there are few roads and transportation is usually by canoe or by foot (*go bae leg* in local Pidgin English). Among the population of 285,000 people, there is an increasing urgency for development—a desire to end the epidemic levels of malaria, to bring education to a people of whom 40 percent over the age of ten have never been to school, to make life in general easier and less risky.

We heard repeated stories of this desire for change in every village we visited during our survey. And to finance this dream, there is one asset that the villagers own which is easily salable—their forests. At the evening meeting in Penjuku, we heard from landowners who were logging their forests themselves, using chain saws. Logs are carted from the forests to the sea and then barged over to a mill on a neighboring island. It is hard work, but it earns cash for their families. "If we had a road, we could reach more trees," they told us. "We've already cut most of the easy forest."

We are told about an international logging company that is about to start a large-scale logging operation across the lagoon, and a discussion begins about the likely impact of that. Some of the village residents are concerned about what will happen to the reef that they fish from. Others argue that with cash from the logging company, people will no longer have to bother with fishing, and the village store will be stocked with canned food, which they will then be able to afford. There is a general understanding about why landowners might want to sell out to a big logging company. It is centered on the desire for cash.

The discussion at Penjuku was echoed in other villages we visited. Most communities want a church, a school, and houses built of timber rather than thatching or bamboo. They want piped water supplies and a well-stocked health clinic. Most yearn for a road to link their village to others and some form of transportation to use it, and an industry to bring continued employment. Individuals talked of their interest in buying fiberglass canoes, which are safer than their wooden dugouts. They want outboard motors, agricultural tools, and a village store full of rice, crackers, and chocolate drink. Younger people told us of their plans for attending one of the few public secondary schools and how that would be impossible without money for school fees and board.

For many villages we visited, the only opportunity to achieve all this is through the sale of trees to logging companies. The government is severely restricted by a developing, and struggling, economy and is unlikely to offer much immediate help to the 3,000 villages in the country. For village residents, forests are their investment accounts, and many have decided that it is time to cash them in. Community knowledge of the natural world and landowners' current dependence on it is frequently not enough to bar the way to change. Nor is an understanding of the environmental impacts of logging or concern about the trustworthiness of swift-talking forest company negotiators. Village residents described to us a determined and clear vision of their future, and leaving behind a total dependence on their fishing, gardening, and hunting skills is part of that future.

On a countrywide scale, the drive for development, coupled with one of the world's fastest rates of population growth and the insatiable appetite of logging companies, is painting a troubling future for the forests and wildlife of the Solomon Islands. The accessible lowland forests are expected to be logged out within a decade or two, causing problems for the animals dependent on these forests for habitat. Overhunting has already resulted in local extinctions of some prized bird species; overcutting of carving timbers such as ebony has led to the loss of these species from the forests close to villages that depend on them for souvenir production.

For several years now, there has been recognition that some forests should be set aside from development, protected to ensure the survival of the unique forest life of the Solomon Islands. But how should this proceed in a country where 88 percent of the land is held in custom ownership (mostly unregistered) by indigenous people? Where people frequently rely on the selling of forests to provide an anxiously awaited chance to develop? Where land, because of its sacred association with its traditional owners, is never for sale?

All of these factors are common to the rest of the South Pacific—including the island countries of Papua New Guinea, Vanuatu, New Caledonia, and Fiji, which, with the Solomon Islands, constitute Melanesia. Because of the common complexities of ownership and development issues, very few protected areas have been established in the region. There is little legislation that enables protected areas to be formally, and successfully, established on customary-owned land.

In the hills behind Honiara on the island of Guadalcanal, there is a graphic illustration of the pointlessness of establishing protected areas without regard to the unique cultural and development context of these countries. Standing on a hilly range surrounded in all directions by degraded grasslands, my Solomon Island hosts argued about the boundary of Queen Elizabeth II National Park. I could understand their confusion. We were supposed to be standing in it—the only national park in the country, established in 1954 to protect a sample of lowland tropical rain forest. Most of the park had long since been cleared for food gardens and then abandoned. We drove along the road that transects the "national park" until we reached the edge of the remaining forest. Here we met some of the indigenous landowners, busy felling trees to provide timber for their family homes in a settlement on the outskirts of the town. This forest was also deemed a "national park," a designation of no concern to the owners. They had not been accounted for when the grand protective title was bestowed on their land. They received no immediate benefits from the protected status of the park but had carried on using the forest to gain access to the useful resource of timber and firewood. The government, understanding the power of indigenous ownership of resources and land, has done nothing further to defend the national park. It is quietly forgotten.

Nor have national parks been a success in most other places in the Pacific. In Papua New Guinea, national park status has been attempted for only 127 square kilometers of land, and these parks are foundering. More popular is a conservation concept born locally and centered on indigenous traditions and landowner control. Known as the wildlife management area (WMA), its success is seen in the 10,000 square kilometers of land that clan groups have requested be protected under its auspices.

The forests of Papua New Guinea are outstanding for their wealth of diversity and the uniqueness of their plants and animals. A large percentage of their flowering plant species are found only on this mountainous island. Ancient egg-laying mammals, marsupials such as rare tree-dwelling kangaroos, giant birdwing butterflies (including the largest butterfly on earth), 200 kinds of frogs, and a plethora of unusual birds are found here. This rich diversity of life is owned and used by the indigenous Papua New Guineans, who, like other Melanesians, live mostly in scattered, remote villages. At traditional sing-sing festivals, headdresses of magnificently colored bird of paradise plumes and the soft pelts of forest mammals adorn village residents. In the cooking pots are the valued meats of many forest animals, as well as birds' eggs or, in villages near the sea, turtle or dugong meat.

Communities that value these assets and that are concerned about the effects of forest clearance, logging, or modern hunting pressures on useful wildlife species are able to establish portions of their land as WMAs. Under a WMA covenant, landowners draw up rules for harvesting animals (frequently based on traditional methods of conservation) and protecting habitat. Importantly, the landowners retain full control over the land and its resources. The government of Papua New Guinea assists with legal recognition of the protected sites.

Whether or not WMAs offer long-term security for hunted animal species is uncertain. An area of habitat protected may be too small to ensure long-term sustainability of the reserve, and landowners may lack sufficient information about the impact of increased levels of hunting using modern technology to make the right management decisions. The hard-pressed Department of Environment and Conservation does not have the resources to provide ongoing ecological advice for all WMAs. Nevertheless, the principle of landowner control over conservation initiatives is an important one for Melanesia, and other governments in the region are expressing interest in applying it in their own countries.

WMAs have usually been established to protect species of economic value to the landowner, such as birds of paradise (for their plumes); megapodes (for their eggs, which are eaten and sold at local markets); and dugongs (locally important as a traditional food source). What happens, though, when landowners control a stretch of forest that would be worth far more to them in cash if it were to be logged or cleared for crops than if it were to be protected for a few animals?

Take the case in Fiji of Litiana Lau and *dakua makadre*. *Dakua makadre* (*Agathis macrophylla*) is an araucarian—an ancient cone-bearing tree that yields valued timber. Most of the forests where Fijian *dakua makadre* is found have now been logged. The last dense stand of *dakua makadre* is found in the wild heartland of Viti Levu Island, in a catchment known as Wabu Creek. Wabu Creek is owned by Litiana Lau.

Litiana Lau lives 50 kilometers from Wabu in a one-room house with her husband and children in the midst of sugarcane plantations on the coastal plains. Litiana is the last descendant of the landowning clan that owns Wabu, but because traditionally owned land cannot be inherited through a woman in Fiji, she is unable to pass on this great natural asset to her sons. She could have it logged, however, and allow her family to inherit money instead. And indeed, Litiana has been offered several hundred thousand Fijian dollars by more than one logging company for the valuable timber of Wabu Creek.

It would hardly be fair to suggest that Litiana Lau should choose to protect Wabu from logging solely for national, and indeed international, conservation interests. As elsewhere in Melanesia, buying the land to create a reserve is not an option—indigenously owned land is not for sale. The answer for this situation is to devise a conservation lease coupled with compensating payments for the value of the timber and for the opportunity foregone for protecting the land. This is exactly what Fiji's government is presently negotiating with Litiana.

The concept of direct compensation for forest protection has been successfully applied elsewhere in the Pacific. In Western Samoa, a Swedish nongovernmental organization facilitated the protection of indigenously owned rain forest in exchange for paying for the local school for the forest owners. The lease that sealed the exchange is valid for fifty years. The fact that the lease is not for perpetuity was an important factor in gaining the landowners' support. Pacific indigenous landowners are reluctant to sign very long-term leases, as this action is seen as a form of alienation from land, tantamount to land sale. They are unwilling to commit their descendants to such binding agreements, which affect the profound relationship between people and their sacred inheritance of land.

Because of the continuing close links between Melanesian communities and their natural resources, most protected areas will need to be established as part of a wider development, resource, and land management program for landowners. The community members at Balai on Malaita Island in the Solomons have initiated such a program themselves. Landowners have drawn up a collective management plan for the tribal land. Part of their land, which they agreed to have logged in the 1980s, will be replanted with tree species useful to the community to provide house- and canoe-building timbers, fuelwood, and fruit trees. The most fertile land that the group owns is being managed for food gardens, and the remaining forested land is to be set aside in a reserve, an area of around 15,000 hectares. Community members have chosen to reserve their forests to protect the catchment above their gardens and behind their reafforestation project, in order to protect habitat for pigs and other useful animals and plants and because they are interested in establishing a nature tourism enterprise, which will involve guiding tourists through the tropical rain forest. Importantly, forest conservation is only part of the overall development package for this community.

It is a fledgling project at Balai. Its long-term success will depend on the cash-generating capacity of the development projects on the land, the commitment and vision of individuals within the community, and the long-term capacity of the landowners to work together. Success over the years to come will require government support to back up the development and conservation initiatives at Balai as well as the continued support of the NGOs that have backed the community until now.

A key to wider success of protected areas in Melanesia will be flexibility in approach. For some landowners, a wildlife management area will adequately address their aspirations; for others, compensation for resource protection is likely to be sought. In other areas, conservation will most successfully be built into landowner-initiated resource management plans. Whatever approach is used, it will have to be deeply seated in the cultural and development milieu that is uniquely Melanesian.

We traveled in the Solomon Islands with the director of the Solomon Islands Development Trust, Abraham Baeanisia. At the evening meetings in the villages, he would describe the development and conservation choices that his fellow Solomon Islanders are facing. His symbol of forests was the coconut tree—that single entity that provides so much to Pacific people. The coconut tree is used for shade, and its leaves are used for thatch. The husk of the fruit is burned for fuel; its dried flesh is sold as copra. The milk of the green nut is drunk, and the tree's trunk is used for construction. It is a veritable supermarket growing in the sand.

"Conservationists come to your village," Abraham would say to the village residents, "and tell you that your coconut tree is the most beautiful they have seen. They describe to you how rare it is and how important it will be for you to protect it. They listen to your legends about the coconut and eagerly note your traditional uses of it. Indeed, a protected area is declared over your tree and you are forbidden to use it. But you wanted to sell your coconut to get cash to start a fishing enterprise. The conservationist goes home, and a coconut merchant comes to your village.

" 'I'll give you cash for your coconuts,' he says. 'Good deal,' you think, 'I can start my fishing business.' The coconut merchant cuts down the whole tree to get your coconuts, and you are left with cash but no tree, no more coconuts, no more thatch, and no more shade.

"You come up with a better plan and go to your friends' village. 'Keep your coconut tree,' you advise them, 'but don't protect it all. Save some of the green coconuts and reserve some of the ripe nuts so you will always have new coconut trees coming on. Harvest some of your coconuts to sell, but don't destroy the whole tree, or you will lose everything.' "

The people of Penjuku Village in the Marovo Lagoon nodded in agreement when they heard this story. Then a discussion began about how to raise the cash for a fishing business.

JOANNA GOULD & ANNETTE LEES

God of the Forest Forever

*Ki te awhina i te tangata whenua ki te tiaki i nga ngahere
motuhake-a-Tane i runga i ona ake whenua.*

*(To help tangata whenua [the people of the land] look after the special
forests of Tane [god of the forest] on their own lands.)*

For hundreds of years, generations of Te Whanau-a-Maruhaeremuri people have
seen the sun rise and set over the forested mountains that belong to them. Their
mana—their spiritual power and well-being—is intricately bound with this land
they call Pohueroro. For generations, they have gathered food from the forest and
used its plants to heal and clothe themselves. Pohueroro, in a remote part of New
Zealand's North Island, is the land over which Te Whanau-a-Maruhaeremuri hold
tino rangatiratanga, the sacred stewardship and governorship over land that is an
integral part of Maori culture.

The inaccessible forested mountains are also important to the survival of two
rare indigenous species, Hochstetter's frog and the kakapo, a large parrot. Ecologically, Pohueroro Forest is part of a valuable corridor that represents a complete
altitudinal sequence of forest, from the coast to high mountain ranges.

Four years ago, the many owners of Pohueroro met and decided that they wanted
to preserve their forest so that their grandchildren and great-grandchildren could
continue to hunt for food there and use its healing powers.

But for the Maori, New Zealand's indigenous people, legally preserving their
land is not a simple matter. The owners of Pohueroro had problems finding an
appropriate way of protecting their land: none of the existing covenants available
through private land protection institutions and legislation addressed complexities
such as multiple ownership or fully respected their *tino rangatiratanga.*

Until recently, because of these problems very little Maori forest was available for formal protection. Yet Maori people own a significant proportion of New Zealand's privately owned indigenous forests. After centuries of forest clearance and burning, only 20 percent of New Zealand's original forests remain; one-sixth of these forests are privately owned, half of them by the Maori.

As a response to the problems of multiple ownership and in recognition of the spiritual and cultural values the Maori attach to their forests, the New Zealand government set aside funding for a special protection scheme for Maori-owned forests known as Nga Whenua Rahui. As Maori landownership is passed down through the generations, it can become quite fragmented, and large blocks of land are owned collectively by many people. Hence, applications for protection through Nga Whenua Rahui are most often made by a trust on behalf of the multiple landowners.

For the owners of Pohueroro Forest, Nga Whenua Rahui was a welcome initiative that enabled them to propose a covenant over their forest in accordance with their own wishes. Under Nga Whenua Rahui protection, the *tino rangatiratanga* of Te Whanau-a-Maruhaeremuri is fully recognized and respected, as are the Maori's traditional uses of the forest and their cultural and spiritual views of what constitutes a high-value forest. The Nga Whenua Rahui fund also provides financial assistance with rates, fencing and pest control, and advice regarding protection mechanisms and future management.

Joe Rua is chairperson of the Pohueroro Trust, which was set up on behalf of the multiple owners of the Pohueroro Forest to ensure that the forest was legally protected in the way they wanted. Traditionally, he said, the forest has been an important food source. "That use is still practiced today, but instead of hunting native pigeons, the main hunting is done on introduced animals—pigs and deer." Weaving materials, such as the indigenous *kiekie* vine, are still gathered from the forest, and even though no timber has been taken out for some time, the Nga Whenua Rahui covenant over Pohueroro gives the trust the flexibility to consider allowing it to be used for cultural purposes, such as carvings for a meeting house. The covenant clearly states, though, that no mining may be carried out and no timber may be used other than for cultural purposes.

Rongoa—traditional Maori medicine using indigenous plants—is an important part of Maori culture, but due to the inaccessibility of some parts of Pohueroro Forest, few people now use it for that purpose. Under the covenant, the owners of

Pohueroro would like to set aside a small, more accessible part of the forest where special healing plants used in *rongoa* would be grown and used to teach traditional healing.

The Nga Whenua Rahui scheme is also a means for landowners to set up income-generating activities to give them the economic independence to protect their forests from alternative uses such as logging. In the case of Pohueroro, Rua said that low-impact tourism initiatives, such as conducting guided walking trips and having a couple of jet boats on the river to take walkers into the forest, may be acceptable uses of the forest.

But from his point of view, one of the more important things about the covenant with the Crown is the spirit of partnership. "We act in good faith to each other and see ourselves as true partners, bearing in mind that at the end of the day, we are the owners of the land and without us there would be no covenant."

Te Whanau-a-Maruhaeremuri feel that they have truly retained their *tino rangatiratanga* over their forest. This is particularly reflected in an important aspect of the Pohueroro covenant that specifies that it is renewable after twenty-five years. Agreeing to protection in perpetuity is not acceptable to most Maori people because as part of the concept of *tino rangatiratanga*, they are unwilling to commit their descendants to binding land use decisions and to risk alienating subsequent generations from their land. "We felt it was important that future generations were able to exercise their *tino rangatiratanga* over their land as we do today. While we would like our decision to remain in perpetuity, we still felt it was the right of future generations to make that decision for themselves," Rua explained. "The indication is very clear, though. The agreement is in perpetuity, but it has a twenty-five-year review clause of the terms, conditions, and continuance. It is not a twenty-five-year covenant."

Applications for forest protection under Nga Whenua Rahui and for the necessary financial assistance are assessed by a committee comprising four Maori and one *pakeha* (non-Maori New Zealander), included for her ecological skills. The committee takes into consideration spiritual, cultural, and ecological values when assessing applications and then passes its recommendations to the minister of conservation for approval. The Pohueroro covenant is in the final stages of approval, with final legal wording still to be decided on.

After fifteen months of operation, Maori landowners are showing cautious interest in Nga Whenua Rahui, with only 11,000 hectares of forest so far being committed to its legal protection. However, when finalized, the Pohueroro covenant will protect another 5,619 hectares and should give faith to many other Maori forest owners that legal protection can go hand in hand with retaining their *mana* and their *tino rangatiratanga* over their land.

SANDRA MBANEFO & HILARY DE BOERR

CAMPFIRE in Zimbabwe[1]

It has been another blistering week in Nyenyunga Village. Onias Mpofu, twenty-five, works his scorched field with little success, harvesting the few dried stalks of maize and cotton not lost to Zimbabwe's worst drought in this century. His wife and children toil alongside him.

A villager, Kaneyengwa Nariti, comes running with bad news: elephants devastated his field last night, eating crops and trampling everything in their path. "I am at the point of suicide!" he shouts bitterly. "Elephants have raided my entire field. How am I going to feed my family?"

Several other villagers have had the same bad fortune that month. The country's growing elephant population means that there are simply too many elephants in the region. They invade farmland in search of food and water, and villagers are forced to endure not only failing crops and hungry families but also destructive and dangerous wildlife.

A few years ago, Nyenyunga's leaders would have demanded that Zimbabwe's Department of National Parks and Wildlife Management kill the marauding elephants. Today, villagers deal with problem animals differently.

Nyenyunga Village is part of a countrywide conservation program called the Communal Areas Management Plan for Indigenous Resources, or CAMPFIRE. The experimental program, which was initiated in the late 1970s and officially established in 1986, is run by the Department of National Parks and Wildlife Management within the Ministry of Natural Resources and Tourism. It is indirectly designed to take pressure off Zimbabwe's national parks by changing the way villagers view wildlife in nonprotected areas.

CAMPFIRE rests on a rural development philosophy, allowing subsistence farmers to manage, and benefit directly from, wildlife in an entrepreneurial fashion.[2] Market forces are used to achieve economic, ecological, and social sustainability. In other words, villagers can now sell access to the wildlife in their areas through either tourism or safari hunting—enterprises that are proving to be profitable and good for both the environment and the participating communities.

The need for a program such as CAMPFIRE is found in Zimbabwe's colonial past, which impaired the traditionally healthy relationship between people and wildlife. In the 1920s, European settlers claimed the best land in what was then southern Rhodesia. While a few thousand white commercial farm or ranch owners prosperously grew tobacco, maize, cotton, and citrus fruits on 40 percent of the arable land, the rapidly expanding indigenous population was confined to "native reserves" or communal lands with poor arid soil. Many black communities were evicted from, or denied access to, traditional hunting grounds, which instead became official wildlife areas. Meanwhile, their new settlements turned existing wildlife havens—previously protected from human habitation by the tsetse fly—into lands for cultivation and livestock.

People and the government clashed when wildlife was declared state property under colonial legislation, making it illegal for rural people to make any use of the resource. The government had a direct say in wildlife management until 1975, when a new Parks and Wildlife Act handed the responsibility for—but not the ownership of—wildlife to landowners.[3]

This was good news for commercial farmers, who increased their wildlife populations, established game viewing areas, and engaged in tourism ventures and limited game hunting.

Subsistence farmers in communal areas did not own their land, however, so authority over wildlife was given to district commissioners. Wildlife management therefore remained in state hands, and subsistence farmers like Mpofu received no incentives for "putting up with" wild animals. Poverty increased, tensions between people and wildlife escalated as the animals encroached on crops, and illegal hunting became commonplace.

Dudley Rogers, a professional hunter who now works with villagers in Nyenyunga, says that in communal areas, elephants, lions, leopards, and buffaloes have become vermin to people. "You can't blame them. These animals destroy their crops, cattle, sheep, and goats—their whole livelihood. Unfortunately, the human population has increased to such an extent that an animal has to be worth its salt to exist. Take away the economic value of an animal today, and you take away its life."

The official introduction of CAMPFIRE in 1986 has given real economic value to Nyenyunga's wildlife. An elephant killed for "pest control" is now worth about

$1,224 from the sale of meat to villagers. An elephant sold to a commercial hunter for safari hunting is worth more than $12,000. In 1991, Nyenyunga Village earned $6,530 net, about half of which was spent on a teacher's house, classrooms, and a solar electric fence to deter wildlife. The other half went into the bank. Other CAMPFIRE communities have invested their earnings in school fees, a community grinding mill, and cash dividends to households.

CAMPFIRE works by encouraging villagers to view wildlife as their own property, which they can sustainably manage. Once a district qualifies for CAMPFIRE status, the government sets a yearly quota of animals that can be "harvested" without adversely affecting total wildlife numbers. Nyenyunga's 1992 district quota was five elephant bulls, thirty buffalo, six lion, seven kudu, two waterbuck, six leopard, thirty-five impala, and six zebra.

Villagers now have options when faced with aggressive wildlife. Mpofu, as Nyenyunga's "problem animal reporter," prepares detailed reports on farmers' fields damaged by wildlife, such as that of fellow villager Nariti. The village then decides whether to use part of its quota by killing the offending elephant or whether to wait until it is hunted—more profitably—on safari.

The enterprise has reduced poaching in districts that have implemented CAMPFIRE, says Dr. Brian Child, CAMPFIRE coordinator for the Department of National Parks and Wildlife Management (DNPWM). In one district, fifty elephants used to be killed every year to protect crops; now, only twenty are killed. "CAMPFIRE is about restructuring the political-economic control of the countryside," he says.

That concept is crucial to the program's success. District councils receive CAMPFIRE status only after satisfying the government of their intention to devolve the CAMPFIRE system to wards and villages under their jurisdiction. Districts must also promote in those wards and villages the development of institutions that aid decision making and a fair distribution of benefits.

It is not always an easy task: the Nyaminyami District Council, in the Zambezi Valley in northern Zimbabwe, took four years to develop its infrastructure to the standards necessary to gain appropriate authority for management of wildlife in the district. It did so with the help and expertise of WWF and two Zimbabwean nongovernmental organizations, the Zimbabwe Trust and the University of Zimbabwe's Center for Applied Social Sciences (CASS).

The Zimbabwe Trust (Zimtrust), a rural development organization, provides institutional support to village CAMPFIRE committees. It organizes workshops on bookkeeping, committee formation, joint decision making, and anything to do with improving villagers' management capability.[4]

Julian Sturgeon, Zimtrust's CAMPFIRE manager, says that if CAMPFIRE is to be sustainable, it must be locally managed. "Therefore, institutional development comes first, and wildlife management second. It's an attempt to decentralize decision-making power," he says.

The trust also works with local schools in raising conservation awareness. In some cases, it subsidizes CAMPFIRE projects by, for example, providing an interim general manager or start-up financing.

CASS is the program's research arm, evaluating and monitoring the social, economic, and cultural effects of CAMPFIRE. The center also provides tertiary training in natural resource management.

WWF works with the DNPWM to advise villagers on resource economics and the ecological aspects of wildlife management—for example, how to deal with "problem animals," how to set up exclusive wilderness areas, how to establish joint ventures with safari operators, and how to monitor wildlife populations.

Some conservationists believe that utilizing wildlife is a better economic option for land use than raising cattle, especially on the marginal soils found on many communal lands. Wildlife and natural areas, for both consumptive and nonconsumptive uses, are worth about $40 million per year in Zimbabwe, with safari hunting earning an estimated $9.36 million from 1,000 safari hunting clients in 1990. Communal land areas participating in CAMPFIRE grossed an estimated $4 million from safari hunting in 1990 and 1991. If distributed equally among each of the 18,000 households involved, that sum would have meant an extra $400 for every household—in some cases doubling their annual income.

Safari hunting also generates income rapidly and without large capital investments. Tourism based on game viewing is obviously biased more toward areas that have particular beauty or abundant wildlife.

CAMPFIRE is still developing, and its successes have not been achieved without obstacles to overcome. Zimbabwe's biggest and most formalized CAMPFIRE project, run by the Nyaminyami District Council, highlights the problems and benefits of the new conservation and development approach.

Nyaminyami, in northern Zimbabwe, comprises three communal lands on the shores of Lake Kariba, surrounding the Matusadona National Park on three sides. Much of its 363,000 hectares is suitable only for extended grazing, yet in terms of wildlife abundance it is probably the richest communal land in the country. In the limited areas where crops can be grown, therefore, wildlife often causes severe damage to crops and injury to people. Its rapidly growing population—partly the result of an influx of new settlers to relieve land pressure elsewhere in the country— is expected to double by the year 2005. Malnutrition and protein deficiency are high, and food aid programs have been necessary for many years.

The district was granted CAMPFIRE status in 1988, having first developed a steering committee in 1985, comprising ward councillors and CAMPFIRE officials, then a wildlife management trust in 1987. The Zimbabwe Trust, CASS, and WWF were involved from the start. Before appropriate authority was gained for the management of wildlife, safari hunting by commercial operators did take place, but revenues went directly to the government treasury. And although the Nyaminyami District Council did subsequently receive almost half of those wildlife earnings between 1982 and 1987, local development projects were often frustrated in their attempts to gain reimbursement.

Now that the wildlife management trust has authority, income is divided equally among the twelve wards in the council area. Nyaminyami earned $133,821 after costs in 1989, including a subsidy from Zimtrust; $99,851 went to local communities, $17,500 was placed in a depreciation reserve, $3,088 was placed in an operating reserve, and $13,382 went to the council in the form of a levy.

Drawbacks lay in the limited transfer of skills to the rural communities, since the expertise and facilities came from, and remained with, the commercial safari operator with whom the trust joined forces. Short-term hunting contracts also meant that the safari operator was disinclined to invest in permanent facilities. An answer appears to lie in the formation of joint ventures between the trust and safari operators—not only for hunting but also for game viewing and photographic tourism. Such ventures, when combined with revenue from other sustainable management activities like culling, cropping, and live animal sales, could earn Nyaminyami a projected $1.3 million over the next decade.

Another cause for concern has been the equal distribution of earnings to wards— a procedure that tends to discriminate against communities that bear the highest social and other costs of the wildlife management scheme. There is an argument that communities and individuals suffering higher wildlife damage and inconvenience should be compensated, and some trusts do operate in this fashion.

Zimtrust's Julian Sturgeon believes that such dissension is positive for institutional development in Zimbabwe. "Through decentralization, we've transferred the conflict between the community and wildlife to tensions between district councils and communities. When people don't get their cash or benefits, they complain to the council. This is healthy, I guess, because communities are beginning to understand their rights."

By 1992, twelve districts had received appropriate authority for the management of wildlife under the CAMPFIRE program, with several others formulating wildlife management plans to gain authority status. In 1993, at least ten districts joined the program, meaning that more than 40 percent of the country's fifty-five districts in communal areas are managing their wildlife under CAMPFIRE. Projects take differing approaches, and comparisons over time should aid future decision making.

For example, the Guruve District Council, which covers the Dande communal land in northern Zimbabwe, bordering Mozambique, employed its own professional hunter to market and operate safaris. Unfortunately, this did not lead to the most effective use of resources or to the expected transfer of skills. Instead, residents of Guruve are now leasing hunting rights to the highest bidder, thus maximizing returns to the community.

Guruve's financial affairs illustrate some of the issues that can arise. In 1989, the district council earned $121,578 from safari hunting—$34,801 from its own operations and $86,469 from private operations. Only 26 percent of the revenue was distributed by the council, and only three of the seven wards received any money, since funds were allocated according to the number of animals shot in a ward. Many local inhabitants thus perceived no benefit coming to them from wildlife, contrary to what they had been led to expect from CAMPFIRE.

However, in the one ward that did receive a substantial sum of money, Kanyurira, the effects were positive. Its eighty-six households each received $103 from the lump sum of $24,350, and the rest of the money was spent on school furniture and construction of a clinic. Poaching by community members was virtually eliminated in 1990, and for the first time in many years, there were no destructive bush fires late in the dry season. The community also increasingly demanded its rights, calling for full proprietorship and for detailed financial accounts from the council.[5]

By 1991, the Guruve District Council had changed its ways and distributed 49 percent of the revenue from safari operations, with all seven wards receiving some income.

The Beitbridge District Council seemed to find the best approach from the start, and it is considered a model CAMPFIRE program. The district, near the Limpopo River, has limited wildlife because of drought, poaching, overgrazing, and extensive livestock management, but nevertheless it joined CAMPFIRE in 1989. Its first hunting quota was sold to a neighboring rancher in 1990, and the following year the council marketed its quota through national newspaper advertising.

In 1990, revenues of more than $49,411 were distributed among five wards and *vidcos* (villages), with $30,882 going to Chikwarakwara Vidco, where most of the animals were killed. Each of the *vidco*'s households was to receive $206, but after community discussion, it was decided that each household would keep $103, giving $88 to build a grinding mill and $15 to the school. Residents learned how to manage money, resources, and businesses, and the grinding mill has proved profitable, earning more money for distribution. The people of Chikwarakwara now say, "Wildlife is our cattle." Poaching incidents are much reduced.[6]

The Binga District Council, in Matabeleland North next to Chizarira National Park, has entered into joint ventures with two photographic safari operators who are building tourist camps—one of the first such ventures to be undertaken by a district council. The Mzarabani District Council has decided on traditional tourism for its Mvuradona Wilderness Area in the Zambezi Escarpment. Rugged terrain and overhunting mean lower wildlife populations than elsewhere, so horse trails, backpacking, hiking, rock climbing, and camping are seen as the best income earners. Effective marketing is the key to the venture's success, and the main markets appear to be local residents on short breaks and budget travelers from overseas.

Yet another approach has been adopted by the Shangaan people in Mahenye Ward (County), traditional hunters who live in southeastern Zimbabwe adjacent to Gonarezhou National Park. The people of Mahenye chose to set aside some of their land exclusively for wildlife areas in return for hunting rights that had been denied them by the colonial government. Two district councils in the area acquired CAMPFIRE status in 1990 and proceeded to set up a wildlife cooperative with a private sector company to market safari hunting. The Shangaan people's traditional wildlife management skills came back into play, replacing a hostility to wildlife that not only had encouraged illegal hunting for food and pest control but also had forged alliances between the people and a notorious group of ivory poachers operating in the park.

The Hwange District Council is following suit, translocating plentiful species such as impalas from Hwange National Park to designated wildlife areas within the communal lands. The council is negotiating with the private sector to develop the tourist potential of those areas alongside the park.

CAMPFIRE still relies heavily on income from elephant hunting, but it should evolve to use more fully the natural resources of Zimbabwe's lands, such as fish and bird life and even silkworms and cocoons, which are marketable. Safari hunting is probably necessary in the short term, however, to provide the immediate financial returns needed to convince rural communities that they can manage their wildlife resources sustainably and profitably. In the meantime, land settlement programs remain an issue: some of the sparsely populated regions most suitable for inclusion by CAMPFIRE sometimes are still seen as convenient relocation grounds for people from overcrowded communal areas elsewhere in the country.

In areas where CAMPFIRE status is appropriate, the main challenges lie in encouraging effective decision making at the ward and village levels. Some councils are reluctant to devolve genuine authority for wildlife management, an attitude that can hamper efficient and equitable distribution of earnings and frustrate communities.

But there is great potential for wildlife tourism in Zimbabwe, with demand growing all the time for access to wild places. Where use of indigenous wildlife is likely to be the most appropriate form of land use, villages have access to readily available resources—with no need for imported technology—and have the opportunity to develop local institutions and encourage genuine participation and sustainable use of natural resources. The CAMPFIRE approach can also help counter the decline in populations of species like elephants and rhinoceroses by making them valuable to local people rather than only to outsiders.

"CAMPFIRE is a good program, and illegal hunting has gone down in our district," concludes Mpofu as he walks along one of Nyenyunga's dusty footpaths. "We still need to learn a lot about wildlife management, but villagers are finally beginning to understand that these natural resources are ours to manage."

Paradise Gained or Lost?
Yanomami of Brazil

On his fourth and final trip to the Americas, Christopher Columbus was convinced that he had come upon one of the four rivers of paradise on earth. It was the delta of the Orinoco, a river that is twin to the Amazon not only in volume of water but also in the role it played in European imagination regarding the New World. As it happens, the upper reaches of the Orinoco in Venezuela—with its vast network of tributaries and its Amazonian counterparts in Brazil—are the homeland of perhaps the most emblematic of South American Indians, the Yanomami.

In recent years, however, Columbus's paradise has become a living hell for the Brazilian Yanomami. Their mountainous territory has been the stage of the most dramatic episodes in the modern history of Indian-white contact in that country, due to the largest-scale gold rush on Indian lands in the recent history of Brazil. Since 1985, successive waves of miners and prospectors have invaded the Yanomami's lands in the tens of thousands, overwhelming the local people, especially in Roraima State, where the Yanomami number fewer than 7,000. Those gold miners are not the first invaders of Yanomami lands, but the impact of their presence has been the heaviest and most harmful to the health and way of life of the Indians, most of whom had previously had little or no direct contact with whites other than missionaries and sporadic visitors.

Despite the forced contact with outsiders, the Yanomami have managed to maintain most of their traditional customs, still little altered by outside influences. Most of the Brazilian Yanomami are monolingual, even in the communities worst hit by mining activities.

Their traditional territory straddles the international boundary between southern Venezuela and northern Brazil in what is known as the Guyana Shield, part of the Amazon rain forest. Soil fertility is extremely low in almost the entire area, but the diversity of fauna and flora is remarkable. Jaguars, giant anteaters, tapirs, copibaras (the world's biggest rodent), black spider monkeys, and giant armadillos all inhabit the area and are hunted for food by the Yanomami.

Extensive groves of cacao trees, found at altitudes of more than 1,000 meters, are a useful food source for the Yanomami, while a variety of palms—some reaching 15 meters in height—are also indispensable as a construction material.[1] The Guyana Shield encompasses about 1 million square kilometers of land and contains about 8,000 species of vascular plants, half of which are believed to be endemic.[2] Of the hundreds of species of birds in the area, several—including the zigzag heron, the harpy eagle, the long-tailed potoo, and the Orinoco softtail—are threatened, mainly by uncontrolled hunting.[3] Under its vast green mantle, the forest displays a rich variety of resources that are unevenly distributed, thus creating an amazing variety of local niches.

Originally upland dwellers, the Yanomami have throughout the centuries spread out and reached the lower valleys to the south in Brazil and to the north in Venezuela. Brazil's Yanomami live in an area of about 94,000 square kilometers in the states of Roraima and Amazonas.

Many Yanomami still prefer to settle on high ground, away from big rivers. For their water supply, the communities use small streams or springs, usually some distance from the villages. Depending on the altitude—some villages are located more than 1,000 meters above sea level—the temperature can be very hot or quite mild, and nighttime temperatures in the higher areas can fall below 10 degrees centigrade.

There are basically two seasons—a rainy season from June to November and a dry season from December to May. Natural resources therefore also vary throughout the year, and the Yanomami are experts at exploiting the ecological and seasonal differences, with their intimate knowledge of animal, plant, and climate behavior. The small streams are especially important in the people's lives. The streams' usually muddy banks display animal tracks, crab holes, signs of hidden enemies, and a whole gamut of clues easily identified by the Yanomami. Along these streams they inscribe their knowledge of geography and history, as if the watercourses represent the veins and capillaries that irrigate the practical and symbolic body of the communities. Along these streams, news is transmitted from village to village. Whole communities engage in collective fishing, and memories of old fields and old village sites are perpetuated and given new meaning, thus feeding into a topographic history that ties various communities into a common trajectory.

Equally important are the trails that link the villages. More direct and faster than the streams, the trails trace paths full of information that is recounted by the Yanomami whenever they go on trips, whether short or long. They tread the forest to fetch raw materials and food or to visit other villages. Walking along in single file, they tell stories about memorable hunts, encounters with spirits, and spotting of hidden enemies. These trails, like spokes of a gigantic wheel, radiate from each village into an elaborate web of tracks that connect the village to new and old gardens; hunting, fishing, and gathering grounds; dry-season camps; and villages near and far. Like nerves, the trails convey the social pulses that keep alive the great chain of relations among communities and render their isolation virtually impossible. Through them, social messages are sent across villages, fields, and forests and among spirits.

The gardens, made and owned by individual families, are not only a space for subsistence. They are also the outcome of joint work and a source of diverse social interaction that includes collective work of felling trees, the privacy of lovers' trysts, and the mild commotion of childbirth. The garden is essentially a domesticated space. Even when far away from the village, it is an extension of it. The garden is not only where one plants the most reliable and abundant food, such as manioc, bananas, and a variety of roots; it is also the locus of well-defined work relations— the man's strength in felling the trees, the woman's expertise in weeding and harvesting, the child's informal learning lessons, the son-in-law's duty to work for his wife's parents. The creation of a new garden is like the opening of a new social file. In the history of every village, the gardens are like cornerstones setting meaningful connections between the past and present.

A family garden is usually cleared in a circle with a diameter of 500 to 800 meters and yields produce for two to three years. After that, it loses much of its productivity because of the poverty of the soil. Weeding becomes so laborious that it is better to invest in a new clearing. Over a span of four years, each village uses an estimated 3 square kilometers of arable land.

The forest, of which the gardens are small, temporary interruptions, is the basis on which a village or group of villages establishes its territorial boundaries, tenuous as these may be. It is the home of spirits and the source of meat, fruit, nuts, honey, and a wide array of raw materials. All of these resources are dispersed over considerable distances, from 3 to 16 kilometers.

It has been calculated that a group of eighty-four people needs a minimum area of 640 square kilometers to provide all the resources needed for subsistence, housing, and other activities necessary for their production and reproduction. That is the basis for the 94,000 square kilometers of territory—an area larger than Scotland—claimed for the Yanomami and officially granted to them in 1991.

The use of natural resources by the Yanomami is the result of a long tradition transmitted through many generations and reaching such an admirable balance that even in soils that are recognizably poor, they have managed to develop a sustained livelihood for centuries on end. The Yanomami have developed a social, political, and economic system that favors a dispersed settlement pattern, for they know that any demographic concentration will lead to resource depletion. If their territory is large, there are very good reasons for it. Their wisdom in preventing such undesirable concentration is apparent in the way they organize their village life, with periodic divisions resulting in the creation of new villages every two or three generations. Political rivalries that arise in a community are very effective mechanisms to draw dissident groups away from the parent community and force them to look for new residence and subsistence sites. As time goes by, social and spatial distance pulls them farther and farther apart. Dispersal thus occurs, and competition for local resources is considerably minimized. At the same time, a vast network of related villages continuously expands to cover the entire Yanomami territory. The average size of Yanomami villages is around 50 to 70 people, rarely exceeding 150.

If the Yanomami are to maintain their traditional standard of living, it is unquestionable that they need the legal guarantee of control over territory. The specific character of their social, political, and economic patterns which have proved to be highly efficient in achieving a sustained livelihood, is even more admirable as we discover the fragility of their ecological milieu.

The Brazilian government created the Yanomami Reserve after a lively campaign both within Brazil and abroad. The long and winding road to protected area status began in 1968 and involved some fourteen proposals to the government from sources both public and private. For more than two decades, proponents of the demarcation alternated constantly between being on the verge of celebration and on the verge of despair. Opponents included the powerful mining lobby, members of government, and the military, which was keen to maintain its authority and power base in the region. The military argued that the Yanomami of Venezuela and Brazil would attempt to create an independent nation if they were granted reserve status. Foreign interests coveted the Amazon's vast natural resources, they said. Then there were attempts to reduce the size of the territory because so many Yanomami had been killed by disease.

The continuous epidemics and tragic deaths brought to Yanomami lands by the gold rush led to an international outcry. Conservation groups threatened to boycott the 1992 Earth Summit in Rio de Janeiro if the Yanomami were not given control of their land. United Nations secretary general Javier Perez de Cuellar telephoned Brazilian president Fernando Collor de Mello to express his concern. The embarrassed president signed the decree of demarcation of the territory in November 1992.

An operation to remove the miners from Yanomami territory took place in 1990–1991, and an emergency health campaign was launched to try to stop the drain of Yanomami lives through pandemic bouts of malaria.

The troubles of the Brazilian Yanomami are by no means over. The Indians will win control of their land only after the government has formally marked out the forest, at a cost of about $2 million. Brazil's constitution requires demarcation by October 1993, and mineral rights are to remain with the government. The Yanomami still suffer the effects of recalcitrant diseases such as malaria, which returns with full force to the communities as soon as a medical team completes a mass treatment. Worst of all, since early 1992, gold prospectors have been returning to places where illegal airstrips had been destroyed and mining equipment and airplanes dismantled or confiscated. The initial impetus to clear the area of invaders has been lost; the air force has withdrawn its aircraft, especially its helicopters, the much-needed tools for evacuation of the miners; and public attention in the country has been too absorbed with the national crisis to pay much heed to the troubles of indigenous peoples. The national health service in charge of Indian health fails to maintain a flow of medicines and other basic supplies to the Yanomami area, involved as it is in the country's political and economic turmoil. Thus, because of constant malaria epidemics and other diseases that are either lethal or very difficult to control, such as tuberculosis, leishmaniasis, calazar, and hepatitis, the Yanomami death rate has not diminished. A survey in May 1991 showed that half of the Yanomami suffered from malaria, a disease previously unknown to them. Mercury poisoning is another great problem—people living miles downstream from gold mines have been found to have unacceptably high levels of mercury in their bodies. Were it not for the heroic efforts of medical teams of the Yanomami Health District (National Health Foundation) and the sustained presence in one specific area of personnel hired by the Committee for the Creation of the Yanomami Park (CCPY), the Yanomami population might be even further reduced.

Chaos is threatening to return to the Yanomami and their forest. Entire gardens have been turned into muddy holes by the power of mighty hydraulic-powered machines and giant hoses; networks of trails have been bisected by mining gorges; streams, trees, and soil have been poisoned by mercury and oil fumes. Once again, the Yanomami need the alert eye of the world to help them protect themselves from the danger of extinction.

JULIO CÉSAR CENTENO & CHRISTOPHER ELLIOT

Forest Home: The Place Where One Belongs

Yanomami of Venezuela

As our small plane banked over the clearing in the forest at Ocamo, the excitement inside was palpable. Pedro García, director general of SADA-AMAZONAS, a special section of the Venezuelan Environment Ministry set up to administer the country's Amazon State, peered intently out a window, his handlebar mustache twitching. We had reached the southernmost part of Venezuela, four hours' flight from the capital, Caracas, and were in the heart of the Alto Orinoco Biosphere Reserve, home to several Amerindian cultures. We were guests of a government mission to meet the Yanomami and Yekuana Indians living in the area to discuss problems and potential solutions.

The 83,000-square-kilometer biosphere reserve, located in the upper reaches of the Orinoco River, is the largest rain forest park in the world. Indeed, it is the second largest park anywhere on earth, after Northeast Greenland National Park. Together with Brazil's adjacent Yanomami Reserve, the Yanomami people have an area totaling 177,000 square kilometers (68,000 square miles). The Venezuelan biosphere reserve was set up not only to protect the rich rain forests of the region, the source and headwaters of Venezuela's most important river, the Orinoco, but also to guarantee the security and livelihood of the Yanomami and Yekuana, who have lived there for millennia.

The Yanomami are the largest group of indigenous people still living their traditional life-style in the Americas. Their falling population is estimated at about 21,000, with 9,000 to 10,000 in Brazil and the rest in Venezuela. About 200 tribes exist in an interdependent relationship, living in harmony with the environment, practicing low-intensity shifting cultivation, fishing, hunting, and gathering.

Urihi and *uli* are Yanomami words for forest. Translated from the Amerindian language, they mean "home," or "the place where one belongs." The green-canopied forests provide shelter, food, and raw materials. They are home to the Yanomami spirits and contain a wealth of historical and cultural information. Their streams and trails link villages, bonding the thousands of Yanomami people living in their traditional territory on either side of the border between Brazil and Venezuela.

The Yanomami's homes have been much under siege over the past two decades. Development, disease, warfare, and now tourism severely threaten "the place where one belongs"—and the very existence of the Yanomami. Years of struggle to protect their lands gained a major success in 1991, when both Brazil and Venezuela established protected areas for the Yanomami. Nevertheless, there are still many serious threats to the Indians, especially in Brazil.

Illegal gold miners, or *garimpeiros* as they are known locally, continue to persecute the Brazilian Yanomami and invade their territories, bringing disease, death, and destruction. An estimated 1,500 Yanomami have died from introduced diseases, including malaria, river blindness, influenza, and measles. A survey carried out in Brazil in May 1991 showed that 50 percent of the Yanomami there suffered from malaria, a disease previously unknown to them.

Contrary to the situation in Brazil, Venezuela's Yanomami have largely been spared from invasion of their territories, mainly because of the isolation of Venezuela's Amazon Territory, which is about the size of Portugal. With little fanfare, the Venezuelan government created the Alto Orinoco Biosphere Reserve in July 1991 by a decree of President Carlos Andres Perez.

As we prepared to land, our group leader, Dr. Wilfredo Franco, who directs the research arm of SADA-AMAZONAS (the Autonomous Service for the Development of the Federal Amazon Territory), told us why the Yanomami are unique among Amerindian cultures. Anthropological studies have shown that the Yanomami have been independent from other indigenous Amazonian societies, in terms of genetics and linguistics, for at least 2,000 years. It is possible that they took refuge in the remote areas where they now live to escape slave raids during the colonial era. The first reported contact with Western civilization occurred in 1787 with the Portuguese Boundary Commission, which was seeking to demonstrate the limits of the Amazon Basin and hence of the Portuguese colonial territory. Although there were intermittent contacts subsequently, including an expedition by Alexander von Humboldt in 1800 and the Franco-Venezuelan expedition to locate the source of the Orinoco in 1951, contacts became regular only in the 1960s, when Christian missionaries launched intense programs of evangelization.

According to missionaries and anthropologists who have lived with them, the Yanomami make very efficient use of the natural resources of the area in which they live, and each community can satisfy its needs without having to stray more than 10 to 15 kilometers from home. One of the mysteries surrounding the Yanomami is their cultivation of plantains, which originate in Asia, not in the Amazon, and are thought to have been brought to the Americas by the Spanish or Portuguese in the early 1500s. How and when the Yanomami began to cultivate plantains, which now form a staple part of their diet, is not known. The Yanomami accord plantains an important position in their mythology, believing that one day in the forest one of their ancestors, Haronanai, stole the plantain from its original owner, Pore.

Yanomami agriculture is based on shifting cultivation, in which small garden plots, or *conucos,* are cleared in the forests and cultivated for two to three years before being abandoned. This system, which may appear wasteful at first sight, is in fact highly efficient because the soils of the upper Orinoco are nutrient poor and become depleted after two to three years of cultivation. Although labor is not strictly divided between men and women, men tend to specialize in hunting, fishing, and the initial clearing of *conucos,* whereas women cook, take care of children, and collect fruit. The French anthropologist Jacques Lizot, who has lived for more than twenty years with the Yanomami, estimates that to feed themselves satisfactorily, the Yanomami work between two and three days per week, depending on the season, which leaves them some seven to eight hours each day free from all work, in addition to the time spent sleeping and resting. Hunters use a log bow up to 2 meters long and immobilize their game by dipping their arrows in curare, a muscle relaxant containing several alkaloids from a variety of plants, including species from the genus *Strychnos.*

The Yanomami have highly sophisticated religious beliefs and mythology. They believe, for example, that there have been three "generations" of humanity. The first was transformed into the animals we know; the second was mostly lost in a great flood; and the third, the survivors of the great flood, constitutes what we know today as humanity.

After we landed on the bumpy earthen airstrip in Ocamo, we were led through the modest Salesian missionary buildings to a meeting area, where we met with Salesian priests and Yanomami representatives. Pedro García introduced himself and the rest of our group and explained that we were on a preliminary mission to gather information on the problems in the area for preparation of a management plan for the biosphere reserve.

Both the Salesian priests and the Yanomami leaders were vocal in saying that their main problem was the army, which had moved into the area in large numbers over the past year in order to stop Brazilian *garimpeiros* from intruding into Venezuelan territory, a regular occurrence. Even though the *garimpeiros* have had devastating effects on the Yanomami in Brazil and strong measures are needed to protect the integrity of the Yanomami territory in Venezuela, the army brings problems of its own. We were told that for a Venezuelan officer, an Amazon border posting like this was more a punishment than a promotion. Thus, the motivation and morale of the officers, and even more so of the soldiers, was poor, and they repeatedly took out their frustrations on the defenseless Yanomami through abuses, including rape. The current concern of the Yanomami was the army's intent to establish a camp at Ocamo, where 150 soldiers would be based, doubling the male population in the area. Although this allegedly would be for their protection, the Yanomami feared the soldiers' presence and could not understand why the army could not build its own airstrip elsewhere and leave them alone.

García was surprised by the opposition of the Yanomami to these government initiatives and had not anticipated the depth of their antagonism to the military. Relations between SADA-AMAZONAS and the army are relatively good, and he had been favorable to the plans for the camp, believing that it would be in the best interests of the Yanomami and would ensure their protection from the *garimpeiros*. At the end of the meeting, he promised to discuss relocation of the post with the head office of the army in Caracas. (We subsequently learned that the post was to be established downriver.)

The other main concern of the Yanomami was the numerous intrusions into their territory by "scientific expeditions." There had been six of these in the past month alone, mostly composed of foreigners, and the Yanomami suspected that the members of these expeditions were tourists rather than scientists. There were reports of these groups climbing *tepuys* (unique "tabletop" geological formations, strictly protected by law); collecting relics from sacred sites; inducing Indians to sell them jaguar skins, as well as parrots, tortoises, and other wild animals; and taking photographs of the Yanomami, who find this practice offensive. "Even if they are scientists," one Yanomami said to us, "we have no idea what they are doing, and we learn nothing from their work." They were also concerned about the diseases and alcohol habits the foreigners brought.

The repeated intrusions of ecotourists seeking a "unique jungle experience" were a common complaint of all the indigenous groups we met during our travels through the Amazon Territory. Part of the problem is lack of proper control and supervision of these groups. Each time we encountered a *bongo* (dugout canoe) gliding up the river, García would intercept it and demand to see the passengers' authorization to be in the biosphere reserve. In every case, the guide leading the group would produce an official-looking document. In one instance, the document had been signed by the governor of the territory; another time, the document bore the signature of a senior officer in the army. In fact, SADA-AMAZONAS is the only institution authorized to issue travel permits for the area, but it does not yet have the capacity to control the situation, and a wide range of officials are happy to issue permits and, presumably, accept the requisite fee. García explained this to the Yanomami, assuring them that he was trying to get the situation under control, but asked them to be patient and not to expect immediate changes.

The third problem of the Yanomami, the lack of health facilities along the upper Orinoco, had been neglected by the Venezuelan government. For example, in the Conference on the Yanomami Culture held in Venezuela in 1991, a Ministry of Health spokesman claimed that malaria was not a major problem in the Venezuelan Amazon and that no deaths from the disease had been reported in the previous year. This assertion was challenged at the conference by Luis Urdaneta, a Yanomami Indian who runs the dispensary at Ocamo. Urdaneta explained that not only was he himself suffering from malaria and hepatitis but also the disease was rampant in the region. During our visit, we saw that the dispensary at Ocamo had only the most basic facilities. Because the microscope did not function properly, blood samples could not be tested there and had to be sent downriver by motorized *bongo* to Puerto Ayacucho, a two-day trip each way. This led to delays in the treatment of diseases that require immediate attention, sometimes with fatal consequences. Physicians rarely visit the region, and when they do, they spend little time there, usually carrying out quick surveys. It was not clear why the Ministry of Health pays so little attention to the Yanomami. Major improvements in health care are clearly needed if the biosphere reserve is to be successful in providing a dignified life for its inhabitants.

One issue that the Yanomami did not raise was concern about the implications of the national park and biosphere reserve for them, although this has been a controversial issue in the past. Proposals for protection of the Yanomami territory have been discussed since the late 1970s. Before then, the Amazon Territory had largely been ignored by Venezuelan society and political leaders. Venezuela, a country twice the size of France and with a population of only 19 million, is rich in natural resources, particularly oil, iron ore, bauxite, and other minerals. Oil is the lifeblood of the Venezuelan economy. The main oil deposits and related industry are mostly located in the coastal areas, where most of the population lives, although large new deposits of heavy oil have been found in the grasslands, or *llanos,* in the center of the country. The upper Orinoco was far away, inaccessible, and not a priority for development. It was not economically viable to extract timber or mineral ore from the region. The consequent neglect of the region had negative aspects, such as the lack of health care, but had advantages when compared with parts of the Amazon in other countries, such as Brazil, which were using their forests as a "pressure valve," encouraging landless farmers to migrate there, with disastrous results.

However, in the 1970s things began to change. Under the government of Luis Herrera Campins (1979–1983), the first mineral exploitation rights were granted in Yanomami territory. This caused considerable controversy, primarily because of the environmental and social impacts that mineral exploitation would have. The government's motives in granting the concession were unclear to many. The region is so isolated that without a major road-building campaign, mineral exploitation would be hopelessly uneconomical. The wisdom of mineral exploitation in the country's major watershed was also questioned. As a result of this controversy, commercial logging in the territory was banned in 1978, and mining was subsequently banned in 1989. SADA-AMAZONAS was set up by the Ministry of Environment and Natural Resources in 1989, with the lead role for conservation and development in the territory. One of the branches of SADA-AMAZONAS is the Alejandro von Humboldt Amazon Center for Environmental Research at La Esmeralda, in the heart of the reserve.

It was not until the 1991 presidential decree that official, permanent protection was granted to the land of the Yanomami and the Yekuana. The form this protection should take had been the subject of numerous discussions. The preference of many anthropologists and of the indigenous groups was for land titling, which would give individuals or communities permanent control over their lands. Only after the governments of Brazil and Venezuela survey and zone the land will the Yanomami gain even partial control of their traditional territory. Under this scheme, scientists and economists are to determine which areas of the Yanomami land in Brazil should be preserved as nature reserves or set aside for traditional hunting and trapping. Additional zones will be used by rubber tappers, and others could be opened to dam and road construction. In Brazil, mineral rights will remain with the government.

"The main thing that we are asking for is title to our land," said José Seripino, a member of the indigenous people's cooperative, SUYAO, in 1991. "We want to live better, without mining. We want to live in peace, without problems." But land titling would have required intricate and time-consuming changes in legislation, with unclear prospects for success.

The proposal for the creation of a national park, overlapped by a biosphere reserve, initially caused concern among the Yanomami. "We don't know exactly what a national park is, and we don't want a national park," said another SUYAO member, Itilio Hoariwe. "Our land will be threatened by the creation of a national park. If they create a national park, where will we hunt?" Pedro García assured the Yanomami that their traditional subsistence (noncommercial) hunting would still be allowed. In view of the legal problems associated with indigenous land titling and the weakness of other possibilities, such as Indian reserves or land titles under the agrarian reform law, the national park/biosphere reserve option was finally chosen by the government as the most immediate and effective way to protect the territory and the people in it.

The decree establishing the Upper Orinoco–Casiquiare Biosphere Reserve and Parima-Tapirapeco National Park recognizes the rights of the Yanomami and the Yekuana inhabitants to land and natural resources. It also establishes measures to protect the Indians' traditional livelihoods and indirectly acknowledges the Indians' rights over their lands by stating that the decree is in accordance with Venezuelan legislation, which recognizes convention 107 of the International Labor Organization.

The reserve was placed under the authority of SADA-AMAZONAS, and a management committee was established to help run the reserve and to prepare a management plan for the area over the next two years. An immediate priority is boundary demarcation on the ground. The committee is to include representatives of relevant government ministries, the Catholic church, universities, the army, and the Yanomami and Yekuana communities. The committee met for the first time on October 19, 1992.

The decree also gave SADA-AMAZONAS the mandate to promote "self-development" in the region, as well as "ethnodevelopment" among the indigenous communities in the reserve, in a participatory manner. Colonization of the area and other interventions that violate Indian communities' rights are prohibited.

The forests in this area are unique both biologically and culturally: apart from being the homeland of the Yanomami and the Yekuana, they include a wide range of habitats, from tropical alpine ecosystems on the tops of isolated sandstone *tepuys,* over 2,000 meters high, down to lowland Amazon rain forests at their feet. The *tepuys* function biologically as islands and are sacred sites for the Amerindians in the area. They are now protected by Venezuelan legislation as national monuments.

The upland areas at the heart of the Yanomami territory divide the enormous drainage basins of the Amazon and Orinoco rivers and form a natural barrier between Venezuela and Brazil. As the source of the Orinoco, the area has major hydrological significance. The river runs in a clockwise loop out of the Amazon Territory, flowing 4,000 kilometers through the country before emerging at the edge of the Caribbean Sea.

Our next stop was in La Esmeralda, a small Yekuana settlement down the Orinoco, which is to be the site for the Alejandro von Humboldt research center for the reserve. It is a well-known center for making curare, which is also used by many Amerindians to coat arrows and darts for warfare.

We were reminded of the rich biodiversity of the rain forest as we came across some Yekuana Indians making a *bongo* from a large log. One of the botanists in our party was intrigued by the log and later identified the species as *Cedrelinga catenaefarmis,* which had not previously been recorded in Venezuela. This tree grows to a diameter of more than 2 meters and can reach a height of 40 meters. Each year, several new species are discovered in the Amazon, and biologists believe that many more—known by the indigenous people—have yet to be named by science.

As we left the reserve, we felt a mixture of optimism and sadness. The cultural and biological richness of the area and the enthusiasm of the SADA-AMAZONAS staff were encouraging. But the group expressed concern that Venezuela's fragile democracy might not be able to guarantee the security of the reserve in the long term. In 1992 alone, there had been three attempted coups to overthrow the government. However, local support for the reserve continues to gain momentum, and international concern and funding are beginning to grow. The Spanish government, through IUCN (the World Conservation Union), and the GTZ (Gessellschaft für

Technische Zusammenarbeit) are preparing management plans and funding training and inventories.

The survival of the Yanomami, and that of the forests in which they have lived for centuries, depends on concerted efforts to ensure that the zoning is carefully planned to prevent environmentally and culturally destructive schemes—and that promises made to the Yanomami are kept.

JOHN CORDELL

Who Owns the Land?
Indigenous Involvement
in Australian Protected Areas

Promises disappear, just like writing in the sand.
YOTHU YINDI

Minga, they call them. Little ants. That is how the tourists look to the Anangu as they rush out of their buses, forming long, winding trails up and down the face of Uluru—to have a look, to say they have done it, have been there, have stood on top and signed the visitors' book. It is an endless passage of aliens. More strangers come and go in a day than there are people in the entire community of Mutitjulu. They come from all over the world, and all are intent on climbing to the top of the rock. Then they scramble back down and disappear into the coaches, never to be seen again.

Dozens of them die doing it. Breathless, hearts racing, they embark on their last act: the heroic ascent of Ayers Rock, one of Australia's most powerful cultural symbols, 9 kilometers around and rising abruptly 300 meters off the desert floor. If you are to get your money's worth, you just have to stand on top of that rock.

The Anangu, an aboriginal desert people who have lived in Australia for centuries, are more than witnesses to this; they are part of the attraction, offering visitors a chance to "see the culture in action"—the indispensable exotic dimension of a unique Australian landscape. Swarms of tourists are the price (a small price, park authorities insist) the Mutitjulu community pays for official recognition of its ancestral estate and a voice in its future management.

For thousands of years, the Anangu have flourished in what to nonaboriginal eyes must seem a place of arid desolation. Yet this parched, red earth is their home, the source of their spirit, and a place of enduring beauty and fecundity. Land that to a stranger might appear as a marginal, featureless plain is to the Anangu a center, plentiful and diverse. The Anangu have no other history as human beings but here, and their homeland is testament to the continuing power and creative force of the Aboriginal Law, Tjukurr.

The Anangu are Yankatjatjara and Pitjantjatjara speakers from the center of Australia. Theirs is an egalitarian, communal society, united by kinship and economic relations of gift and service. Their subsistence production, like that of other aboriginal groups, depends on profound knowledge of natural resources—not just the location of intermittent water supplies but also plant and animal stocks and their kind and season, distribution, and behavior.

The Anangu have developed flexible, open systems of group affiliation and membership that allow for a necessarily high degree of personal mobility and that provide real security in an uncertain environment. Spiritual practices hold the peoples of the desert in strong networks of responsibility and custodial relationship to the land and to one another. This land is not wilderness, and Anangu knowledge cannot be commoditized. It is inalienable, owned by those who must use it to live each day.

Uluru–Kata Tjuta National Park is aboriginal land, an integral part of the ancestral estate of the Anangu people. For indigenous people, this fact is incontestable. It has always been so. Yet it was not until October 1985 that the Australian government was prepared to give any form of recognition of ownership to the Anangu. Under the Aboriginal (Northern Territory) Land Rights Act of 1976, title was granted to the Uluru–Kata Tjuta Aboriginal Land Trust, but only on the condition that the land be leased back to the Australian government as a national park. After decades of struggle, the Anangu actually held the title for about thirty-five seconds before relinquishing their ancestral rights to the state for the next ninety-nine years.

Some Anangu are deeply critical of the ninety-nine-year lease, seeing it as a denial of self-determination; they feel that they should be free to negotiate the continued existence of the park itself. The history of the Anangu mirrors the colonial miseries of all aboriginal peoples, who remain the poorest people in Australia, with the worst health and lowest life expectancy, the lowest level of mainstream education, and the highest imprisonment rates. Yet despite lack of recognition of their legal, cultural, and human rights, aboriginal peoples continue to assert claims to their ancestral estates, to sovereign authority over their cultural domains, to their land and law.

Two World Heritage sites, Uluru and Kakadu National Park, are lauded as Australian success stories of indigenous involvement in protected area management. As partners in this joint venture with the Australian National Parks and Wildlife Service (ANPWS), aboriginal people receive the acknowledged right to live on their lands, are free to practice their culture, have majority representation on park governing boards, and are protected by strong lease provisions, through which they receive rent and a share of the parks' income from tourism.

Places like Uluru and Kakadu, however, are only part of the Australian experience of indigenous comanagement. They are reputed to be the best part, providing a measure of accommodation of indigenous interests. Yet compulsory aboriginal participation embodied in the Northern Territory comanagement compromises can hardly be held up as a formula for self-determination. Nor do the agreements for comanaging Kakadu and Uluru represent any coherent national strategy to integrate and protect indigenous values or rights in protected areas. This is in spite of the fact that protected areas are being touted as one of the primary vehicles for what Australia calls its process of "national reconciliation," the Labor government's progressive, though somewhat vague, plans to repair the two centuries of injustice and suffering that have been inflicted on aborigines.

Compared with the early history of national parks in Australia, which largely excluded indigenous interests, not to mention customary tenure and land claims, opportunities for indigenous participation in a range of conservation initiatives have increased dramatically in parts of the country today. However, a closer look at the political economy of protected area development in Australia may reveal why policies of comanagement in conservation areas, like reconciliation, promise a lot more than they can deliver, as explained in Sheila Davey's introduction to part four of this book. These euphemisms for deeper indigenous concerns, namely, land justice, may ultimately be rejected by aborigines and Torres Strait Islanders as so much "whitefella" dreaming.

Before succumbing to British colonialism in 1788, virtually the whole of Australia was owned and occupied by aborigines. The reality and antiquity of aboriginal settlement and ownership of the continent, greatly predating the arrival of Europeans, stands in stark contrast to the legal fiction of *terra nullius,* or "land belonging to no one," a doctrine recently struck down by Australia's High Court. Tribal and clan territories, today often referred to as "clan estates," extended over land and sea, in some cases quite far offshore. With European expansion, despite widespread dislocation and dispossession of people from their home "countries," many

A black crinoid perched on gorgonian
coral with a school of small fish,
Micronesia, Pacific Ocean.
Courtesy WWF/Jack S. Grove.

A Papuan with a dress of bird of paradise plumes and a necklace of
tree kangaroo skin, New Guinea. Courtesy WWF/Duncan Poore.

A young Zimbabwean woman harvesting her crops, Gokwe District, Zimbabwe. Courtesy WWF/Sandra Mbanefo.

Two Zimbabwean children try to scoop water from an almost-dry riverbed in Gokwe District, Zimbabwe. Courtesy WWF/Sandra Mbanefo.

Dehorning of a rhino, Zimbabwe, 1992. This program was developed to take the mounting pressure off rhinos. Courtesy WWF/Michel Gunther/BIOS.

A Yanomami woman rests in her hammock while roasting an armadillo.
These forest dwellers depend on hunting for their survival.
Courtesy Victor Englebert/Time-Life Books.

Yanomami village, Amazon rain forest, Brazil. Courtesy Victor Englebert.

Yanomami Indians in a jungle garden in the Amazon. A woman is loading bananas onto her back, and the boy is eating sugarcane. Courtesy Victor Englebert/Time-Life Books.

Yanomami child in the Brazilian Amazon.
Courtesy Victor Englebert/Time-Life Books.

Lotus, Blue Lagoon, Lakefield National Park, eastern Cape York Peninsula. Courtesy Kerry Trapnell.

Aboriginal gallery site, Laura sandstone escarpments.
Courtesy Kerry Trapnell.

A man mending fishing nets, Torres Strait Islands, Australia.
Courtesy Kerry Trapnell.

Traditional Hatam house in the village of Kwok, Arfak Mountains Strict
Nature Reserve, Irian Jaya, Indonesia. Courtesy WWF/Ian Craven.

Hatam villager in the buffer zone of Arfak
Mountains Strict Nature Reserve with a butterfly
from his ranch. Courtesy WWF/Duncan Neville.

aboriginal groups were able to maintain a strong sense of belonging to land and sea areas. Continuity of tenure, on a scale that is still not appreciated by government authorities, is constantly being renewed and experienced by both urban and remote communities as individuals and families move back and forth between town and bush. In aboriginal thinking, tenure customs—and not simply what researchers construe as "environmental knowledge"—must be the foundation for involvement in protected areas. This tenure connection is not something that people feel they ever lost, whether or not their traditional claims are ever completely acknowledged in land rights legislation. The well-meaning conservationist, disillusioned when aborigines come across as less than grateful or enthusiastic about a park gazetted for comanagement, fails to grasp the irony involved in according traditional owners the Western science status of "resource managers" on their own lands.

Practically no area of public policy in Australia today is more rife with speculation, misconceptions, and stereotypes than the question of indigenous peoples' involvement in conservation. "Greens" are highly polarized on the issue of whether blacks living in protected areas should be allowed to engage in so-called traditional hunting, fishing, and gathering. A national debate rages over what economic activities can be classed as traditional for purposes of environmental legislation. Political conflicts and cultural misunderstandings spring from historical divisions between blacks and whites in Australia, compounded by the gulf that separates those charged with managing parks and resources from those who must live with management regulations.

Current political events in Australia, epitomized by the ruling in the landmark *Mabo* case (explained in "Boundaries and Bloodlines," the introduction to this part), hold out the promise of increasing aboriginal control of protected areas. Parallel to this, environmental managers are becoming more sensitive to aboriginal concerns and more conscious of the long-range environmental benefits of customary ways of "caring for country." However, there is still a pressing need to convey to protected area managers a better understanding of aboriginal land and marine tenure and all that it implies.

Among other impediments, progress on this front is hampered by some basic problems of cross-cultural translation. Aboriginal tenure carries special obligations to protect and sustain ancestral territory that go beyond "possession" in a strict legal sense. Customary law ranges from ritual burning of the countryside during the annual round to careful control of the comings and goings of outsiders (including other aborigines) so that they do not stray into dangerous zones, or "poison places."

There are no Western equivalents for many kinds of sacred sites and the elaborate ceremonies that must be observed to safeguard them. Aboriginal cosmologies locate sacred sites and related "storyplaces" along "dreaming tracks" created in the distant past (the Dreamtime) by supernatural beings. These beliefs convey and reinforce the aboriginal spirit and perception of interrelatedness of all things in the natural world. Aboriginal people find it inconceivable that they could be isolated in any way from the responsibility of caring for their home countries.

Deciphering tenure relations—the custodial connection between kin and country—is proving a formidable task for protected area managers in Australia. People who can properly "speak for country" must be identified before any meaningful consultation can take place between the owners of clan estates and protected area authorities. Most indigenous communities are represented by some form of community organization, whether it be a local corporation, a housing cooperative, or a council. These organizations are essential for political action, but they are not necessarily the loci of decision making when it comes to the distribution and uses of clan resources. Comanagement deals cut in the back room or at public meetings with aboriginal council leaders do not necessarily carry the consent of traditional landowners. One thing that can make life miserable for Australian protected area managers is the extreme atomistic character of postcolonial aboriginal society, in which communities compete, often as warring factions, for government goodies and there are no indigenous umbrella groups or federations (as in Latin America) with the authority to represent a cross section of communities.

Given the intricacies of aboriginal tenure, how successful—indeed, how useful and generalizable—is the Uluru model for shared management of protected areas? What are its strengths and shortcomings? A more critical look at how joint management has evolved on the ground sets the Australian cases in perspective.

In 1976, the Northern Territory (N. T.) Land Rights Act made it possible for aborigines officially to regain ownership of the areas that were eventually to be declared Uluru and Kakadu national parks. After more than ten years of negotiation with the Commonwealth, aborigines now legally own and share power on the governing boards and in the day-to-day operations of four N.T. parks: Kakadu; Gurig National Park, on the Cobourg Peninsula; Nitmiluk (Katherine Gorge) National Park; and Uluru.

Uluru–Kata Tjuta and Kakadu became the first aboriginally owned national parks in the country after the Commonwealth obtained commitments from the Anangu and Jawoin peoples that they would automatically lease their lands back to the government as national parks. According to some observers, the lease-back and comanagement provisions that were drawn up constituted state-sanctioned "greenmail" legitimized by the Federal National Parks and Wildlife Conservation Act of 1975.

A relatively powerless N.T. administration, faced with the prospect of further alienation of lands either from successful land claims or from the possible declaration of federal national parks, has itself been forced to negotiate generous park deals. Nitmiluk and Gurig are two cases that list among their provisions recognition of traditional ownership, strong comanagement arrangements, annual rents or fees, and some guarantees of long-term indigenous interests in the lease.

In addition, it is not simply the separation of powers between Commonwealth and states that explains the relative strength of indigenous rights in conservation in the Northern Territory. Its national parks are very much part of Australia's resource frontier, and the relative scarcity of capital development in the region has meant fewer competing uses for land, in contrast to the situation in more densely populated areas of Australia's eastern coast.

Not all of the figures are in on the Uluru model; it has its pros and cons. For the ANPWS, comanagement translates into greater access to spheres of traditional knowledge for managing country, aboriginal assistance in conducting environmental research and in interpreting cultural and natural history information, and revenue sharing from tourism. The idea is that overall, the "blackfella" presence is supposed to enhance the visitors' experience. Significantly, the Uluru approach does contribute to greater land tenure security for aboriginal people, in lieu of national land rights or a treaty. Comanagement arrangements include funding for a range of community projects, housing, roads, health and education benefits, income from tourism, control of cultural sites, and, finally, support from environmental agencies for the continuity of traditional resource management practices. On the down side, the national park lease-back status is conditional; it precludes certain development avenues that would otherwise be open to communities. Nor do aboriginal owners have the choice of closing or degazetting the N.T. parks. At Uluru, where population pressure threatens to overwhelm cultural practices, the Anangu are able to exercise little control over the influx of tourists.

Moreover, evidence from Kakadu and elsewhere indicates that tourism is of marginal economic benefit to indigenous people. It may even leave them worse off. At Kakadu and Nitmiluk, there are no aboriginal controls on tourism growth, although, as at Uluru, custodians have some power over access and use. There are, however, strong and persistent criticisms from aboriginal people over the invasion of privacy, the taking of photographs, and intrusion onto sacred and significant places. As one Anangu leader put it: "We still worry for photos. *Minga* come and take photos anyway, not listening to Anangu. Take photos of *miilmiilpa* [sacred areas], take photos of Anangu. *Kura mulapa nyangatja*. [That's really wrong.] I say to them, '*Mamu wiya ngayula. Anangu ngayulu*.' ['I'm not a monster. I'm a person.']"

In late 1992, the Anangu were embroiled in a bitter dispute over access rights to the park. Having refused permission for a large social club gathering at Uluru, the Anangu found themselves invaded by more than 300 drivers, who overran barricades and asserted their right to go wherever they liked in the "lucky country." The drivers have since been strongly supported in their actions by the chief minister of the Northern Territory. Clearly, the Anangu can be forgiven for having grave concerns for the future of their lands.

Disputes of this kind are now an ongoing part of life for the Mutitjulu community. Tourists wander where they have been told not to go, to places where aboriginal women and children would never be allowed, and debase powerful and revered places.

On another level, judging from Kakadu and Uluru, aboriginal involvement in protected area management is on the verge of degenerating into Smokey Bear–style ranger training, in which the role of traditional owners is simply to add an interpretive and marketable ethnic element to running the parks.

In Kakadu and Uluru national parks, the two principal forms of aboriginal involvement are employment in the mainstream park service or in the tourism industry, amounting to a kind of compulsory incorporation into a commercial economy. The development of federal policies of joint management in protected areas has, at least in part, been motivated by the Aboriginal Employment Development Policy scheme (AEDP).

Other tensions and incompatibilities are evident: between the indigenous social economy and wage labor, between family and clan obligations and jobs. Now, even though the Anangu have ownership, they find that they still cannot control tourists, and, like it or not, they find themselves forced to participate in the commoditization of their culture. Nor is there any guarantee that their participation will ensure that visitors learn respect for their culture.

Events unfolding elsewhere around Australia point to an alternative approach to indigenous involvement in protected areas: indigenous community initiatives. This movement is not about community-based conservation, so popular in international conservation circles. It may not make many waves beyond western Oceania, but it has the potential, ultimately, to render both Queensland and N.T. comanagement innovations obsolete. What is happening is that communities themselves are seizing the initiative and declaring their own indigenous, tenure-based protected areas without waiting for official recognition. By presenting government agencies with a *fait accompli,* this strategy shifts the burden and cost of negotiating any challenges or disputes to the state. In any case, communities traditionally act informally to protect sacred sites, control access to territory, and resolve resource management conflicts. But certain marginal, disenfranchised communities are finding it especially exhilarating and empowering to begin consciously to take resource management into their own hands, as owners of their clan estates.

A pioneering effort in this regard is being made by the Kowanyama aboriginal community on western Cape York Peninsula. Kowanyama's lands are currently administered as a 1,000-square-kilometer Queensland aboriginal DOGIT (deed of grant in trust) territory. Kowanyama residents contest ownership of only a relatively small section of a nearby national park. However, the community is gradually gaining respect and a reputation as an innovative land management agency. Its resource management initiatives include negotiated closure of commercial fishing in ancestral fishing grounds in the Mitchell River Delta; community-oriented interpretive and educational projects designed to integrate traditional environmental knowledge in the schools; creation of a watershed management network consisting of aboriginal and nonaboriginal user groups; and a ranger program responsive to local cultural and natural resource preservation priorities. The Kowanyama Council is conducting its own cultural site mapping program and developing its own geographic information system (GIS) to help manage its lands and fisheries. The collective visions of Kowanyama's elders concerning the scope of environmental management go well beyond the standards for national parks. The council points out that "it would be a sad thing indeed if the only land people cared for in the future were national parks and protected areas."

Australia's other indigenous minority, the Torres Strait Islanders, whose distinctive Melanesian cultural heritage differs from that of the aborigines, in fact has much in common with aboriginal coastal communities in terms of subsistence hunting and fishing and exclusive, clan-based land and marine tenure. Islanders are also generating a range of community conservation initiatives in their quest for government recognition of home island, reef, and sea rights.

Much of the Islanders' maritime domain does not qualify as a marine park.

Rather, it is a special kind of transnational protected area, known as the Torres Strait Protected Zone. In 1978, the Torres Strait Treaty between Australia and Papua New Guinea established the protected zone, primarily for regulating fisheries. It allows for the continuation of "traditional fishing" and free movement by Torres Strait Islanders and Papuans and defines commercial fishing areas and seabed jurisdiction between the two countries.

The treaty looks good on paper. However, it establishes no rights of indigenous people per se. Similarly, no treaty-related Commonwealth or Queensland jurisdiction (which encompasses Torres Strait) recognizes indigenous fishing rights. Not long ago, the realization that Islanders had no rights whatsoever to their home seas and islands really hit home. This is largely what prompted Eddie Mabo and others to pursue their High Court petition, as explained in the introduction to this part.

Consequently, in May 1991, foreshadowing the High Court ruling that quashed *terra nullius,* Islanders organized to lay down their own principles and objectives for the future of Torres Strait. This charter is embodied in MASTS, the Marine Conservation Strategy for Torres Strait. Significantly, a centerpiece of MASTS is establishment of a set of indigenous protected areas, supported by the basic premises that Torres Strait Islanders are the traditional and current users of the marine environment and that securing customary tenure is a prerequisite to protecting resources, improving livelihoods, and encouraging the sustainable development of the unique and vulnerable environment of the Torres Strait region. Islanders will settle for nothing less than identification and confirmation in law of land and sea rights in a manner enforceable through Australian and Queensland courts.

Mick Dodson of the Northern Land Council injects a philosophical note in speaking of the implications of *Mabo:* "Mere possession of land or sea is a critical first step, but not the whole answer in overcoming our woes. Ideally, other things will come with landownership, i.e., people will gain more control over their lives, housing, health, jobs, etc. A settlement that involves self-government and self-determination in the fullest sense is what is needed, not just land and sea rights. The nation and justice would be far better served, rather than facing a landslide of post-*Mabo* litigation, if the federal cabinet would sit down with us and negotiate a treaty, something we sought long before the *Mabo* decision."

So, for a really Australian experience, what could be better than heading for the outback and mingling with the "blackfellas"? *Coolamons* and dances. Wisdom of the elders. Fetishized indigenous images to help save the environment. ESD (ecologically sustainable development). Even the Royal Commission into Aboriginal Deaths in Custody recommends more aboriginal involvement in protected areas.

Notwithstanding Australia's improving track record in accommodating indigenous peoples in protected area management at home, aboriginal people and Torres Strait Islanders were conspicuously absent at the recent IUCN Fourth World Congress on National Parks and Protected Areas in Caracas. In the end, the congress's "people and protected areas" theme was in many ways about the people who were not there—the customary owners of many of the world's "tropical biodiversity hot spots," biosphere reserves, and parks.

One wonders, Would things have turned out differently had the option of traditional tenure holders to bar outsiders, or at least to regulate their activities, been retained in places like Uluru and Kakadu? This is just one of the questions raised by the brand of protected area partnerships taking shape on indigenous homelands in Australia. Is the Uluru and Kakadu model equitable for indigenous peoples? Have two hundred years of dispossession been reversed? Is it really "no worries, mate"? Or, in deconstructing the political economy of national parks in Australia, are we seeing the lengthening and tightening of green fingers around black lands?

Butterfly Ranching

For the isolated Hatam people living beside the Arfak Mountains Strict Nature Reserve in Irian Jaya, Indonesia, any reliable source of cash income is difficult to find. Unless they move to town, where employment possibilities are few, most of their income comes from garden produce or the exploitation of forest resources. Garden produce has to be transported to town, a two- to three-day journey by foot. Given the effort expended just to reach the market, the income received is low.

The Hatam are a subsistence farming and hunting people. Both men and women are well adapted to the rigors of walking up and down mountain slopes in search of game and in tending their gardens. Their leg and back muscles are comparable to those of the finest athlete. Nevertheless, most are poor and undernourished: they deprive themselves of adequate food in order to sell it in town. Their simple diet is based largely on sweet potatoes with carrots and greens.[1]

The Hatam have no tradition of raising animals in cages or pens; domestic animals, such as pigs and chickens, run free and are normally reserved for special occasions or sold. Protein therefore comes from wild animals like deer, tree kangaroo, wild pig, and birds, hunted with bow and arrow or air rifle. Their shifting-cultivation vegetable gardens involve the destructive practice of slash and burn, requiring a great deal of land.[2]

In 1986, WWF, working alongside the Indonesian Directorate General of Forest Protection and Nature Conservation (PHPA), began a joint management strategy for the Arfak Mountains Strict Nature Reserve. The reserve has had some protected status since 1957 but became an official protected area in 1982, with full protected status achieved in 1992.[3] The plan was to formulate a management strategy that would gain local landowners' approval for the reserve by allowing the Hatam to continue to use natural resources to support themselves. An aim was to encourage the Hatam to replace their slash-and-burn agricultural practice with a more sustainable method by introducing new farming techniques and alternative sources of income.[4]

Butterfly "ranching" was considered a viable option.[5] The Arfak's Rothchild's birdwing butterfly is found nowhere else in the world; four additional birdwing butterflies are also ranched here, and collectors in Japan, the United Kingdom, France, Germany, and the United States are willing to pay a handsome price for these and other Indonesian specimens. Since 1975, the Insect Farming and Trading Agency (IFTA) in neighboring Papua New Guinea has helped villagers benefit from marketing their local natural resources, including butterflies. In Arfak, small-scale agricultural projects have also been developed to complement the butterfly-ranching scheme.[6]

The Arfak Mountains Strict Nature Reserve comprises 68 square kilometers in the Bird's Head region of Irian Jaya.[7] It lies within the Manokwari Regency, about 25 kilometers southwest of the town of Manokwari, with its population of 40,000, and rises steeply from the coastal plain to an altitude of more than 2,800 meters. Three tribes live in the region—the Hatam, the Soughb, and the Meyahk—but the reserve itself lies entirely within Hatam lands. The Soughb and Meyahk have access to the coast by way of footpaths across the Arfak Mountains.

The establishment of projects attempting to link management of protected areas with local social and economic development faced considerable challenges. The management strategy was based on the idea that there must be acceptance from the Hatam landowners—not an easy feat, given that Hatam decision making is based on consensus: it is customary that all people involved must agree before a decision is implemented. Nine different Hatam dialects and traditional warring factions among villages also had to be overcome. Then there was the challenge of getting local people and government personnel to work together. The government of Indonesia has ultimate authority over land, so protected areas can, in fact, be planned and implemented without reference to local people. After two years of consultation—involving seven visits with the Hatam elders before they agreed that their traditional lands could be included in the reserve—the Arfak Mountains Nature Conservation Area Irian Jaya Management Plan 1988–1992 was approved.[8]

"Marking of the reserve boundary was done in three stages between December 1987 and early 1991 and proved a challenging task," says Ian Craven, former WWF project leader and one of the collaborators in the creation of the management plan. "But we had a commitment from the Hatam to respect the boundary and maintain the resources within the protected area while still retaining the right to hunt and to use the forest in traditional ways. It was a very important compromise."[9]

The first big challenge was to identify a boundary for the reserve. WWF insisted that the Hatam be involved in identifying boundaries. It realized that employing local skill would facilitate drawing of the boundaries and would stimulate local respect for the reserve. Government boundary marking usually involves a small team hand-cutting a narrow trail, guided by only a map line drawing, followed by the placement of concrete posts every 50 to 100 meters—a formidable task.[10] The Hatam brought hundreds of years of traditional family landownership to the discussion table.

The reserve and adjacent outlying lands were partitioned into nature reserve management areas (NRMAs). Initially, there were twelve NRMAs, but intervillage arguments made sixteen necessary. The size and boundary of each NRMA were defined by the extent to which each collective group of landowners was willing to work together. A committee of influential people, such as village heads and church leaders, who may themselves be landowners, was assigned to manage each NRMA in accordance with tribal customs and community decisions. The committee was responsible for identifying the official landowners and overseeing the correct marking of the length of boundary running across their lands. However, there were still problems. For example, a landowner might want the boundary high up the hill, while a neighbor might want it lower down. And the eastern boundary was marked before the system was established; thus gardens and even houses were to be erroneously included in the reserve.[11]

The system works on the theory that the boundary falls under multiple jurisdictions, allowing rapid identification of landowners and outsiders should there be a violation of the reserve's regulations. The Hatam were allowed to retain enough land outside the reserve for future gardening needs.[12]

An important part of the NRMA system is the fact that each committee is provided with government-sanctioned powers to enforce the reserve's regulations within its area.[13] The committees were also very involved in implementing economic incentives and other development projects in their areas. The NRMA committees ensured that no permanent houses or gardens were established. Other regulations stipulate that firewood may be collected, but standing trees may not be felled; hunting is permitted only with traditional bows and arrows (not with air rifles or firearms); birdwing butterflies and other protected wildlife may not be collected for sale; trees may be felled for tribal needs but not for sale; people from one community may not take forest resources belonging to another community without first obtaining permission from that village committee and the landowners; and fires may be built for cooking and comfort but not to aid hunting.[14]

While the regulations allow the continuation of Hatam traditional use, outsiders face much stricter rules. They are not allowed to hunt, to make temporary shelters from forest materials, or to remove animals, plants, or trees.

If the rules are flouted—for example, if someone kills a bird of paradise in the reserve—he or she receives a warning from the committee. Ignoring the warning may lead to a fine paid to the owner of the land where the bird was shot and/or confiscation of bows and arrows and the bird. The reporting system and direct intervention by the committees have proven very successful. Several hunters have been caught, and people who moved into the reserve to build gardens and houses have moved back out without incident.[15]

There were problems in the northern part of the reserve, where members of the Soughb tribe pulled up twenty markers because of jealousy that their land did not fall within the defined reserve boundary. Minor boundary changes were also made where local landowners were unhappy because the boundary cut through their gardens.[16] As of 1992, boundaries around villages within the reserve were still being demarcated.[17]

As the reserve was being put into place, butterfly ranching began in earnest. Because the Hatam people have never kept caged animals, butterflies are raised in the wild. Butterfly "gardens," a low-technology solution, tie in nicely with the Hatam tradition of gardening. No handling or care is needed, and the method is cheap: butterfly gardens use natural forest cover, so the Hatam need only transplant the birdwings' preferred food plants into their gardens. WWF is promoting a sustainable activity, providing a direct link between a protected area, where wild butterflies spend most of their lives, and local people, who receive economic incentive without damaging the natural forest. Ranching may also help replenish birdwing populations, much reduced by coastal trading dating from the mid-1970s.[18]

Since 1989, WWF has worked with the Hatam communities along the reserve's western boundary, planting the food vines of *Aristolochia* and *Rhododendrum* spp. to attract *Ornithoptera* birdwing butterflies—*Ornithoptera priamus poseidon, O. goliath, O. paradisea arfakensis, O. tithonus, O. rothschildi*—and *Troides oblongomaculatus*. The latter species feeds on the fast-growing vine *Aristolochia tagala* and has a low market value but is considered an excellent product for the live pupae market. "Butterfly houses," large enclosures where adult butterflies fly freely, are good potential markets because they require a steady supply of good-quality pupae. About 820 farmers were registered by late 1992 in the butterfly scheme, although not all were actively participating.

Butterfly gardens range in size from several square meters to 2 hectares, each with an appointed leader who monitors the garden's development and butterfly activity. In areas where vines do not grow so well, WWF field staff members provide consultations and advice on local growing conditions, such as soil type, drainage, and light conditions.

Ranching and marketing of birdwings requires careful organization and control. *Ornithoptera* are protected under Indonesian and international law, so permits are necessary. A group of farmers holds a permit covering all of its members, and photographs for identification cards are regularly updated. Only farmers holding identification cards are allowed to sell to the WWF-authorized collection office; there are reports of local people transporting larvae from other gardens to their own for the official inspection required before identification cards are issued.

"Illegal collection of pupae from the wild should be containable," says Duncan Neville, a butterfly expert with the project. "To be realistic, it is certain that people will continue to collect [illegally] these pupae from the wild, but we hope that a strict inspection system and good extension services will minimize this." Illegal collection may not seriously affect wild populations. The Arfak Mountains are difficult to get to, and *Aristolochia* vines grow very tall. The larvae generally feed and pupate high in the vines, making searching and collecting difficult.

WWF has built a collection office at the village of Mokwam, just outside the reserve's western boundary, where butterflies and pupae will be purchased and packaged. "Mokwam's 1,200-meter elevation makes its cool climate more suitable for hatching out adults," says Neville. "Then they can be killed, packaged, and labeled by species, origin, date of emergence, and agency stamp and sent to Manokwari for selling." The office will also be used as a training center for local people, and its garden will serve as an open-air study laboratory for butterfly food plants. Tourists will provide extra income from produce sales, and local people will serve as guides.

An adult birdwing is light and easily stored and transported, but expert handling and packaging for overseas mail delivery are crucial. Ranched adults are killed on emergence from the pupae and thus earn more than wild-netted adults; wholesale prices for birdwings range from about $1.50 to $60.00, depending on species, sex, and condition, but individual sales can earn twice as much. It is hoped the Hatam ranchers will receive as much as 60 percent of the wholesale price. In 1992, the first year of ranching, between 1,500 and 2,000 *O. priamus poseidon* pupae were expected, as well as about 500 pupae of other species.

The marketing system involves a local charitable foundation called Yayasan Bina Lestari Bumi Cenderawasih, which acts as management agent. Initial exports of the butterflies will take place through a partially state-owned company, P. T. Inhutani II, but Yayasan is applying for an export license and is expected to take over all aspects of the business within three years.

The United Kingdom's CITES[19] Scientific Authority for Animals is debating a special derogation to permit imports to the European community of at least some birdwing species—a crucial step in the project's future success. As Duncan Neville stresses: "If the people don't see some money coming in very soon from the pupae and butterflies they are collecting, support for the reserve and its boundary may fail. This could lead to an anticonservation and even an anti-WWF feeling." Nevertheless, there is still strong local support for the scheme. The Hatam know that the butterflies are valuable, and they feel that local traders have been taking advantage of them for years.

WWF is experimenting with other sustainable projects to help increase local people's incomes. Attempts to increase the number and diversity of local food plants by establishing home gardens were not always successful. The Hatam are unfamiliar with home gardening, generally planting crops and leaving them until harvest time. Also, pigs dug the gardens up, and the financial returns were poor. Experiments with pig-proof fences made from oil palm leaves have, however, proved an effective and inexpensive way of controlling pig damage.

Peanut growing was tried as an alternative and has proved very successful; peanuts give a quick return and need little maintenance. In late 1991, four farmers' groups harvested 80 to 232 kilograms of peanuts from their gardens with seed supplied by WWF. About 30 kilograms was set aside by each group as seed stock for future planting, and the rest was sold for 1,800 rupiah (about 85 cents) per kilogram. Most groups wanted to distribute the proceeds individually as an immediate reward, but the Angressi group decided to use its money to start a small cooperative shop. The venture had a successful first year, and other areas are trying to set up similar shops.[20]

Onion planting is being experimented with successfully as well, as Manokwari imports most of its onions and transportation is unreliable and expensive. And WWF has been involved in efforts to improve the genetic stock of local village chickens. Disease wiped out the new stock in the first year, so subsequent efforts will concentrate on education, inspection, vaccination, and extension work.

Terracing, already a common practice elsewhere in Indonesia's hilly, mountainous terrain, is also being introduced in Irian Jaya to prevent erosion of fertile topsoil on steep slopes. WWF began experimental terracing of slopes and planting of leguminous crops in late 1991 in three communities north of the reserve, which faced increased land clearing for dry rice production. The aim is to increase gradually more site-stable agriculture, using methods such as terracing and leguminous crops such as peanuts and mung (soya) beans. If farmers can get more use from their land, the rate of opening new land should decrease. However, transformation of the region's agriculture will obviously be a long process.

The success of the reserve's experimental small-scale agricultural and birdwing butterfly ranching projects depends on local understanding, agreement, and involvement. The main components of each project depend on "ecoconservation development": the project must be directed to meet the basic needs of local people first; it must encourage self-reliance of local people; and it must enhance natural resource sustainability. Income-generating projects for local people must be in as close a symbiotic relationship with the natural resources of a protected area as possible. Opening of markets and application of marketing strategies are immediate tasks for the coming future, according to Ian Craven. Improvement of the standard of living through economic returns is an essential ingredient of the project.

"The Hatam are enthusiastic, even excited, about what's happening," says WWF's Duncan Neville. "How can it not be successful?" Like a butterfly undergoing metamorphosis, the Hatam in the Arfak Mountains in Irian Jaya are undergoing changes that they hope will help alter positively their way of life.

PART THREE

Nature in the Crossfire

Nature in the Crossfire

Parks and protected areas are supposed to be havens of tranquility and peace. Unfortunately, they are often places where conflict occurs. This frequently involves protection of park resources on the one hand and local development needs on the other. As the examples in this book indicate, conflicts relating to parks are often manifestations of enormous and intractable problems such as poverty and global environmental degradation. In a world in which the biophysical environment and sociocultural systems are changing rapidly, conflicts involving parks and protected areas are inevitable.

Conflict erupts mainly when people with competing interests and different values interact. This process can be useful and is an ever-present function in a dynamic society. Depending on the way in which problems are identified and solved, progress may be achieved. However, as we all know so well, many conflicts become counterproductive and destructive, leading to unwanted results and bad relationships. The challenge that park managers face is how to manage park conflicts so that the unproductive consequences are avoided while human welfare is safeguarded and the natural environment is protected.

The descriptions in part three of this book reveal that there are many reasons why conflicts arise in parks and protected areas. In almost all of these examples, the conflicts relate to (1) people in nearby communities having substantive needs that have come into direct opposition to the needs of the park (e.g., people's needs for grazing land, firewood, building materials, fodder, medicinal plants, and land for hunting) and (2) not enough attention being paid to the process of involving local people in decision making and park management. The approaches described in the chapters that follow all involve responses made to the substantive needs of the people engaged in conflict *and* the way in which the people whose interests were at stake were involved. Conflict management efforts that deal with only one of these dimensions are not likely to succeed.

A major challenge in resolving conflicts is to get the conflicting parties to abandon their positions long enough to examine the interests that are really at stake. Interests are people's fundamental needs and concerns; positions are the ideas put forward to try to protect interests. Often, a variety of different positions will serve the same interest. As an illustration, suppose that a farmer near a park has an interest in producing food from his or her fields. If this interest is being violated by the fact that grazing animals from the park are coming into the fields to eat the crops, the farmer may adopt a position that the animals should be shot. An alternative position might be that a fence should be built around the field.

A conflict management effort in which all interests are addressed is much more likely to result in a lasting and satisfactory resolution for everyone (i.e., a mutually agreeable outcome) than is an effort in which the interests of only one side are addressed. In conflict management terminology, a mutually agreeable outcome is sometimes called a "win-win"—all parties believe that they have gained something. The reason why conflict participants do not always strive for a mutually agreeable outcome, of course, is that to do so usually involves some amount of compromise. Unfortunately, therein lies the root of what so often makes conflict destructive and enduring.

It is important to emphasize that working toward a mutually agreeable outcome does not necessarily mean sacrificing the interests of either side. Replacing overt conflict with the stability and predictability of a mutually agreeable solution is often the best way to serve everyone's interests in the long run. In the context of park management, allowing some use of park resources may ultimately serve a park's interests better than keeping the park in strict reserve status. The alternative— perhaps uncontrolled poaching or outright warfare—could be worse.

Another critical element in conflict management is recognition of the power that various stakeholders have. Power comes in many forms:

- Power of position (having authority; having influence with decision makers)
- Family power (being from a well-connected family)
- Power of knowledge (having information)
- Personal power (being personally forceful or persuasive)
- Economic power (having financial resources)
- Political power (having a constituency)

- Legal power (having a "good" legal case and/or expert legal counsel)
- Coercive physical power (having police or military backing)

Some power is real (i.e., it exists); some is perceived (it does not really exist, but someone thinks that it does). When managing conflict, it is important to understand the relative power, both perceived and real, of the parties involved in the conflict. Each party's decisions about how to approach the conflict will depend a great deal on that party's view of the power balance. There are often extreme differences in power between parties in park conflicts. Park neighbors are often rural, poor, and less educated than urban park constituents. Parks themselves are often relatively powerless in dealing with conflict because of lack of staff, equipment, training, or outside support.

The examples in the following chapters illustrate a variety of approaches for dealing creatively with the substantive and procedural dimensions of conflict in parks, for addressing the interests at stake on all sides, and for dealing with the balance of power. While there are many common themes in the approaches taken in these cases, each has unique aspects as well. Conflicts occur and must be addressed within a cultural, ecological, political, and historical context. Each requires a specialized approach, one that is appropriate for the people involved and the situation at hand.

In spite of the uniqueness of each case, the similarities are striking and important. Most of the cases include (1) attempts to address conflicts by providing local communities with benefits from the park; (2) attempts to include people in park decision making and management; (3) education; and (4) information gathering and research. These four elements can form the basis of most efforts to manage park conflict.

The benefits provided in these chapters vary, but the concept is the same in each situation—opposition to the park, including overt conflict, will be reduced if people perceive that the park serves rather than contravenes their interests. For example, in Khunjerab National Park ("Survival in a Vertical Desert"), an attempt is being made to reduce conflict with the Shimshali people by providing them with a portion of the fees collected from hunters. Employment in a park is another benefit that can help reduce conflict, as illustrated in Mingma Norbu Sherpa's chapter on Sagarmartha National Park in part one.

Conflicts in the Manas Tiger Reserve in India ("Mayhem in Manas") and the

Sierra Nevada of Colombia ("Aluna: The Place Where the Mother Was Born") are being dealt with through comprehensive, long-term programs that address health, education, and economic development needs of the people. In addition to the direct benefits provided, these two examples show how a holistic approach to improving living standards of the people may help reduce their dependence on park resources—when dependence is reduced, so are the conflicts that often result. Another strategy for reducing dependence on park resources is to find alternatives so that the park resources are no longer needed. For example, in the Aïr-Ténéré National Nature Reserve in Niger ("People in Blue"), local people are shown how to use mud bricks instead of poles for the roofs of their houses, thereby reducing deforestation in the reserve. Another kind of benefit is to compensate local people for damage done to their crops by animals ranging from the park, as is the case in Khunjerab National Park.

Providing benefits to local people is usually a means for addressing the substantive dimensions of the conflict. However, as mentioned earlier, there is another, equally critical dimension—the procedural one of including local people in park decision making and management. One obvious reason for taking this procedural step is that it provides a means for understanding the substantive needs of the local people. Including people also gives them a sense of ownership, which is a precursor to stewardship. When people's interests are unknown and ignored, and when they lack any sense of ownership, the predictable outcome is opposition and conflict.

A powerful way to include people is simply to ask them what they think about the park, what they want from it, and what their concerns are. "Conflict in Cameroon" vividly illustrates this approach. Of course, the act of asking the questions carries with it some responsibility to try to do something with the answers. The Shimshali case is one in which conflict was exacerbated when the questions were asked and promises were made (to provide compensation for predation) but then broken. The chapter on Sagarmartha National Park provides a positive illustration of several different ways to include local people in park decision making: including them on advisory committees, hiring them into the park leadership, and giving them enforcement authority.

Another approach to including people in park management and decision making is to revive or adapt traditional forms of stewardship. Examples of this approach are provided in several of the case studies, most notably in the description of the Karen people of northern Thailand in "The Winds of Change."

The Sierra Nevada case suggests that involvement at a very personal level can also be effective in responding to and avoiding conflict. Juan Mayr-Maldonado, who does monumental work in a particularly trying situation, somehow seems to know almost everyone around the protected area personally. His ability and willingness to invest the time to develop individual relationships with people of all points of view may be one of the keys to his accomplishments. It may be difficult, of course, to know or to include everyone who has an interest in a park. An alternative to trying to reach every single person is to rely to a large extent on community leaders. The Sierra Nevada and Sagarmartha cases both offer examples of how this can be accomplished by working with elders and religious figures who have authority and credibility in the community.

When conflict is particularly adversarial, when the situation is extremely complex, when there is a great deal of mistrust, or when communications among stakeholders have broken down, the use of a neutral, respected mediator may be helpful. As an example, mediation was used to develop a management plan for a newly designated and highly controversial "wild and scenic" river in the United States. The stakeholders, who included Native Americans, fishermen, powerboat operators, kayakers, private landowners, and several government agencies, were assisted by The Keystone Center, an NGO that specializes in mediation, to develop a plan that everyone could accept.

The third conflict management element in most of the examples in this book is education. Local people and park users may not be aware of the conservation values associated with a park. It is unrealistic to expect them to support park protection measures (particularly those that affect them personally) or accept compromises that may be necessary to resolve a conflict unless they have a sense of those values. In "Tourism versus Turtles," education is the cornerstone of efforts to save endangered turtles and seals in the Greek islands.

Research is the fourth element in many conflict management efforts. For example, research may be critical to the development of substantive solutions to conflicts. In "Dance of a Thousand Cranes," research on the habitat and food needs of the cranes (perhaps these could be called the cranes' interests) was a necessary precursor to developing a plan for their protection.

Given the difficulty, complexity, and variety of conflict situations that occur in parks, is there a general approach that can be used to get to mutually agreeable and satisfactory outcomes? The answer, of course, is that each situation will require a specifically tailored approach that recognizes and adjusts for the cultural, legal, and social context and the particular dynamics of the conflict. What is proposed here is a framework and a description of a few options rather than any sort of prescribed solution or approach. The framework is most directly applicable for parties who have the authority to deal with conflict and the responsibility to do so (e.g., park managers), but it could be useful for any other stakeholder who wants to play an active role. Undoubtedly, the framework is neater than the real world and should not be relied on too greatly!

Assessment

Conflicts are uncomfortable for most people, especially when it is their interests that are at stake. A constructive first step for embarking on a conflict management effort is to take a mental step away from the situation and to try to assess it as objectively as possible.

The assessment may be as simple as writing down, in an organized fashion, what is already known about the conflict. Other assessment tools include consultation with knowledgeable colleagues, interviews with stakeholders, questionnaires, environmental and social impact assessments, public hearings, roundtables, and advisory groups. Assessment is, of course, an ongoing process. The initial assessment almost always reveals the need for additional information, which will need to be acquired as the conflict management effort proceeds.

The following are some useful questions to ask in the assessment:

- What are the issues in the conflict?

- What has been the history of the conflict so far?

- Who are the potentially affected stakeholders? What is their role in the conflict? What are their underlying interests, both substantive and procedural? What positions have they adopted? What other positions might serve their interests?

- What ideas do various stakeholders have about how to resolve the conflict?

- What are the relationships among the parties? How well do they communicate with one another?

- What is known and what is not known about the scientific, ecological, and technical aspects of the conflict?

- What is the institutional-legal context for the conflict, and what institutional and legal avenues exist for resolving it?

- What resources are available to deal with the conflict (financial, human, and institutional)?

- Is there any other pertinent information?

Developing a Conflict Management Strategy

After conducting an initial assessment, the next step is to use the information obtained during the assessment to develop and implement a strategy. The strategy should address both substantive and procedural interests that are at stake in the conflict, and it should address needs for education and research. It may be necessary to have both short-term and long-term strategies. It will always be necessary to recognize the challenges and limitations of any conflict management effort. In cases in which the park conflict is related to issues like poverty and factional warfare, it may take years and a multitude of incremental steps by many people and institutions before the conflict is truly resolved.

A few options that might be considered for addressing the procedural and substantive interests of stakeholders are as follows.

ADDRESSING PROCEDURAL INTERESTS

- Develop personal relationships with individual stakeholders.

- Develop relationships with community leaders.

- Hire local people to manage and/or staff the park.

- Involve local people in technical research or social impact analysis.

- Establish a management committee.

- Set up a roundtable or dialogue.

- Appoint a liaison officer to maintain relationships with local people.

- Involve a neutral mediator or other respected third party to assist.

ADDRESSING SUBSTANTIVE INTERESTS

- Look for ways to give local people some of the benefits of the park.

- Provide compensation for damage or loss.

- Establish zones with varying kinds and intensities of protection and use.

- Develop alternatives so that people do not have to be dependent on park resources that need to be protected.

• Revive or adapt formerly used traditional methods of stewardship (this can also be a way to address procedural interests).

This conflict management framework is intended only to serve as an introduction to the topic and to provide a context for the examples that follow.[1] The chapters offer a wonderful array of creative ways to approach a wide diversity of conflicts. While none of these conflicts is fully resolved, each demonstrates progress toward balancing human well-being and protection of park resources.

Aluna: The Place Where the Mother Was Born

In the beginning, there was blackness. Only the sea.
In the beginning there was no sun, no moon, no people.
In the beginning there were no animals, plants. Only the sea.
The sea was the Mother.
The Mother was not people, she was not anything.
Nothing at all.
She was when she was, darkly. She was memory and potential.
She was aluna.

THE KOGI HISTORY OF CREATION

As our Jeep swung onto the highway, a column of tanks rolled past us toward the Caribbean town of Santa Marta. The camouflaged vehicles were armed with soldiers, their uniformed bodies studded with hand grenades and rockets. Machine guns were mounted on the tanks, ready to open fire. Colombia was at war—and we were navigating our way through the war zone, as we had done for the past week, in the hope of bringing together the disparate groups of the Sierra Nevada of northern Colombia so that they could begin work on a conservation strategy for the strife-torn region.

Our leader, Juan Mayr-Maldonado, who has dedicated the past seventeen years of his life to conserving the cultural and biological diversity of the battle-scarred area, did not flinch. He and his team of seventy environmentalists, who have been promoting sustainable development among the region's inhabitants, are accustomed to working with and mediating among nervous troops, guerilla fighters, narcotics producers, worried farmers, and oppressed Indians. "Tomorrow will be a very interesting day," he commented, as we watched the convoy fade into the darkness.

In the morning, we planned to penetrate the guerilla-held territory along the Río Frío and drive to El Congo, one of four conservation and educational stations that the Fundación Pro–Sierra Nevada de Santa Marta—founded by Juan in 1986—has built at strategic points in the remote mountain region, which encompasses two national parks and two indigenous reserves.

Like a monolith, the Sierra Nevada massif rises sharply from the shores of the azure waters of the Caribbean to the sacred snow-capped peaks of Colombia's highest mountains. At an altitude of 5,775 meters, it is the highest coastal mountain range in the world. Its rushing rivers and crystal-clear streams tumble down the pyramid-shaped mountains in a striking array of waterfalls and rapids until their life-giving waters are absorbed by the parched plains of the valley. The survival of some 1.2 million people depends on the Sierra's rich tropical forests and the watershed they maintain.[1]

For thousands of years, the Law of the Mother has ruled the indigenous people of the Sierra Nevada. This complex code, developed by the pre-Colombian Tayrona people, regulates human behavior in harmony with regional plant and animal cycles, astral movements, climatic phenomena, and the sacred geography of the mountains. Three groups of indigenous people who have been the traditional guardians of the ancient Law of the Mother are the Kogi, Arsario, and Arhuaco Indians. Before the arrival of the Spanish in 1502, they numbered around 700,000. Today, the survivors, who retreated from the conquistadores into the remotest middle and upper reaches of the Sierra Nevada, number around 20,000.[2]

The Kogi, who are the least acculturated of the three groups, helped Juan and his team to design the Fundación's four ecological stations and community centers, using Kogi architecture. Drawing on the knowledge of their Tayrona ancestors, who built the great stone cities and intricate communication network of stone paths that crisscrossed the treacherously steep slopes of the Andes, the Kogi people have helped the Fundación to restore abandoned sites, destroyed over the years by tomb robbers and dense jungle foliage.

The Kogi people's contribution to cultural and biological diversity is unprecedented. They are transferring—both to local farmers and to tribes that have lost their traditions—the ancient technologies of the Tayrona chiefdom, including sophisticated systems of agriculture, terracing, and irrigation. This transfer is unique to the Fundación because the Kogi, who call themselves the Elder Brothers of

Humanity, do not want interaction with people outside their immediate group, whom they consider to be the Younger Brothers. With the support of the Fundación and other government and nongovernmental agencies, they are reclaiming lost villages and recovering ceremonial sites in the two national parks and indigenous reserves on the lands to which they recently regained title. In 1989, the government of Colombia returned approximately 25 percent of its territory to its indigenous people.

El Congo, our destination this morning, was the second environmental training and health center built by the Fundación. Like the other three stations, it serves as a conservation model for local farmers and indigenous people living in and near the national parks and indigenous reserves. As executive director of the Fundación, Juan had organized a meeting at El Congo to which he invited all factions from the conflict-ridden region. The Fundación hoped that representatives of the three indigenous groups, government agencies, nongovernmental organizations, and leaders of local farmers' societies would meet to discuss a conservation strategy for the Sierra Nevada of Santa Marta.

Reaching agreement on such a strategy poses a monumental challenge for the Fundación because it requires consensus among thirty-five different agencies, ranging from departmental representatives of the three statelike territories that share jurisdiction over the Sierra Nevada (Magdalena, César, and La Guajira) and federal officials from Bogotá to leaders of farmers' (*campesinos'*) cooperatives and governors of the three indigenous groups. Jurisdiction often overlaps, causing confusion because so many groups have opposing goals and objectives.

"This meeting in El Congo today is the first of its kind in the country because it is in guerilla territory," Juan said. "We have worked at the Río Frío for four years in El Congo. Everybody trusts us. The local population is supporting our work, they are benefiting from it, and they are using the technology we have developed."

As we veered off the main highway, Juan wondered whether the guerillas would arrive unexpectedly and whether the Arsario people, whose leader had been murdered three weeks earlier, would come at all. A military roadblock answered his first question. Each person moving up the mountain pass was stopped and questioned about his or her destination. The soldiers were armed with grenades, rockets, and automatic machine guns. (For years, the guerillas have been fighting the military, which they say keeps the rich oligarchy in power. In mid-1992, during my second visit to Colombia, the guerillas stepped up their attacks.) After several minutes, we were allowed to continue toward El Congo. Along the route, Juan waved and called to every family we met. Farmers on horses and mules, the main mode of transport in the steep terrain, stopped and chatted for a few minutes before our Jeep continued, groaning, up the muddy slopes.

Juan, a tall, jovial man, exudes confidence and inspires it in his team members, who live and work in some of the most dangerous and demanding conditions in the world. And he demands the same of visitors. When I arrived in Santa Marta for the first time in February 1992 to research this book for WWF and IUCN on the changing relationship between people and protected areas, I discovered that Juan, who was to have been my guide, was busy in Bogotá. He arranged for one of his team members to accompany me to the Alto de Mira Ecological Station and nearby Kogi and Arsario villages. On the first day, to reach the station we trekked ten and a half hours in temperatures hovering around 35 degrees centigrade, at an altitude averaging 1,500 meters, on moss-covered rock ledges no more than 20 centimeters wide. There were no plateaus—just peaks, ridges, and valleys. It took us three days to reach the nearest indigenous village.

The Fundación's ecological station at Alto de Mira was discovered by Juan in the 1970s when he spent two years in the Sierra. In 1986, the Fundación bought and began to restore the abandoned Tayrona village, whose surrounding land had been used for years by a rancher. The station—the first established by the Fundación— is about a six-hour trek from Ciudad Perdida, the Lost City, discovered in 1976. Located at the headwaters of the Buritaca River at an altitude of 1,100 meters, the center's stunningly beautiful setting is one of the last remaining areas of tropical rain forest on an ancient archaeological site in Colombia. The station was set up to serve as a research base where scientists could study the area's rich biological diversity and varied ecosystems as well as learn about the Kogi's traditional knowledge of environmental conservation. The ecological station at Alto de Mira, like the one at El Congo, demonstrates the Kogi's practice of soil conservation, irrigation terracing and drainage, slope exposure, and agricultural production. The station's researchers are involved in the conservation of Sierra Nevada de Santa Marta National Park, and their presence lends protection from the settlers, who are constantly trying to move inside the park's boundaries. Thus, the station is also used as a base for work with Colombian *campesinos* who farm in the buffer zone of the park, and it has become a center for land regulation programs for local communities.

The park, covering 675,000 hectares, was created in 1964 and extended in 1977. The indigenous reserve, established in 1980, overlaps 70 percent of the protected area. In 1979, UNESCO accepted the Sierra Nevada of Santa Marta as a biosphere reserve.[3] Only the Indians are supposed to live, hunt, gather, and engage in subsistence farming inside the park. The Kogi used to keep their population density in balance with the carrying capacity of their territory, but their numbers are increasing. As their population grows, so does their need for more land. Since the *campesinos* already resent being removed from the national park, disputes over the exact location of park boundaries are common.

Today at El Congo, the Fundación, under the leadership of Juan, was attempting to break new ground in Colombia and bring the hostile groups together so that they could begin peaceful discussions for a conservation plan for the Sierra Nevada.

"Look down there," Juan said, pointing toward an invitingly picturesque river. "That is the Río Frío, where the guerillas blew up the oil pipeline last night, for the second time this year." Worry lined his normally smiling face. "I might not be able to fly to Bogotá tonight either. The guerillas have destroyed radio communications in Medellín, which means there may be no night flights from Santa Marta to Bogotá." We later learned that some 6,000 barrels of crude oil had been spilled and that four oil workers repairing damage to another pipeline from a previous blast had been injured. One man had lost a leg; another had been blinded.

Juan was driving the recalcitrant old Jeep up the rugged mountain pass. "On our left, you can see a field where marijuana was grown. It has just been burned," he said. "Half the forest in the Sierra Nevada was smoked, mainly by North Americans. Beginning in the 1970s, around 100,000 hectares of land was cleared for marijuana plantations. Then our government intervened. They sprayed the crops with herbicides, but without helping the local people find an alternative source of income. In the eyes of the farmers, the government was the enemy, which came in helicopters and wiped out their only source of money. Some people replaced the marijuana with coffee, whose price has plummeted to an all-time low, and others planted coca. It is not surprising that guerilla groups found allies among some of the angry farmers, but others armed themselves against the guerillas. The Sierra is a land in crisis," he said, sighing.

"It was because of the spraying that I found El Congo in the first place," Juan explained. "I was at home one evening and the military police knocked on my door. They told me that they had been spraying the marijuana crops in the western Sierra and that they had found a place with stones overgrown by the jungle. They wanted to know if I would like to fly over the area to see if it was an archaeological site. The next morning, we flew by helicopter into the Sierra to the spot with the stones. The police told me they would drop me off and return in two hours. I jumped from the helicopter and watched it fly away, the huge letters of POLICÍA NACIONAL shining brightly in the sun. Suddenly, someone shot at me from the other side of the mountain. I lay flat on my stomach in the field of marijuana and shouted loudly, 'I am only here looking at the stones.' As you can imagine, they didn't believe me. They thought I was from the police. Finally someone came to collect the marijuana, and I repeated that I wanted to explore the ancient ruins and look at this magnificent site. I don't know how, but I convinced him. I had landed in El Congo."

That was 1984. By 1987, a year after the Fundación was officially inaugurated, it conducted a comprehensive socioeconomic survey of the El Congo microbasin on the western slope of the Sierra Nevada in order to evaluate the needs of the settlers. The group made contact with the local population of farmers and chose to build El Congo in one of the remaining pockets of forest lying over an important pre-Columbian settlement. Members of the Fundación assessed the risk of working in a zone of guerilla activity and decided to go ahead with their plan. They also strengthened ties with some thirty-five state institutions with jurisdiction in the area, including SES (the Foundation for Higher Education), INDERENA (the National Institute of Natural Resources and the Environment), and HIMAT (the government water authority). Discussions with HIMAT have included a proposal for a water tax as a source of funding for maintenance of the Sierra Nevada watershed, which is critically important for Colombia's economic development.

Together, these very different groups are trying to meet the ambitious common goal of restoring the ecology of the Río Frío Basin, the main tributary of the Prado-Sevilla irrigation district in the low-lying banana-growing area. These plains surrounding the Sierra Nevada are the setting of the fictional Macondo in *One Hundred Years of Solitude* by Gabriel García Márquez. They are some of the most fertile lands in all of Colombia. In addition to bananas, they produce other tropical fruits for export and are used as palm and cotton plantations. But in times of drought, these agricultural centers, on which the largely impoverished farmers rely, dry up. In the rainy season, massive amounts of water stream uncontrollably into the cities and towns, washing away roads and bridges and flooding the fields below. These floods are the result of continuing deforestation in the mountain watershed.

After analyzing information gathered through months of research, largely among the farmers, the Fundación drew up a project for El Congo based on local requirements and funding availability. Before beginning any work, the Fundación invited indigenous communities to visit the site and asked their permission to begin restoration. The high priests, or *Mamas,* said that they had to divine with the spirits before giving their decision. When they returned to the ruins, which had been seriously disturbed by grave robbers, they blessed El Congo. An interdisciplinary group was formed, and the first excavations were made in cooperation with the national archaeological institute, ICAN. Drawing on its experience at Alto de Mira, the Fundación rebuilt El Congo, using indigenous architectural techniques and local forest materials.[4]

At the summit of the pass, we came upon a farmers' market. Horses, mules, Jeeps, and a few trucks were parked on the roadside. Dogs lingered near the meat stall, hoping that a few scraps would drop off the scale, where farmers were weighing the parts of a freshly butchered cow. Juan parked in the shade of a tree and leaped from the Jeep. He was greeted by a round of handshakes with the farmers and passengers emerging from trucks and buses. Among them were two Indians: Ramon Gill, who is part Kogi, and another, identifiable by his white, rectangular-shaped hat, who was a member of the Arhuaco tribe. They were accompanied by Amparo Jiminez Luque, director of the Ministry of the Interior's Office for Indian Affairs for the departments or territories of Magdalena and La Guajira. She and Juan descended the steep path leading to the station of El Congo as a long trail of people followed.

As we gathered in the main house in the center of the station, I noticed that Juan and most of the participants looked quite shaken. They had not expected to be stopped and questioned at a military roadblock. Juan opened the meeting and gave the floor to the five *campesino* leaders, who represented thirty communities throughout the Río Frío Basin. A woman was the first to speak. She announced that she could not stay and attend the meeting because she, like the other farm leaders, feared for her life. The last time the group had tried to meet in San Xavier County recently, everyone going to the meeting had been stopped and their cars searched for weapons. Some had been charged as guerilla collaborators. She expressed her disappointment over losing the opportunity to make contact and work on the Fundación's conservation strategy for the Sierra Nevada. The other farm leaders stood up in turn and expressed a similar message to the entire group. After they had finished, each of them walked around the room, shaking hands with everyone, and apologized for leaving the meeting. Suddenly, the entire group agreed to disband, except for several participants who stayed and wrote a statement of protest. The peace representative at the meeting agreed to deliver the statement to the local government.

As I watched the disheartened *campesino* leaders hike back up the trail to the main road, I realized why the Arsario people had not sent a representative to El Congo. I remembered how only five days earlier we had met a group of Arsario Indians as they were leaving a special emergency gathering of the three indigenous groups of the Sierra Nevada. The Arsario had told us that it was too soon for them to be meeting after the death of their governor, Jose Luiz. They were still in mourning—and they were afraid for their lives.

We spent the next two days in a Kogi village with the Kogi and Arhuaco people. The *Mamas* allowed me to interview them at their "earth summit," which coincided with the official opening of the Earth Summit in Rio de Janeiro. They, the Elder Brothers, gave us the following message for the thousands of Younger Brothers who were assembling in Brazil:

> You have to know the place where thinking was born—*aluna*—the creation, the beginning of life, where everything was born. *Aluna* is where the Law of the Mother began; it is the place of the spirit, of the mind, of intelligence. It is the place of thinking. But the white man is trying to take away our thinking. . . . The world was created in *aluna,* in the Sierra, so the white man was created here, too, but he has robbed himself. That is why we had a very long summer; that is why the snow peaks are shrinking and coming to an end. For example, one of the mountains near Alguacil is teaching us. It is sacred because everything was born there. You can bless food and everything there . . . but all the time the white people are coming and putting their feet everywhere. In one of the upper lakes many white people left a lot of garbage. Many strangers have been to our snow peaks, making photographs, studying them. We see that the place is affected, and that is why the *Mamas* and the indigenous philosophy of the Sierra forbid the entry of foreigners to these places. This is an indigenous law of all the country and all the world. They have to respect these rights. . . . The white people have an economic principle. They want to get as much money as possible, and it does not matter if they destroy culture, environment, or sacred sites. They are coming from everywhere with every kind of passport, and they are staring at us as if we were just a beautiful part of the landscape. As a result of this and their greed, they are creating an imbalance between man and nature that is affecting the world. There is time to analyze and correct this. We believe it is necessary to respect our rights and to begin to learn from us, a society that is living in harmony with nature. So that the air can be clean again and the water can continue to be abundant, so that all life that exists on the planet, the sun, the heat of the sun and the cold of the night, all that is in this world, can return to its natural state. . . .

What is remarkable is that the message of the indigenous people to the Earth Summit was almost identical to statements that had been made by nearly 100 *campesinos* at a meeting convened by the Fundación just two days earlier. The farmers had stated publicly that they wanted help in restoring the ecological balance of the Sierra Nevada. They, like the Indians, who also till the land, said that their greatest common concern was the lack of water in the mountains. They wanted the government to help them plant trees and to educate them and their families, who barely had enough to eat. That meeting, like the one with the two indigenous groups, was extremely uplifting compared with the letdown we experienced this morning at our meeting in El Congo.

Juan, who was used to setbacks of this type, closed the session and offered to show me El Congo. Together with Guillermo Puyana, the Fundación's legal advisor, he guided me through the station's impressive grounds. Guillermo, like most people who work with the Fundación, had spent several months at a field site. His choice was El Congo, the most outstanding of the Fundación's educational stations. The local settlers are beginning to model their homesteads after El Congo and to build irrigation terraces for their "kitchen gardens," an innovative idea demonstrated at the Community Assistance Center. This voluntary program, supported by SENA (the National Training Service for Apprentices), has improved the nutritional status of families in the area. The concept has also been a catalyst for productive gardens, which are a source of cash income for local people, as well as medicinal and herb gardens. Contributions from HIMAT have helped the Fundación to start a community reafforestation program. Nurseries for raising fruit trees and commercial timber species were established near settlers' houses and are managed mainly by women and children. Thousands of trees have been planted, with a survival rate of about 75 percent. In order to market produce and timber products, a consumer-producer cooperative has been established, the first of its kind in the area. In association with SENA, training is being given in cooperative management. Also with the assistance of SENA, the Fundación built the first training center in the Sierra at El Congo. It was in the training auditorium, which holds as many as 100 people, that we had met this morning. The training center also can house as many as thirty trainees or workshop participants in its network of small circular huts located throughout El Congo's 30 hectares.

A health post, serviced by a nurse who lives in the area full-time, has also been built at El Congo. Established with assistance from the national Hospital Fund, the post was constructed mostly from local materials and now serves as a primary health care and family planning center. The only health center for miles around, it takes care of eight rural population centers.

"Our path has been fraught with difficulties," Juan said quietly as he mounted a stairway of beautifully restored stone steps through the remnant patch of forest that encircles El Congo. He paused, dwarfed by a gigantic liana twisting around a tree at least 40 meters tall, and declared, "This is like a virgin forest, and we saved it with El Congo." For centuries, indigenous people have lived throughout the Sierra, and in the 1950s, 120,000 settlers moved in, so it is unlikely that this or any patch of forest could have remained untouched.

"It does look like a primary forest," I agreed when we reached the top of the hill. From above, the golden thatched roofs of El Congo stood out in contrast to the rich green layers of trees, where they seemed to belong as part of the landscape, in the shape of the mountains themselves.

On the way to the valley, we found that the roadblock had dispersed. However, soldiers still stood sentry along the route for about a kilometer at strategic points overlooking the Río Frío. Once we had passed them, Juan drove down the mountain quickly toward the Santa Marta airport. "My plane," he cried. "It's there. It's flying to Bogotá. If I am going to the Rio summit, I have to get that plane." The jet's engines were already running, the propellers whirring rapidly. Juan parked the Jeep and rushed for the check-in counter. "Do you have your passport?" I shouted after him. He nodded and leaped forward, prepared to charm his way onto what might be the last plane of the day for Bogotá.

We rushed to Juan's father's house and grabbed his luggage. When we returned to the airport, we found that he had left for Bogotá, with only the clothes he was wearing and his *mochila*, a hand-woven pouch worn by the Kogi. Fortunately, a special plane was scheduled, and Xavier, a friend of Juan's, flew to Bogotá that afternoon and took him his luggage and materials for presentation at the Earth Summit. I hoped that Juan's voice and the message of the Kogi would be heard among the throngs of people there.

I stayed behind and traveled to another part of the Sierra Nevada the next day. I was at an "earth summit" in what the Kogi call "the heart of the world." According to the Law of the Mother, this was the universe.

Survival in a Vertical Desert

At 4 A.M., the yaks leave the camp to begin the tortuous 500-meter ascent of a mountain still shrouded in darkness. When we follow half an hour later, the peaks that stud the horizon are a soft, luminous white—the sole relief to the eye in a landscape as barren and desolate as the moon.

It is springtime in 1991, and we are headed for the Pamir, a range of pasturelands on the roof of the Himalayas, where the Shimshali people of northern Pakistan have grazed their animals for hundreds of years.

Every April, half the population of 1,000 leaves Shimshal Village to make the pilgrimage. It takes two days of dawn-to-dusk marching across two mountain passes and rivers swollen into torrents by the melting glaciers to reach a place where there is enough grass to sustain the Shimshalis' livestock—and their way of life.

But it is a way of life that the Shimshalis believe is under threat. Much of their traditional grazing land is within the boundaries of the proposed Khunjerab National Park, which lies alongside the Pamir. The park is home to one of the world's only remaining populations of Marco Polo sheep and what is believed to be Asia's stock of snow leopards, creatures of almost mythical stature among conservationists. It also contains rare Tibetan asses, brown bears, blue sheep, and ibex.

For Pakistan, Khunjerab National Park is a matter of prestige, tourism potential, and, possibly, the country's first World Heritage listing for a natural site, something it has sought for the past ten years. In addition to its unique and endangered species, the park boasts an incomparable setting, at the intersection of four of the world's mightiest mountain ranges—the Himalaya, Karakoram, Pamir, and Hindu Kush—and at the crossroads of central Asia, where Pakistan meets China and Afghanistan.

For years, the government had been determined to have an international-class national park based on a Western model—banning all grazing of domestic animals and other human activity. But by the early 1990s, recognition was dawning that this stance, which has pitted the people of Shimshal and other villages against park officials and pitted conservation groups against one another, is untenable and is endangering the park itself. WWF-Pakistan is now trying to help find a solution to the impasse. The affair offers a classic example of the difficulty of meeting conservation goals in the Third World if the development needs of the people are neglected.

In the barren mountains of northern Pakistan, conservation is a high-stakes game. Unlike the Nepalese and Indian Himalayas, which lie in the path of the life-giving monsoon, more than half of the area is covered by bare rock or glacier, and only 4 percent is forested. It is literally a vertical desert and, for the 800,000 people who live there, one of the harshest climates on earth. G. M. Khattak, Pakistan's foremost forestry expert, says that natural resources are under too much stress to afford the luxury of blocking off a piece of land exclusively to protect wildlife. "There is not a hectare of land that is not being used," Khattak says. "You can go to the most barren, remote patch of land, where you think no one could possibly live, and put a fence around it, and you'll have ten people appear from nowhere seeking compensation."

The geology of the area is treacherous—it is struck by frequent earthquakes, rockfalls, and catastrophic floods from the rapidly shifting glaciers—and so are the politics, which have immensely complicated the Khunjerab park issue. As territory disputed by India, Pakistan administers rather than rules here, and the population has no representation in Parliament. For many people in the Northern Areas, Pakistan is a foreign, hostile country. Villagers are so distrustful of Islamabad's ability to manage natural resources on their behalf that in one valley the local population expelled the forestry department and set up their own manned barrier to prevent exploitation.

Pakistan legally established the 2,300-square-kilometer park in 1975, following a proposal by the noted American biologist George B. Schaller. But few resources were put into it. Even today, the park has a field staff of just fourteen, none of whom has training in wildlife conservation. Park staffers live in stone huts without electricity and have only a few sets of binoculars among them. The only vehicle is the park ranger's motorcycle.

Dawood Ghaznavi, director of WWF-Pakistan, which is funding the $50,000 project to develop a management plan, says that park officials are almost powerless to police the park. There was widespread poaching of wildlife by construction workers during the building of the Karakoram Highway, and even though hunting is banned throughout the Northern Areas, it is widespread, including hunting by Pakistani army soldiers, who have been known to go on machine gun shooting sprees from helicopters.

Ghaznavi says that villagers saw no reason why they should abide by the rules of the park because they were convinced that whoever was in charge would "pocket the money, cut down the trees, and provide hunting for his pals." As Qurban Mohammed, spokesman for another group of villages that graze their animals in Khunjerab Park, said in 1991: "We are interested in developing Khunjerab National Park, but the management of the park should be in local hands. The government will take the profit without involving the people. They just want to take all this beautiful land away and leave us empty-handed."

When Dr. Per Wegge, a Norwegian wildlife conservationist, surveyed the park for IUCN in 1988, he found that the Marco Polo sheep population was almost wiped out and the other species had significantly declined, mainly due to illegal poaching and grazing pressure from domestic animals.

At a conference on Khunjerab in 1989 organized by the U.S. National Park Service and IUCN, Wegge said that the area should be reclassified, expanded, and developed into a multiple-purpose conservation area similar to the Annapurna Conservation Area in Nepal. That plan would allow grazing in some areas and controlled trophy hunting in others, with some of the income from the permits going to the villages that have traditional grazing rights. Shimshal would also be developed as a tourist center.

At the time, the government rejected the approach, saying that a management plan for the park must be drawn up to phase out all grazing over a number of years and eventually to ban all human activity. Like many developing countries, it was aspiring to create a "Yellowstone model" park (see "In Search of a Home," the introduction to part one), which was, according to a growing number of park managers, inappropriate for the Khunjerab.

To help alleviate tension and find a way to resolve the conflict, a planning team, funded by WWF-Pakistan, attempted to begin work in 1990. But the team had to suspend the project due to opposition from the Shimshalis and people from six other villages along the Karakoram Highway, who for hundreds of years have held rights to graze their animals and collect firewood in the park.

John Mock, an American social anthropologist who was a member of the team, reported: "Clearly, no one is happy with the current situation. A unique wildlife population is on the verge of extinction. The local people are organized in opposition, and the park is an embarrassment for the international conservation organizations involved as well as for Pakistan." He said that the government's insistence on sticking to its protective stance "would seem to guarantee the failure of the park."

To understand the depth of opposition to the park, one must make the three-day trek by foot into Shimshal and then a further journey up to the Pamir. After walking for days along a treacherous mountain path, clinging to steep mountain slopes of buff-colored sandstone, shale, and scree, one emerges into a verdant oasis. Here, green and gold fields of barley, wheat, and peas ripple in the desert breezes, crisscrossed by a complex grid of irrigation canals built hundreds of years ago to wring water from the glaciers that overhang the valley on every side.

Most other villages in the Northern Areas were brought into the cash economy in the 1960s and 1970s, when the carving of the Karakoram Highway through the mountains linked the region to China in the north and the Pakistani capital, Islamabad, in the south. But the people of Shimshal remain self-sufficient, completely dependent on agriculture and produce from the thousands of sheep, goats, and yaks they keep in the Pamir during the summer.

For them, the national park does not exist. They have refused to let park officials even visit the Pamir, and they continue their lives as always—hunting blue sheep and ibex for meat and killing wolves and snow leopards that threaten their livestock.

The morning we arrived at Shuwert, the Shimshalis' summer grazing headquarters, the fresh carcass of a wolf was on display on a rock in the center of the village, and Shahgul Baig, Shimshal's premier hunter, was crouched in a stone hut nearby, cutting up an ibex and two blue sheep, which were later distributed throughout the village. Baig said that a pack of wolves had been carrying off five or six sheep and goats each day since the Shimshalis had moved their livestock up there in May.

I later sat with Shambi Khan, the thirty-nine-year-old son of the village headman, on ibex skins in the dim, smoky interior of his family's stone hut. While his mother prepared a meal of unleavened bread and yogurt made from goat and yak milk, I asked whether the road planned to link Shimshal to the Karakoram Highway would not bring new income to the Shimshalis and lessen their dependence on grazing here.

Khan shook his head. "You can see, Miss Terry," he said, "we have rugs and dung from the yaks and *choga* [wool coats] and hats from the sheep. We have meat, cheese, and butter. If we do not have the Pamir, we will not be self-sufficient." Khan conceded that the road would bring more tourism and allow the village to enter the cash economy for the first time. "But the Pamir is our insurance policy," he said.

Dulat Amin, headmaster of the school in Shimshal Village and president of the local village organization, was more blunt. "First they can kill us, then they can come and make it a national park."

Emotions have also run high among the six villages south of the park in Gojal, which hold grazing rights, but the villages lie in the tourist belt along the Karakoram Highway, and most villagers can see the potential for tourist income. For them, the main issue has been money.

The villagers say that when the park was formed, they were promised compensation for lost grazing rights but received nothing. They went to court seeking compensation for not grazing in the only area in the park where rules against grazing and hunting have been enforced: a 12-square-kilometer area once considered most important for Marco Polo sheep at the Chinese border.

After the courts awarded the Gojali villagers the right to continue grazing elsewhere in the park until the compensation issue was resolved, the graziers forced their way into the 12-kilometer zone in October 1990, bringing in yaks that they had been grazing elsewhere and occupying the area in a show of defiance, until police forced them out in May 1991. A strike was immediately called throughout the six villages, and people poured out on the streets, tying up traffic on the Karakoram Highway for a day before cooler heads prevailed.

The government finally realized that a strictly defined park may not be possible. For one thing, the graziers could not be legally forced out of the park until there was a court finding on the compensation claim. Ashiq Ahmad, a wildlife management specialist at Peshawar University who had headed the management planning team for WWF-Pakistan, was given the job of trying to find a solution to the impasse.

Ahmad said that one of his main problems was that there was such a level of distrust that the Gojali villages would not agree on three people to represent them in negotiations. There was fear that the negotiators would be "bought off" by the government and would not represent the villagers' interests.

Finally, in January 1992, Ahmad managed to get the Gojali villages, the park directorate, and the Northern Areas administrator to sign an agreement that will form the basis of a management plan very much like the one envisaged by Wegge.

Under the agreement, grazing would continue in the park but in a controlled fashion, so that range resources would not be destroyed by overstocking of animals and wild species would not be disrupted. It would also be the responsibility of the Gojali villages to patrol the park and outlying areas to protect wildlife from hunting.

In exchange, 80 percent of new employment opportunities in the park would go to local people. There would also be spin-off jobs generated by the extra tourism: guides, porters, and canteen services would be needed. Once wildlife stocks had increased, the government would also consider changing the law that currently prohibits hunting throughout the Northern Areas to allow hunting of specific animals in a game reserve outside the park boundaries, for a hefty license fee. Seventy percent of the proceeds would go to the local people.

WWF-Pakistan's Dawood Ghaznavi believes that once the management plan is in place, the government will be looking for foreign sources of funds so that the park can be properly administered. He says they are hoping to tap into the World Bank's $1.5 billion Global Environment Fund for biodiversity protection.

But large question marks hang over the issue of whether the agreement can be turned into a viable management plan. Distrust of the government still runs high. While the Gojalis have already begun to police themselves, subjecting any villager caught in illegal hunting to a social boycott of his business, they are incensed over the fact that government officials have been caught coming up to the Northern Areas on shooting sprees.

But the main barrier to the park remains Shimshali opposition. Ahmad said that he is going to proceed with a management plan for the area excluding Shimshal, in the hope that the Shimshalis will eventually see how the Gojalis have benefited and will want to become part of an agreement. "It is most important to develop confidence between the people of Shimshal and the park authorities," he said. "They must understand that we don't want to take away their grazing. We just want to rationalize it."

As for the Shimshalis' having to give up their age-old practice of hunting to protect their animals and to obtain meat, Ahmad points out that they would have to give it up eventually anyway because hunting is illegal. Park officials themselves will drive predators outside the park boundaries, where they can be killed, and the villagers will be entitled to compensation for any animals they lose to wolves. He said that many Shimshalis already understand how they will benefit from the development of pastureland through the national park and from the employment opportunities. Half of the new jobs in the park will be earmarked for Shimshalis, he added.

But Aban Marker Kabraji, Pakistan's representative to IUCN, said that beyond the considerable difficulty of overcoming the hostility of the people in Shimshal, she thinks that the government lacks the trained staff, institutions, political will, and imagination to tackle seriously the issues surrounding the park. "On top of all that, no one yet has done a comprehensive survey of the park. I think it's a very, very important park from a World Heritage point of view and from a biological diversity point of view, but until the mess is sorted out, no one's going to know what's there," she said.

Jeffrey Sayer, former head of IUCN's Forest Conservation Program, who is currently working for the World Bank and who was in Khunjerab in August 1992 looking at its prospects for a World Heritage listing, agrees. He said that even if Ahmad succeeds in putting together a management plan for the park, there is no guarantee that it will succeed. The important thing is ongoing consultation with all parties involved, he said. "You can have excellent management with no plan, and an excellent plan with no management. At the moment, you have neither management nor planning. . . . I'm afraid it's being treated as an academic exercise."

Sayer also said that the park would be more likely to obtain a World Heritage listing if its boundaries were expanded to encompass adjoining parts of China, Afghanistan, and Tajikistan. "Getting more than one country involved could really get the area on the map," he declared. "I think it's a fascinating area in terms of biodiversity, and it would be a real shame if something weren't done to conserve it."

ELIZABETH KEMF & VO QUY

Dance of a Thousand Cranes

In Vietnamese mythology, west is the direction of paradise, and the crane is the bird sent from heaven to fetch those destined for eternal life. If legend rings true, the residents of Tram Chim, one of Southeast Asia's most important wetlands, should benefit from good fortune and immortality. There, in one of Indochina's wettest corners, in southwestern Vietnam near the Cambodian border, local farmers and scientists have made a remarkable rediscovery of one of the world's rarest birds. In 1988, for the first time since the end of the Vietnam War, more than 1,000 eastern sarus cranes were counted at Tram Chim. The bird, whose range once stretched from South China to the Philippines, is believed to have been extirpated in the wild elsewhere in Southeast Asia, except in neighboring Cambodia and Laos.[1]

Long revered as a symbol of fidelity and longevity, the crane has been a source of inspiration and hope for mankind since ancient times. To enjoy the privilege of counting more than 1,000 is believed to bring good luck into one's life. The cranes—which vanished along with thousands of other birds and animals during the Vietnam War, when U.S. troops cut two huge drainage canals across the basin, then defoliated and napalmed what was a refuge for Vietcong soldiers—began their return to Tram Chim (Bird Swamp) and the Dong Thap Muoi floodplains in the early 1980s.

In 1986, the eastern race of the sarus crane (*Grus antigone sharpii*) was sighted by the Vietnamese Wetland and Waterbird Working Group, founded by one of the authors of this chapter, Professor Vo Quy, a trained ornithologist and director of Vietnam's Center for Natural Resource Management and Environmental Studies (CRES). Uniformly gray in color, the eastern sarus crane is smaller than its cousin, the Indian sarus crane, which is strictly protected in India and numbers at least 25,000 on the Indian subcontinent. Although scientists in the Philippines, China, and Thailand (which has a captive breeding program for the eastern sarus crane) have been actively searching for evidence of the bird in the wild, the eastern sarus crane has not been officially sighted in its traditional range with regularity except at Tram Chim. First visits to the site indicated that approximately 100 cranes were living in the area and that the cranes had an ally named Muoi Nhe, who was born in a village near Tram Chim in what is now Dong Thap Province. When Muoi became president of the province in 1975, he began rehabilitating the wetland back to its former condition.

After the war ended, in 1975, Muoi was the driving force behind the construction of 42 kilometers of dikes around the former wetland to prevent monsoon rains from spilling into the drainage channels during the dry season. Thousands of acres of forests were replanted, and the "healing began," says George Archibald, director of the International Crane Foundation (ICF) at Baraboo, Wisconsin. Archibald surveyed the wetland for the first time in January 1988, counting 300 to 400 eastern sarus cranes. In March of that same year, Derek Scott, compiler of the *Directory of Asian Wetlands,* counted 400 to 500 birds. By the time all of the cranes had arrived and the 1988 census was conducted, more than 1,000 cranes had been recorded.[2]

The number of cranes and other birds began to climb steadily after local residents turned in their crane traps and restoration of the wetland was escalated. Without the cooperation of the local people, the project could not have succeeded. After local residents began to understand that preserving the birds could also benefit them, they stopped using poisoned bait and began helping the conservationists.[3]

When the cranes were rediscovered in 1986, the provincial authorities created the Tram Chim Crane Reserve. Since then, an initial protected area of 5,000 hectares has been extended to 9,000 hectares. Unfortunately, not everyone is pleased with the expansion of the crane reserve. For the first time since the end of the Vietnam War, conflict has erupted in the Plain of Reeds in South Vietnam. Some local representatives want to reduce the size of the protected area and turn it over to rice and fish cultivation, while conservationists would like to see the area declared a national reserve. Vietnam's prime minister, Vo Van Kiet, is said to be backing the latter initiative. However, impoverished fishermen and farmers, who have been moving into the area steadily since 1975, want to drain the reserve during the dry season in order to plant rice and to fish more easily. They say that they do not have enough to eat; their children have difficulty getting to school by the only means of transportation, human-powered sampans; and insects have plagued their rice crops for the past few years. They do not have the money to buy motors for their sampans or even wire to construct fish traps. Meanwhile, wardens of the reserve stand by helplessly, trying to discourage other, richer, fishermen who have mounted motors on their sampans from shocking fish with electric wires and encroaching on the crane's feeding grounds.[4]

By 1990, the hope and elation felt when the first 1,000 cranes were counted had begun to fade slightly. An international sarus crane and wetland workshop, sponsored primarily by Germany's Brehm Fund for International Bird Conservation and organized by the International Crane Foundation and CRES, was held in Tram Chim. Its main objective was to help resolve the conflict and find a way to satisfy the needs of the local residents, who had already dug a new drainage canal two-thirds of the way through the heart of the reserve.

Advice was offered by the aforementioned groups as well as by IUCN (the World Conservation Union) and the Universities of Hanoi, Ho Chi Minh City, and Can Tho, and a management committee was established. More important, participants at the conference, who represented the views of the residents of Tram Chim and surrounding villages, agreed that all human activity inside the reserve would be stopped for one year in order to carry out additional surveys and begin development of a management plan. Technical advisors included the president of the district of Tram Chim, who was elected chairman; village leaders; Muoi Nhe; Jeb Barzen of the ICF; and Dr. Le Dien Duc from CRES. One year later, in early 1991, a second international conference was held during the Gulf War. Both conferences were financed by the Brehm Fund and held at Tram Chim's educational center, which is soon to be used for teacher and adult conservation education. According to conference chairman Jeb Barzen, a draft management plan was presented that would allow restricted human activity in the reserve. "The Vietnamese wanted to continue digging canals in buffer areas of the protected area. And they wanted to finish digging the big canal down the middle of the core reserve, which they said was needed to manage intensively rear mangrove [or melaleuca] forests, sarus cranes, and fish," said Barzen.[5]

Discussions between conservationists and needy rice farmers and fishermen were long and sometimes heated, but consensus among the groups was reached. They agreed that construction of the huge canal would be stopped. If natural methods of management failed to meet local needs, ditch digging could continue. Under the leadership of the management committee, human activities inside the core and buffer of the reserve were to be modified.[6] Fish harvesting was limited to areas immediately surrounding water control structures, and it was recommended that fishermen avoid disturbing nesting birds.

Completion of the dike system around the 4,000-hectare extension to the reserve, which will enable water retention during the dry season, is under way, but a great deal of work still needs to be done. A water management plan for the reserve is being developed, including construction of guard stations for dikes as well as planting of vegetation bands to protect selected dikes from deterioration. It is hoped that artificial islands will also be built to provide a refuge for other wildlife and raised grounds where the cranes can "dance." Elaborate courtship dancing that pairs of cranes perform involves spectacular leaps, bows, and graceful wing flapping and is an essential part of the birds' life, preparing them for breeding. Older local residents say that they have not seen the cranes dance for decades, but it is hoped that the new islands will encourage the cranes to breed in Tram Chim as they did thirty to forty years ago, before the effects of war took their toll on the area and its inhabitants.

Archibald, one of the few people who has ever "danced" with cranes, is mounting a drive to raise funds to help the Vietnamese complete construction of the dikes, canals, and sluice gates in order to restore and maintain the reserve. So far, substantial grants from the Brehm Fund and the John D. and Catherine T. MacArthur Foundation have financed salaries for a full-time staff at the reserve and for installation of four water gates in the dikes that surround the reserve. Now water flows from these gates into the reserve rather than over the dikes, minimizing erosion of the dikes. Flow from the reserve during the dry season is managed to simulate prewar hydrology.

Archibald is quick to point out the need for Tram Chim to become self-sufficient and the fact that multiple use of the restored Tram Chim wetland is vital if the wildlife and the local people are to live in harmony. In order to ensure the livelihoods of local people, he recommends carefully controlled fishing, duck trapping, lumbering, grazing, and bird-watching vacations. Plans are under way for construction of a guest house and for environmental teacher training and adult education at the information and conference center built by the Brehm Fund.

In addition, local authorities, with the assistance of CRES and apiary experts in a neighboring province, are hoping to develop improved methods of beekeeping (see the chapter titled "Honey for Sale," on Malawi's beekeeping clubs). This would involve planting melaleuca (*Melaleuca leucadendron*) and marketing melaleuca products, including oil, medicines, timber, and honey. Melaleuca forests once covered 250,000 hectares in Vietnam's Mekong Delta, but today only some 116,000 hectares remain.[7] Otters, pythons, crocodiles, eels, shrimp, crabs, turtles, and primates still inhabit the mangrove swamps, along with a rich variety of bird life, and are also a current source of food and a potential source of income. Melaleuca trees are one of the few species of plants able to survive in the highly acidic soil of the Mekong Delta. Replanting and maintaining these forests can therefore yield direct economic benefits to local residents, both from the sale of products and from creation of a cautiously developed tourist industry. Already Earthwatch, an environmental charity, has led its second study tour to Tram Chim in cooperation with the ICF. In 1992, Earthwatch volunteers interviewed eighty residents near Tram Chim, including people in the nearby town of Tam Nong. These volunteers, who pay to join the ICF's research and education efforts in and near the reserve, have helped in the restoration and maintenance of Tram Chim by supporting the upkeep of the new Brehm Center for conservation education.

During the course of their interviews with local people, Earthwatch volunteers discovered why some villagers have resisted melaleuca replanting as a viable source of income: they must wait three to five years for the first returns on their investment. After ICF and Earthwatch volunteers left Tram Chim in the spring of 1992, some 16 hectares of melaleuca forests were burned. The reasons for the destruction are not clear. The fire could have been started accidentally, by honey collectors trying to smoke out bees or by residents attempting controlled burning to create fire breaks. However, it also could have occurred because rice farmers wanted to clear the land for agriculture. An increase in sustainable activity in the reserve's buffer zone is essential if the reserve is to maintain—indeed, continue to gain—the necessary support of the local residents.

So far, restoration work has been carried out in 15,000 hectares of the 30,000-hectare floodplain area. Shortly after U.S. troops nearly destroyed the natural flood basin of the Dong Thap Muoi (Plain of Reeds) wetlands, of which Tram Chim is a part, the area dried out, acid sulfates in the soil rose to the surface, and the pH dropped to 3.9. The pH level in the canals plummeted to 2.8, rendering the water undrinkable and causing the virtual disappearance of all wildlife. "Even the mosquitoes died out!" says Derek Scott. Thanks to Muoi Nhe's efforts at replanting melaleuca forests and the construction of dikes to retain water in the floodplain during the dry season (which flushes the acid sulfates from the soil), the soil's pH value has risen to 5.8. Fisheries have also recovered, and sulfates have disappeared from some of the surface soils. An abundant supply of potable water is available again, and areas formerly unsuitable for cultivation are being planted with a floating strain of rice.

In addition to these benefits, cranes and other birds, including 20,000 to 30,000 ducks, mainly *Anas querquedula* and *A. crecca,* are rapidly increasing in number. Many rare species of birds continue to return, including the black-necked stork (*Xenorhynchus asiaticus*), the lesser adjutant (*Leptopilos javanicus*), and the painted stork (*Ibis leucocephalus*). Two pairs of Bengal florican (*Eupodotis bengalensis*) were sighted in 1990, for the first time in decades.

No one is quite sure where the cranes go when they leave Tram Chim every summer, but it is believed that they migrate across the border to the most unspoiled wetland site in Indochina, Cambodia's Great Lake. Considered Southeast Asia's richest and least-known wetland, it lies just 10 kilometers south of the ancient ruins of the Khmer empire, Angkor Wat. Surrounded by a belt of swamp forest, the lake is the largest permanent body of fresh water in Southeast Asia.

Long considered the "heart of Cambodia," the Great Lake is 160 kilometers long and 35 kilometers wide and measures some 250,000 to 300,000 hectares during the dry season (December to May). With the onset of the summer monsoons, the Great Lake swells to fifteen times its normal size, flooding the forests and fields around it for a radius of 300 kilometers. When it recedes, it leaves the rice paddies full of fish. In addition, a residue of rich silt covers the fields, providing a natural fertilizer for crops and at the same time irrigating the paddies.

During this dry spell, peasants wade through the paddies, scooping out the flopping fish with ease. So far, more than 850 species of fish have been counted in the lower Mekong River and the Great Lake area. It is believed that hundreds more exist, but the local people eat primarily ten species. Formerly, some 40,000 families depended on the lake for their income, living on houseboats floating on the lake or in small homes perched on stilts at the water's edge. Giant weirs more than a kilometer long are used to trap the abundant fish. Today, the lake produces an average of 57,000 metric tons of fish per year, having fallen from an estimated 99,800 metric tons in the late 1960s. In former times, the lake provided about 70 percent of the protein in the people's diet, but that has fallen to between 40 and 60 percent. However, the bountiful amount of fish is still impressive, particularly when one considers that the combined annual yield of the Great Lake and the Mekong River is between 150,000 and 200,000 metric tons of fish per year, making it one of the most productive inland fisheries in the world.

It is believed that thousands of birds also make a stopover at the Great Lake and along the flooded banks of the Tonle Sap and Mekong rivers on their migratory winter routes. Scientists suspect that a variety of birds that may have become extinct or endangered in other areas of Asia still abound on the Great Lake. These include the rare giant ibis and the white-shouldered ibis, the milky stork, the greater adjutant, and the white-winged wood duck.

CRES, which drafted an international agreement among Vietnam, Cambodia, and Laos to protect migratory species—including the eastern sarus crane and one of the world's rarest bovines, the kouprey—hopes to work with Cambodian scientists in developing a management plan for the Great Lake. Since only a handful of scientists remain in Cambodia, most of them having been killed during the war when the Khmer Rouge enacted a genocidal policy toward professional cadres, no one has yet conducted a reliable survey of the wetland. During the reign of terror of the Khmer Rouge (1975–1979), many prisoners were forced to work at the Great Lake, harvesting the wide variety of fish. Chan Sarun, one of the few forestry officials to survive the reign of the Khmer Rouge and now head of Cambodia's forestry department, lived during the war in the dense swamp forests that surround the Great Lake in a broad belt some 20 to 30 kilometers wide. In January 1988, Chan Sarun was one of several representatives of the three countries of Indochina who met in Hanoi to discuss how environmental cooperation among Southeast Asian countries can be improved.

Although the rich riverine forests of the Mekong and those bordering the Tonle Sap have been proposed as a nature reserve, they are decreasing in size because of clearing for firewood, agricultural land, and fish ponds. To date, there is no wetland legislation, and little scientific research has taken place since 1970. Clearing of the freshwater swamp forests surrounding the Great Lake is also accelerating, and conservationists fear that this could have disastrous effects on fish populations and cause serious siltation, leading to a reduction in fish numbers and species as well as a reduction in the size of the lake itself.

In January 1989, we interviewed villagers along tributaries of the Tonle Sap, who said that the eastern sarus crane migrated along their waterways. We also learned that the cranes were kept as pets by people living along the Tonle Sap. In 1992, George Archibald made a revealing discovery that offers hope for the survival of the crane in Indochina. Thai scientists have confiscated twenty-three eastern sarus crane chicks from wildlife dealers in Thailand, who secured the young birds from northern Cambodia, near the Laotian border. WWF scientists saw a pair of cranes in southern Laos near the border of northern Cambodia in the spring of 1991, confirming their presence in that region.

"During our years of work in Vietnam, we often wondered what the wetland basin must have been like before the whole environment was transformed by war. Having circled Tonle Sap in a small airplane in 1992 and observing the colonies of birds below us, we flew along the Tonle Sap River east to its junction with the Mekong south toward the border with Vietnam. It was one of the most thrilling moments of my life to look down and see vast expanses of natural wetlands, pristine habitat for cranes—and people," Archibald exclaimed after his first aerial survey of crane habitat in Cambodia. During this trip, the ICF signed a memorandum with the Cambodian Department of Forestry outlining plans for the training of Cambodians in wildlife management in Thailand in 1992 and for their training in the United States in 1993. According to Archibald, approximately 5.2 percent of Cambodia is still covered by wetlands and grasslands.[8]

Scientists such as Archibald and Chan Sarun and wildlife enthusiasts, including Cambodia's vice minister of agriculture, Dr. Mok Mareth, expect that surveys of the country's six forest reserves and its one national park, Angkor Wat, will be stepped up soon. It is to be hoped that before long they and the people of Cambodia can count 1,000 cranes on the Great Lake once again—a sign that good fortune and peace have returned to the heart of Cambodia.

Mayhem in Manas
The Threats to India's Wildlife Reserves

The crackle of gunfire broke through the morning mists lying over the dense forest in the Manas Tiger Reserve in northeastern India. Startled wildlife guards, just finishing breakfast and preparing for routine patrols, grabbed their shotguns and leaped to the windows of their timber guard post. Shouts from the surrounding vegetation told them they were surrounded. The Bodos were attacking. In the gun battle that ensued, the guards were overcome. There were only about a dozen of them, and the attackers were in the hundreds.

When armed police rushed to the scene the next day, the Bodos melted away into the forest. The guards were rescued—demoralized and terrified, but unhurt.

It was February 1988 at Lafasari Camp. Guard posts elsewhere in Manas were also overwhelmed by the Bodos; three guards lost their lives. The attackers looted arms and radios and burned buildings and equipment. The Assam State government ordered guards to concentrate at range headquarters. Even though the guards were still in the reserve, the management system was completely disrupted. Within a short time, illegally felled timber began to appear in markets, venison turned up in restaurants, and reports spread of tigers and deer killed and rhinos slaughtered for their horns.

Manas, one of Asia's finest wildlife reserves, designated as a World Heritage site, had fallen victim to political turmoil of a kind active or latent all over the world. Events there represent a worst-case scenario, but other reserves in India have also suffered incursions by violent extremists, and all are threatened by growing population pressure on the natural resources they are meant to protect. Almost everywhere, villagers around reserves have exhausted their basic resources in striving to maintain a meager standard of living. Wildlife protection laws have deprived them of the right to use the resources in the reserves, and the laws provide for punishment if they are defied. Official and citizens' group programs have recently been launched in an attempt to ameliorate the conditions and to encourage the villagers to take pride in protecting India's rich wildlife.

Manas Tiger Reserve extends over 2,800 square kilometers of land at the foot of the eastern Himalayas, where the Manas River flows out onto the plains to join the Brahmaputra. A relic of the vast forests that extended all along the foot of the 1,500-kilometer Himalayan chain, Manas is a sanctuary for one of the principal concentrations of India's surviving wildlife. The forests, grasslands, and marshes are home to elephants, one-horned rhinos, tigers, leopards, clouded leopards, marbled cats, wild dogs, sambars, swamp hogs and barking deer, gaurs, giant squirrels, sloth bears, hoolock gibbons, golden and capped langurs, and pythons, as well as hornbills, eagles, and a host of other birds, and its rivers contain gharial crocodiles and river dolphins. No fewer than twenty-two species on India's list of endangered mammals live in Manas. It is almost the last hope for the wild Asiatic buffalo (progenitor of the hundreds of millions of domestic water buffalo), pygmy hog, and hispid hare.

The importance of Manas has long been recognized. The core area around the river was declared a sanctuary as long ago as 1928, and in 1973 it became one of the first of India's special tiger reserves. Apart from forests extending east and west beyond the reserve boundaries, Manas forms part of an ecological block with an adjoining reserve of the same name in the hills of Bhutan to the north.

But like most of the world's wild places in modern times, Manas is not isolated from the human world. It falls within the homeland of the Bodo people, who make up about one-third of the 30 million population of varied communities in Assam State. A large proportion of the people of Assam consists of immigrants from elsewhere, some resident for many generations, others still arriving. The struggle for a decent living and political power among these communities has made Assam a turbulent area. The Bodos, claiming that they were deprived of their lands and incorporated into Assam during British rule, launched a campaign in the mid-1980s for autonomy or a separate state of their own.

Following a long tradition, students formed the most militant campaigners. Some of them, members of the Bodo Students' Union, turned to violence, attacking government offices and killing officials. What better refuge was there than the great forests of Manas in the heart of their country, where Bodos made up the bulk of the villagers? Furthermore, the extremists could expect fraternal sympathy from their own people in the villages, who also nursed grievances against rules to protect wildlife and habitat, which inevitably restricted their traditional way of life.

Rivalry between opposing political parties in power in the central government in New Delhi and the state government in Assam, along with the onset of the wet season, held up action to drive out the Bodo extremists and restore order in the reserve. Meanwhile, the extremists, who killed a total of twelve guards in all, were destroying bridges and culverts to handicap action against them. Wildlife staff members at all levels, who had taken pride in conserving the wonders of Manas, were demoralized and bewildered.

During 1990, progress was slowly being made in restoring the management regime in Manas, with the help of armed police. But in September of that year, yet another range headquarters was attacked and looted, and a young forester was killed. Fortunately, this turned out to be an isolated burst of extreme violence. Political efforts to negotiate a settlement with the Bodo leaders were in hand, and since then the situation has been relatively quiet. The wildlife administration has been able to reestablish its control at strategic points.

But Manas still lies deep in the shadows of uncertainty. A political settlement of the Bodo claims has still to be reached, a necessity for restoration of stable conditions in Assam and reestablishment of full management of the reserve. Despite damage to government property, estimated at 50 million rupees (about $2 million), aerial reconnaissance indicates that habitat has not suffered to any great extent. This has yet to be confirmed on the ground, where wildfire guards still have not been deployed in many areas and communications remain disrupted.

Poaching in the absence of control may have depleted some animal populations. Nevertheless, poaching has never been easy in Manas because of inaccessibility, dense cover, and poor ground-level visibility.

In the event of such political turmoil in any area, it is not unusual for wildlife management to become a casualty. In such hours of crisis, only a strong, commanding leadership backed by a toughened field staff may be able to repulse an offensive. Unfortunately, at the crucial point of the crisis in Manas, the leadership buckled under pressure, and the tough ground force gave up the fight. However, an able leader of proven worth has now been posted to Manas who not only should be able to restore the morale but also may be able to fight back if that again becomes necessary. The political situation has improved considerably, though the clouds have not yet fully cleared. Thus, the danger appears to have been averted.

But a question remains: Is this area safe? To answer this question, many more aspects must be considered. With strong political will and necessary resources made available, no objective may be beyond achievement. But then, what is the depth of this political will? Will it be sufficient? These are questions that cannot be answered easily or directly.

The main threat to Manas in the long run could be from the population living on the fringe of the reserve and its poverty. The southern tracts of Manas consist of flat terrain with extremely fertile land. Many determined attempts have been made by fringe people to cultivate these areas. In all of these cases, where encroachment has been supported by interested political groups, encroachers have been expelled only after violent clashes. The pressure on land will rise further in the future, keeping pace with the rise in the human population. Naturally, this will lead to further complications, although at present the legal status of the reserve is sound and strong.

During the late 1970s, Manas was threatened by a proposal to build a massive dam on the Manas River in Bhutanese territory, upstream of the Indian tiger reserve. The waters were to generate power, irrigate agricultural land, and control floods in the Indian state of Assam. A 100-kilometer canal was to be cut through the tiger reserve to transfer the water to another dam on the Sankosh River to the west.

The Ministry of Environment and Forests objected strongly on the grounds that the project would change the hydrology and ecology of the area and severely damage the reserve. The World Heritage Committee of UNESCO supported the objections, and the late prime minister Rajiv Gandhi's government dropped the project. There appears to be little likelihood of its being revived in the foreseeable future. The Indian government is well aware of public reaction on conservation matters and associated legal and political problems, and this was not the first time that Indian administrations have been forced to revise proposals. The Bhutanese government is not known to have any development plans.

To contain pressure from people around Manas in the years to come, an extensive ecodevelopment plan has been formulated to cover the target population. The original plan, prepared by one of the authors of this paper, has been further developed and has been taken up by WWF. It is likely to be executed as soon as the political clouds clear. The plan envisages the improvement of all socioeconomic aspects of the life of the fringe people by reducing their dependence on the forest and by making use of environmental education combined with their traditional wisdom. This whole plan has to be executed by the wildlife authorities, with contributions from other departments and disciplines.

Since relations between the royal government of Bhutan and the Assam government are more than cordial, management of both areas runs smoothly. They could be cited as an example of excellent international cooperation.

Unfortunately, Manas is not the only Indian wildlife reserve suffering from population pressure and political turbulence. All of India's nearly 500 protected areas are virtual islands surrounded by villages and agricultural land, where people are desperately short of the basic resources of life, such as firewood, building materials, and grazing areas for their livestock. Inevitably, they invade the reserves and come into conflict with the authorities. Poaching of animals, timber, and other forest produce is rife, and cattle and goats are found in most reserves. Resentment at the wildlife authorities' attempts to control the situation has exploded in violence against officials and guards. In Nagarhole National Park in southern India, local people put to flames more than 20 square kilometers of forest after a suspected poacher was found shot dead, even though the evidence clearly showed that wildlife guards could not have been responsible.

Violent political extremists, like their Bodo counterparts, use the forests as safe retreats. Sikh terrorists have invaded Corbett and Dudwa tiger reserves in northern India, killing guards and paralyzing the administration. Left-wing extremists, called Naxalites after the area of West Bengal where their insurrection began, have sought refuge in many forest areas, terrorizing guards and encouraging poaching by forest dwellers, whom they champion.

Only recently have those in official circles realized that survival of India's wildlife reserves can be ensured only with the goodwill of the people who live around them and that such goodwill can be obtained only by amelioration of the lives of those people. Pioneering work has been carried out by citizens' groups, such as the Ranthambhore Foundation and WWF. Both have been working in villages around the high-profile Ranthambhore Tiger Reserve, located only 200 kilometers from Delhi and world-famous for its spectacular views of normally secretive tigers.

Programs have involved provision of medical and family planning facilities; rehabilitation of derelict land; protection of surviving forests from cattle grazing, which prevents regeneration; planting of trees for fuel and building material; establishment of fodder plots; assistance for women to increase family incomes by marketing their skills at making the colorful regional dress; provision of high-yielding milking buffaloes, which can be stall-fed to replace low-producing grazing cattle, and help in setting up dairy cooperatives; and environmental education, which included introducing children to the beauties of the reserves, which they had never before seen.

Around Manas, WWF has initiated an ecodevelopment program, conducting interviews with three-quarters of the local villagers to find out their problems and needs. Local officials, university students, and resident youth groups have cooperated with WWF staff members in carrying out the surveys. As at Ranthambhore, the project aims at minimizing pressure on the reserve for fodder and thatch grass, fuelwood and building wood, and livestock grazing, as well as improving health care and income generation.

It is hoped that all of these efforts will be boosted by a World Bank plan to grant $12 million for ecodevelopment around India's tiger reserves and major wildlife sanctuaries.

SERI THONGMAK & DAVID L. HULSE

The Winds of Change
Karen People in Harmony with World Heritage

I know, one day, I may lose to the winds of change. For generations, our people have built homes in the mountains. In a bamboo shack roofed with grass, we are free.

The world has changed, and things will not return. I dream of our ancestors traveling from the end of the sky to find a land of peace.

I know, one day, I may lose to the winds of change. But I will stand tall. I will tell other peoples that in the land of the mountains, it is not us, but you, who are the intruders.

POH LEI PAH, KAREN ELDER AND POET[1]

When a Karen child is born, the father of the newborn takes the placenta and umbilical cord and walks deep into the forest, where he selects a large tree and offers to it the afterbirth by placing it in the crook of a branch. The tree, which exemplifies both life and longevity, becomes a lifetime reminder to the Karen child that his or her own health and well-being are related to the health and well-being of that tree.

As the father walks back to the village, he picks wildflowers to give to his wife and the baby girl, thus transferring the beauty and sweet smell of the flower to his newborn daughter. If the child is a boy, the father selects a long, straight branch, which he whittles smooth and presents to his son for use as a toy to play with while growing up, giving his son strength and vitality.

When the child is old enough to walk and understand, the father will guide his daughter or son to the forest to see her or his "life tree" and to know that she or he must nurture and care for this ancient being. No Karen would dare to cut down any large tree, since it surely is the life tree of a family member or a village neighbor. This simple and poignant ritual initiates at birth the direct connection that Karen people have throughout their lives with the forests and mountains surrounding their villages.

Unfortunately, fewer and fewer Karen fathers are able to walk directly from their village homes and into thick primary forests to find suitable life trees for their newborn children, for much of the land that the forest-dwelling Karen occupied in the past has been cleared and settled by other groups. Consequently, the Karen tribal people have lost substantial tracts of their traditional forestlands to concessions and government resettlement programs and from expanded cash crop cultivation and development in the Thai provinces of Kanchanaburi and Tak. Karen people living on the Burmese side of the border are even less fortunate, having been engaged in a bitter, four-decade struggle for greater autonomy from the government in Rangoon.

The Karen are a tribal people living in the highlands of Burma and Thailand; around 2.5 million inhabit the forested mountains of Burma, and 250,000 live in Thailand. There are four major Karen subgroups: Pwo, Skaw, Thongsu, and Kayan. No one knows for sure where the Karen who live in and around the Huay Kha Khaeng and Thung Yai Naresuan wildlife sanctuaries came from or how long they have been in the Thai border area adjacent to Burma, but it is generally believed that they have lived there for at least two centuries, long before the lowland Thais migrated to the foothills. Today, the Karen, like many hill tribe minorities, are under pressure to leave their forest homes.[2]

One of the few remaining refuges where the Karen have been free to uphold their simple ceremonies and environmentally harmonious life-style is inside Thailand's Thung Yai Naresuan Wildlife Sanctuary, where six villages are home to a remnant population of 1,100 Karen. Yet even in Thung Yai, the survival of the Karen is under threat, not from developers or loggers but from well-intentioned conservationists who seek to evict the Karen from the forests that they have been occupying and protecting for centuries.

The debate over removal of the Karen from Thung Yai escalated in 1991, when Thung Yai, along with the adjacent Huay Kha Khaeng Wildlife Sanctuary, was declared a World Heritage site by UNESCO. With the inclusion of recent extensions and combined with Huay Kha Khaeng (257,464 hectares), Thung Yai is the largest conservation area in mainland Southeast Asia, covering a total of 622,000 hectares. In addition, Thung Yai adjoins Umphang Wildlife Sanctuary to the north (251,600 hectares) and Bung Kroeng Kawia Non-Hunting Area (51,200 hectares) and the proposed Khao Laem National Park (122,300 hectares) to the south.[3]

The royal Thai government was justifiably proud that Thung Yai–Huay Kha Khaeng was the first natural site in Southeast Asia to be declared worthy of World Heritage status. However, this also meant that officials in the Royal Forest Department and some wildlife conservation experts felt obliged to recommend enforcement of the laws governing wildlife sanctuaries, which restrict human habitation inside the gazetted sanctuary boundaries. There has been particular concern among some officials that an increasing population of resident Karen in Thung Yai could lead to nonsustainable utilization of the forest and wildlife resources. Advocates of the Karen point out that the population of rural Karen in Thung Yai has remained stable over the past several decades due to a small but consistent out-migration of Karen who choose to live and work in the urbanized areas of Thailand, giving up their traditional village life-style in the forests of Thung Yai.

Thung Yai's wildlife conservation laws were written with the clear intention of preserving Thailand's diverse fauna, which at Thung Yai Wildlife Sanctuary includes viable populations of Asian elephants, tigers, clouded leopards, serows, gaurs, bantengs, five species of primate, and some 400 resident or migrant bird species, including four species of hornbill and the magnificent green peafowl. Yet a strict preservationist approach to wildlife and forest conservation does not take into account the positive role that resident forest peoples such as the Karen can have in preserving and protecting the dynamic forest ecosystem. The Karen receive their cultural, spiritual, and daily food sustenance from the old-growth forests, and their long claim on the forestlands of Thung Yai has ensured that other groups who practice destructive agriculture and timber harvesting have been kept out, to the benefit of the forest.

The Karen's struggle for survival in Thung Yai has been noticed and championed by a loose coalition of grass-roots and conservation groups. The groups first joined forces in the 1980s to protest government plans to build a major hydroelectric facility on the Nam Choan River, which would have submerged a large portion of Thung Yai Wildlife Sanctuary and the traditional forest homeland of the Karen. The dam's 75-square-kilometer reservoir would have split the sanctuary into three smaller areas, greatly reducing the long-term survival prospects of the larger mammals living in the reserve.[4] Watershed protection in both Thung Yai and Huay Kha Khaeng is conservatively estimated to be worth some $13.8 million annually.[5]

One of the prominent groups in the coalition is Wildlife Fund Thailand (WFT), the Thai associate organization of WWF. This NGO has been promoting environmental education and basic extension activities for villagers living in and around the Thung Yai Naresuan–Huay Khaeng wildlife sanctuary complex in western Thailand since 1986. The WFT extension staff, initially headed by Nikom Putta of the innovative and well-recognized TEAM (The Environmental Awareness Mobilization) Project, an integrated environment and community program at Khao Yai National Park, which lies 100 kilometers northeast of Bangkok, soon realized that the Karen villages were different from those of the lowland Thai and Hmong residents of the same region.

The first evidence of this difference was found in the contrasting conditions of the surrounding forests. Karen villages, which had often been in the same location for decades and sometimes centuries, were enveloped by thick groves of primary forest rich with birds and wildlife, while the villages of the lowland Thais, who had migrated to the area within the past ten or twenty years, were typically encircled by denuded lands marked by burned-out tree stumps and eroded hillsides. While the Thais were planting cash crops such as cassava, pineapple, and sugarcane for sale in the provincial market, the Karen undertook subsistence rice and vegetable farming. They supplemented their income by collecting natural forest products such as cardamom, which they could sell for 200 baht (about $8) per kilogram, creating an important source of cash revenue. The Karen's agricultural practices were documented by Ketty Faichampa, a Thai graduate student at the Yale School of Forestry, when she spent several months working with the WFT community extension staff on a WWF-supported research grant in 1988.

Anthropologists and agricultural researchers have found that the Karen, who are mistakenly grouped by Thai government officials and other outsiders into the category of primitive and destructive slash-and-burn agriculturalists, have developed an elaborate succession of rules that dictate their natural agricultural practices. According to these traditions, farmers never plant rice over a natural spring, on opposite banks or at the fork of a stream, in an area populated with rare birds and wildlife, or on top of a hill. The latter is observed because in Karen folklore a hilltop resembles the back of a turtle, and to degrade such an area would slow down the progress of the turtle and of life itself. One family never plants more than three plots of land, and the Karen select the location of their rice and vegetable plots only after the bamboo shoots have come up, so as not to disrupt the natural forest cycles.[6]

The Karen's system of multicropping rice with bananas, potatoes, sesame, and millet maintains a balance of nutrients in the soil. Planting several different varieties of rice in the same field protects the crop from pests and disease, and the use of natural fertilizers ensures that the Karen are not reliant on expensive chemical inputs and hybrid seeds, even though these modern techniques are promoted by government agricultural officers.

In fact, the Karen people protect and defend their forestlands from impurities because they look to the forest as the guardian of their fortune and livelihood. In an annual ceremony of thanksgiving and contrition referred to in the Karen language as the Request for an Extension to Existence, the villagers pay homage to an ancient tree that has been specifically selected for its expansive size and girth. Following a brief prayer of gratitude and a confession of their past and future sins against nature and the spirits of the forest, the respectful worshipers prepare mounds of earth and pebbles on the ground surrounding the tree, cover the mounds and the earth with flowers, water the roots, and brace the trunk and lower branches of the tree with seven bamboo poles, representing the seven days of the week, with each person assisting according to his or her day of birth. The villagers seek forgiveness from nature, for they fully realize that they depend on the forest for their sustenance and that it is an offense against nature every time they gash the soil to raise crops or cut fruit from a tree.

Although not all Karen follow the strict vegetarian regimen of their monks and temple abbots, most villagers' diets consist almost entirely of grains, vegetables, and fruits. The sources of animal protein are fish and small animals such as bamboo rats and jungle fowl, which are trapped in the streams and wooded areas of the forest. Thai government agricultural extension programs have recently promoted the rearing of chickens for local consumption; however, due to their aversion for killing, the Karen did not traditionally raise farm animals. This profound respect for life is extended to all forest creatures. The Karen utilize animals only when needed for survival, and many species are considered sacred. For a Karen, to injure or kill a hornbill is a sin equivalent to executing a holy man, and traditional folklore predicts that any hunter who shoots a gibbon or tapir, even if by mistake, will surely die as punishment for this grave error.

The endemic cultural beliefs of the Karen are the foundation for an environmentally sound and sustainable life-style in Thung Yai. Many Karen villagers are now puzzled over the fact that after many years of peaceful coexistence with the forests, they could be moved out because the Thai government wants to protect Thung Yai. A village elder illuminates the frustration and confusion of the Karen:

"When we moved to these forests over two centuries ago, Bangkok was just a small village surrounded by lush vegetation. Over these many years, we Karen have protected our forestlands out of respect for our ancestors and our children. Maybe if we had cut down the forests, destroyed the land, and built a great city like Bangkok, we would not now be faced with possible eviction."[7]

Only when the conservation community begins to appreciate more fully the role of forest-dwelling people as an inherent part of nature rather than as intruders, and makes appropriate changes in project design and protected area management schemes, will the special niche of communities like the Karen be preserved. As Nikom Putta explains: "Our main objective as conservationists should be to save Thailand's remaining natural habitats and ecosystems. Intricately woven into this objective are the realization and understanding that people are an integral part of these natural ecosystems and they cannot be left out of any of the projects to protect and conserve these areas."

Wildlife Fund Thailand's work on behalf of the Karen is only a first step in the preservation of Karen culture at Thung Yai. One of the authors of this chapter, Seri Thongmak, who is the WFT extension officer working on the Community Extension Project at Thung Yai Naresuan Wildlife Sanctuary, recalls that it took nearly a year to gain the trust of the Karen residents of Saney Pong Village, which lies a few kilometers inside the sanctuary's boundary. "At first, the villagers thought I was one of the sanctuary forest guards, and they were hesitant to speak openly with me about their concerns and beliefs. They were fearful that I was collecting information in order to move them out of the sanctuary. Only after I took the time to walk with them to their fields in the forest, to sleep many nights on the floor in their homes, to share their meals, and to chew betel nut with the abbot of the local temple did they begin to see that I was different."

Many of the village leaders were equally surprised that Seri sought their permission to work with Wildlife Fund Thailand on a community development project and that he solicited their input and ideas before the project started. "They told me that none of the government officials who previously visited their village had acted as I did or had shown a genuine interest in the Karen culture."

Fortunately for the Karen, not all government officials disregard or misunderstand the Karen people's interactive role with the forests. The sanctuary chief, Weerawat Theeraprasart, has worked at Thung Yai since the area was declared a wildlife sanctuary in 1974. He has become a strong advocate of the Karen villagers, and he has persistently argued for their continued habitation inside the boundaries of

Thung Yai, even though this opinion runs contrary to Thai government policy. His efforts won the Karen a temporary reprieve in April 1992, but their future at Thung Yai remains uncertain.

It is a bitter irony to the Karen that the forests they have striven to protect and preserve for centuries are worthy of UNESCO World Heritage designation, yet some government and conservation officials do not recognize the Karen's unique and indigenous culture as an inseparable part of that heritage. The WFT and other NGOs continue to work closely with the Royal Forest Department and provincial government officials to develop acceptable compromises to ensure that the Karen can maintain their traditional life-style inside the Thung Yai Naresuan Wildlife Sanctuary. Even though land and forest policies change with successive governments, and the 1992 decision allowing the Karen to remain in Thung Yai may be only temporary, the Karen's eloquent interaction with the forests of Thung Yai remains their lasting contribution to a world heritage.

STEPHEN ELLIOTT & OOKAEW PRAKOBVITAYAKIT BEAVER

A Mountain for Profit

A red taxi swings into the extensive new parking lot at Ban Doi Pui, Thailand's most heavily visited hill tribe village. The tourists who emerge from it push their way through a horde of trinket sellers and climb the steep, potholed street, lined not with traditional houses but with souvenir shops, in which exotic products like bears' paws, ivory, tigers' teeth, wild boars' tusks, and aromatic medicinal herbs compete with handicrafts, T-shirts, and Coca-Cola for their attention. Some take snapshots of children dressed in the traditional costume of the Hmong tribe, the inhabitants of the village, while others wander into a dingy bamboo shack with a sign outside proclaiming it to be a "hill tribe museum." It contains nothing more than a few unlabeled, decaying relics and a miserable kalij pheasant—a species listed as vulnerable to extinction—calling plaintively in a tiny cage. "It's disgusting," says one of the tourists. "I would never have come if I'd known it was going to be like this."

That the culture and environment of the village have been completely over-whelmed by about 200,000 annual visitors is disturbing. The fact that it lies at the heart of a so-called national park makes the situation all the more deplorable.

Doi Suthep–Pui National Park (*doi* means "mountain") provides a spectacular backdrop to Thailand's second largest city, Chiang Mai. The park covers an area of 261 square kilometers, and its main attraction, Phra That Temple, is one of the most sacred sites in the country. The park also contains some of the most diverse dry tropical forest known to science. Near streams, there are about 150 tree species per hectare, a figure that makes Doi Suthep's deciduous forest comparable to the rain forest of Borneo. J. F. Maxwell, a botanist at Chiang Mai University's biology department, has recorded more than 2,000 species of vascular plants in the park, more species than occur in the whole of the United Kingdom. Animal species include 326 birds, 61 mammals, 28 amphibians, 50 reptiles, and about 500 butterflies and 300 moths. Doi Suthep is also an important refuge for several species threatened with extinction, including the crocodile salamander, found at only four sites in Thailand. Fifty of Doi Suthep's orchid species and twenty-two birds are listed as rare, vulnerable, or threatened with extinction.

Such diverse flora and fauna have attracted scientists since the turn of the century, making Doi Suthep's forest one of the most intensely studied in Thailand. About 275 plant and 60 animal species first became known to science from specimens collected from the mountain.

The park is also northern Thailand's most important tourist attraction, receiving more than half a million visitors per year.

Situated so close to Chiang Mai, Doi Suthep has always suffered from disturbance. Settlers were present long before the area was designated a national forest reserve in 1967 and upgraded to a national park in 1981.

"We were here first," explained a young man selling gemstones at Ban Doi Pui. "It is the national park that has encroached on our land, not the other way around. The Forestry Department is no good. It won't let us have electricity here, and we have to get permission even to put toilets in our houses."

In 1964, a survey revealed 369 people living in the area. They were permitted to stay for the remainder of their lives but were not allowed to sell their land. Only 148 people insisted on staying, but they were soon joined by immigrants, arriving in droves to cash in on the tourism boom, so by 1981 the number of people living in the park had increased to 1,956. There has been no attempt by the authorities to relocate the village outside the park. Occasionally, illegally built houses have been ordered demolished, but this has not prevented Ban Doi Pui from doubling in area over a three-year period in the early 1990s.

The Hmong are by no means the only encroachers in the park. A survey published in 1988 revealed a total of 13,694 people belonging to four ethnic groups living within the park or on its boundary, about 60 percent of them claiming to have been born there. Large resorts financed by wealthy businesspeople have mushroomed around the edge of the park; in 1991, five such resorts were ordered demolished. Government organizations, including agricultural research stations, television transmitters, and police and army posts, also occupy large areas. Altogether, about 44 percent of the park has been cleared of forest by encroachers.

The governor of Chiang Mai advocates taking a pragmatic approach to the encroachment problem by bringing encroachers to court on a case-by-case basis rather than employing draconian measures to expel them all. However, such legal

Snow peaks in Colombia's Sierra Nevada de Santa Marta National Park
provide much-needed water to millions of people. Courtesy Juan Mayr.

Kogi *Mama* high priest in Sierra Nevada, Colombia.
Courtesy Juan Mayr.

Ciudad Perdida (the Lost City) is a sacred site for the Kogi people.
Courtesy Juan Mayr.

A Kogi Indian village at a high elevation,
Sierra Nevada de Santa Marta, Colombia.
Courtesy WWF/Juan Mayr.

A young Arsario boy collects shrubs in Sierra Nevada de Santa Marta National Park in northern Colombia to make brooms for sweeping the village school yard. Courtesy WWF/Elizabeth Kemf.

The El Congo ecological and educational station near Santa Marta was modeled after Kogi architecture and was restored and rebuilt with the permission and help of the Kogi. Courtesy Juan Mayr.

The headwoman of the Shimshali tribe at the Pamir. Courtesy Luke White.

This roadside shop on the Karakoram Highway, traversing Khunjerab from
Islamabad to China, sells drinks and other necessities to weary travelers.
Courtesy Luke White.

Ibex horns mark the pass to the Pamir (Roof of the World). The horns are
placed here as a totem or monument to this animal, which the Shimshali people
both hunt and worship. Courtesy Luke White.

Patchworked sails power sampans on a waterway in Vietnam.
Courtesy Elizabeth Kemf.

A fishing net at Tram Chim, Vietnam. Courtesy Elizabeth Kemf.

A female soldier planting mangroves in the Mekong Delta to replace those destroyed by Agent Orange during the U.S.–Vietnam War. Courtesy Elizabeth Kemf.

Vietnamese women fish in a rice paddy. Courtesy Elizabeth Kemf.

A Karen woman cutting palm fronds for roofing material.
Courtesy Acacia/Edward Milner.

A Karen tribal man fishing in a river with set net and traps.
Courtesy Acacia/Edward Milner.

A Karen mother and child digging for crickets in a sand bank along a river in
the dry season. Courtesy Acacia/Edward Milner.

A Tuareg girl in ripening wheat, Zomo, Aïr Mountains, Niger.
Courtesy WWF/John Newby.

Cooking for guests at a project gathering, Niger, March 1989.
Courtesy WWF/John Newby.

A Tuareg mother and child with a goat, Temet, Aïr Mountains, Niger.
Courtesy WWF/John Newby.

Watering camels from a shallow well, Wadi Iglodlef, Aïr Mountains, Niger.
Courtesy WWF/John Newby.

Fiskardo Village and harbor, northern part of Kefalonia Island.
Courtesy WWF/Michel Gunther/BIOS.

Researchers measuring turtle tracks, Zakynthos, Laganas Bay.
Courtesy WWF/Michel Gunther/BIOS.

Loggerhead turtle swimming in the Mediterranean. Unchecked tourism threatens the survival of this species. Courtesy WWF/Michel Gunther/BIOS.

battles are lengthy and are complicated by interference with the boundary markers of the park and ambiguous land documents, often acquired illegally with the connivance of corrupt officials. Several thousand such court cases would have to be fought to remove all encroachers from Doi Suthep. Between 1987 and 1991, only sixty-seven were successfully prosecuted and ordered to leave.

Another major threat to the park's integrity, again undertaken to satisfy the demands of tourism, is a road improvement program. Work is to begin shortly to widen the main highway from Chiang Mai to Phra That Temple, and survey work has been completed to extend the road that runs over the sensitive summit areas of Doi Suthep and Doi Pui to provide a circular route for motorists. Dirt tracks all over the park, previously used mainly by hikers, are being widened and upgraded into surfaced roads to open previously inaccessible parts of the park to tour buses.

The mass tourism currently being promoted within the park simply cannot be sustained, and the tourists themselves do not seem to want it. A recent survey by Chiang Mai University's biology department showed that the majority of visitors to the park are satisfied with the existing road system, while 72 percent complained about lack of guidebooks and maps of walking trails and 75 percent complained about the complete absence of facilities for viewing wildlife. Most visitors also felt that the park had been spoiled by deforestation and too much tourism development (69 percent and 58 percent, respectively). An overwhelming 82 percent thought that construction of tourist facilities, such as roads, resorts, and souvenir shops, should not be permitted inside national parks. As tourism is Chiang Mai's most important industry and Doi Suthep is its main attraction, such results have important implications for the continued economic prosperity of the city.

Only a complete change of attitude will save Doi Suthep and its diverse forest from complete devastation. One grass-roots organization helping to bring about that change in attitude by raising awareness of the cultural and scientific importance of the mountain is the For Chiang Mai Group, which in 1987 successfully campaigned against construction of a cable car system that would have whisked tourists from Chiang Mai Zoo to Phra That Temple. In 1991, the group organized a seminar that brought together for the first time villagers and government organizations involved in the park's management. A constructive dialogue was begun. Now the group is producing educational materials for distribution to schools around the park. Chiang Mai University, which hosted the 1991 seminar, is also playing an active role in conserving the park. The university plans to build a nature education center at the foot of the mountain. The faculty of the social sciences department is assisting the Royal Forest Department to update maps of the park by using satellite images, and the biology department plans to establish a tree nursery to provide seedlings to restore the natural forest ecosystem to degraded areas. Such initiatives are a small start, but they show that Chiang Mai's citizens are not all prepared to sit back and watch Doi Suthep be sacrificed to the tourism industry.

HANSON L. NJIFORTI & NGANKAM MARTIN TCHAMBA

Conflict in Cameroon [1]
Parks for or against People?

"These parks were created for white men, who can still hunt in the parks, who can go into the parks and do whatever they want." This was the general feeling from almost three-quarters of the villagers we interviewed around three national parks in northern Cameroon in 1990 and 1991. "We didn't even know the parks existed until the authorities started sending our people to prison for hunting. That was when we found out that we couldn't hunt where we used to hunt and that we were not allowed to hunt the wild animals that were killing our livestock. Why didn't anyone ask us what we thought? Then we might not have these problems."

We were as surprised as most of the villagers were when we set out to interview them about the growing conflict they were experiencing with the park authorities. The Wildlife Program of the Institute of Animal Research (IRZ) in Cameroon had noticed a great deal of strain in the relationship between park authorities and most villages surrounding the national parks. Several people had been sent to prison for poaching, and there was even open combat between game guards and poachers. A special program was set up to investigate the source of conflict, with a team of researchers carrying out interviews in sixteen villages around the national parks of Faro, Bénoué, and Bouba-Njida.

The parks, in the north of the country, are the only three of Cameroon's seven national parks to be surrounded by hunting zones. These zones, rented almost exclusively to foreigners for commercial safari hunting, have exacerbated tensions as villagers continue to live on the land and attempt to farm or graze it. Rapidly expanding human populations cause additional pressures.

Fari, at 330,000 hectares, is the country's largest national park, while Bénoué—one of the oldest nature reserves in Cameroon—covers 180,000 hectares. Bouba-Njida, with an area of 220,000 hectares, became a game reserve in 1948, then a national park in 1968. The people living in the hunting zones are mostly of Fulani and Fulbe origin—traditionally cattle breeders—with a mixture of native Bandu tribes, who practice agriculture and fishing. Before the parks were created and the people were resettled, hunting was also an important tradition.

The research project gave villagers a chance to discuss such issues. The interviews normally started with a visit to the *jaoro,* the chief of the village, for a briefing, after which village men and women were interviewed. Employees of the Ministry of Tourism, which is responsible for the management of national parks, were excluded from the interviewing team, since the villagers seemed disinclined to talk when ministry personnel were with us on our first two visits.

One *jaoro* was surprised that we had taken the trouble to come to his village. "How come you have trekked all this distance just to ask us what we feel about the national parks?" he asked. "This is the first time somebody has come here to ask our opinion." He looked around at the village elders, who had gathered when they heard that strangers were around. They nodded as if to confirm his statement. "Come," he said, rising from his wooden chair, which was covered with the skin of an antelope. He led us through a back door and we walked to the middle of the village, stopping near a baobab tree. "Look," he said, pointing to a flock of sheep grazing on a farm nearby. "We have to keep these animals because it is our tradition. It is also our main source of income." He paused, then looked in the direction of the park. "You cannot count how many of our sheep, cattle, and goats have been taken by wild animals from over there. What do the park authorities say?" "*Babou* [nothing]," the elders answered in chorus. "If they come to our village," the *jaoro* continued, "it is to arrest somebody because he has hunted or grazed his animals in the park."

"Oumarou," he called, looking at a young man standing a few meters away with several others who had gathered to hear our purpose. "Go and bring my bow and arrows." The young man returned from the chief's house with a bow that looked at least twenty years old. The arrows were carried in a special bag made of skin, too old to distinguish the species of origin. "Look," the chief said, taking the bow and arrows and holding them high enough for all of us to see. "This is what I was using to hunt when I was just like that young man over there. We used to go hunting where you now call it a national park. It was our tradition that a young man train himself to aim correctly. How many of these young men can do so?" "*Babou,*" the elders echoed. "Those white men who come to hunt here every year, don't they have to practice sighting in their countries before coming here?" We said that they did.

"Then why do they not want us to teach our own children, or does it mean that only white men can hunt nowadays?"

We began to explain the complex subject of wildlife conservation as the scientists saw it. We said that the government had to regulate hunting so that some important species would not become extinct. "Can I ask you a question?" said an elder. "When Fritzo was moving around this country carried on human shoulders to choose where to create national parks, I was a lot younger than now. Why did he choose our land? Was it not because there were many animals there? Were we not hunting? Are you telling us that we cannot hunt because some animals will 'finish,' as you said? When the white men come here and hunt every year, why don't the animals get finished? Does it mean that it is only we who can make the animals finish?"

In another village—this time near Bénoué Park, which receives as many as 2,000 visitors each year—we spoke to an old man called Saibou, who had lived in the area from birth. We arrived at 3 P.M. Saibou was the oldest man in the village, already too old to go to the farm. He was sitting on a mat under a tamarind tree near his house, about to have lunch. We wanted to wait for him to finish, but he insisted that we join in. His elderly wife brought another mat and more food—millet cake and smoked fish in *folere* sauce, made from a type of wild okra. As we were eating, a couple of young men came and joined in without invitation. We later learned that people had the right to participate in any meal without waiting to be invited. When we had finished eating, the old man apologized for the poor quality of his meal, which had, in fact, been fine. It had become difficult to have even fish, he said. "The fish we just ate was sent to me by my first son, who lives in Lagdo." Lagdo is the site of a hydroelectric plant some 70 kilometers from Bénoué; many fishermen settled there after the dam was filled. "We have no more fish in this village because the only way we can get them is to go to the river. That is now in the park, and it is forbidden for us to fish there." How did he know that we wanted to talk about the park?

We told Saibou how we were investigating the source of conflict between people and national parks. He listened to our story without interrupting, then asked: "Why do you come to me? Why not go to the man who has the national park?" He meant the game warden. We explained that we had been to the game warden but thought it was important to talk to people like him, who had lived in the area for a long time.

It was nearing 4 P.M., and women and children were returning from the farm. Most of the children carried logs on their heads, and the women were carrying maize, millet, or vegetables. By now our group had increased by five more men. "Aisatou! Aisatou!" Saibou called. His wife came out of her kitchen and walked slowly to us. "Look at this woman," he said. "How much farming can she still do? You must have noticed that she did not go to the farm today. What really worries me about your so-called park is the fact that we sometimes almost go without food because baboons have raided our farm. Our three living children have settled out of this village, so we do not have anybody to guard our farms. My wife and I are too old to pass the day in the field chasing monkeys. When the small farm she works is invaded by monkeys, what do we do? We have to depend on charity from other people in the village." He stopped, then added, "That is what the park means to us."

We were ready to wrap up the interview when a newcomer joined us. "I am a traditional healer in this region. In the past I gathered my medicine from all over this place, but now I can't get some drugs because I am not allowed to gather medicine in the park. When people decided that we should not get anything from the park, did they know that we do not have a hospital? If somebody falls ill now, he will run to me, but sometimes I cannot get the medicine because of the park. If you were in my place, would you let the person die, or would you go to that park and gather the medicine?" We said that we would ask the warden for permission for him to gather the medicine. "Good," he replied. "And if you don't meet him, or if he is sleeping, or if he refuses?" We could not answer that. It was 6 P.M. before we left for our campsite, thinking about how complex conservation problems could be.

When we visited another village the next day, the story was almost the same. We arrived at 4 P.M. Small groups of men were sitting on mats, either under a tree or in sheds. We went to the house of the village chief, and even before we had exchanged greetings the entrance was filled with curious people. It is not every day that a car drives up with four people asking for the *jaoro*. The chief's wife brought us mats. When we sat and explained the purpose of our visit, the chief called to one of his sons to bring us some *bilibili*, a traditional drink made from millet and maize and a variety of tree barks that are believed to give the drink medicinal properties.

Our conversation ranged from their everyday problems to family issues. (It is a tradition in northern Cameroon to ask about visitors' and hosts' wives and children.) When we finally came to the subject of the national park and its problems, we asked the *jaoro* what he and his people thought of Bénoué National Park. "Nothing," he said. "Why should I be thinking of the park?" We tried to explain the importance of the park and why conservation measures should be enforced to preserve wildlife. "I don't understand what you people call conservation," said the *jaoro*. "Does that mean that people should not farm, hunt, or rear animals?" We said no, but part of the land had to be kept aside for the wild animals so that future generations would have what we have today. "I see," said a middle-aged man, who later identified himself as Hamman. "So you think that for our future generation to see what we are seeing, we don't have to eat. How will this future generation come about, anyway, when people are dying of hunger?" All our efforts to answer this question only resulted in laughter from our hosts.

The *jaoro* spoke. "I don't know why people think that creating a national park and making people suffer is a good thing. We had always lived with these animals, and there were no problems until your national parks came. Do you know that what is now the Bénoué National Park used to be the private hunting ground of the *lamido* of Ray-Bouba?" The *lamido* (local ruler) of Ray-Bouba is a very powerful chief in the region, and most of the *jaoros* are under him and appointed by him. "When it was still under the control of the *lamido,* we had to make sure that people didn't hunt there without his permission. He had to give approval for anybody to hunt there, and defaulters were punished by our traditional laws. People were not allowed to hunt certain animals because they were reserved for the chief. When anyone did, the carcass was taken immediately to the palace. Since the national park came, who knows what is happening?"

In another house, we were told how things were in those good old days. "While we could not always hunt in the *lamido*'s hunting ground, we could hunt somewhere else. We then had a chief hunter, who had to perform traditional rites to the gods before we could go hunting. He also gave advice on when we could hunt and what not to hunt. People generally had to obey him; those who did not could easily be killed by wild animals." We gathered from other villages that fishing had been regulated in the same manner. It was amazing to learn how tradition could help in conservation.

When it came to interviewing the game wardens of the three parks, we found that most had similar complaints. There was a lack of adequate manpower and too few basic working tools. The three parks had no operative vehicle at the time of our visit. The game guards had received no new uniforms or camping equipment for about eight years. The guns at their disposal were old rifles, some of which had not been fired for the past ten years. There was no means of communication in an emergency.

The park authorities were concerned about poaching in the parks by, and in collaboration with, the villagers. The people were also accused of searching for gold, firewood, and medicinal plants in the parks without permission.

The wardens were troubled by the unwillingness of some safari hunters to co-operate with them. These hunters, who rented the hunting zones surrounding the parks, were supposed to present their kill to the wardens before it left the country. Some simply refused to do so, and the wardens had little power to enforce compliance. Some hunters seemed to feel that their relationship was with the Ministry of Tourism, in the capital, rather than with the wardens. There was even a case reported in which a hunter destroyed a small village near his hunting zone, arguing that the villagers were grazing their cattle and poaching in his hunting zone. We were told that the administration reacted then because the villagers were planning to riot. The safari hunter was asked to compensate the villagers.

These were our experiences in the three national parks. The stories told in the villages all had the same message: the national parks have no value to the villagers. Our conclusion was that many measures must be taken to get villagers involved in the management activities of the national parks. It then becomes a question of organization and funding: to the best of our knowledge, there are no projects from organizations like WWF and IUCN in the three parks. There is, however, a great diversity of species in this region, including rare species such as the black rhinoceros (*Diceros bicornis*), to merit such projects. There are institutions in the area that can carry out studies—for example, the Wildlife Program of the IRZ; Wildlife Schools Garoua; and the Center for Environmental Studies and Development in Cameroon. The work force is not limited, but the means are.

One way of solving the conflict in this region is to organize village sessions during which villagers are introduced to the concept of and the need for conservation. Access laws and management strategies for parks and hunting zones could be revised to give more benefit to local people. Research could be carried out on traditional methods of nature conservation and ways of reviving them. To remedy the already deteriorating situation, we recommend that a mechanism of compensation for damages to crops and domestic animals also be established. What is clear, however, is that whoever attempts to solve the problems between the national parks and the villagers should be prepared to explain to the villagers why foreigners can hunt in the hunting zones while they are not allowed to hunt as they always did.

JOHN NEWBY & ALISON WILSON

People in Blue
The Tuareg of Niger

In the winter of 1992, Alassoum Oumarou, director of the WWF/IUCN Aïr and Ténéré Conservation and Development Project, went to the Blue Mountains in northern Niger to confirm the sighting of a group of rare addax in the interior of Africa's largest Saharan nature reserve. He and his five companions have not been seen since. It is known that they were kidnapped and taken hostage by Tuareg rebels.[1]

A month later, a band of dissidents attacked the village of Iferouâne, at the park's project headquarters, and took four project vehicles, radios, tools, tires, and another hostage. A few days after this, at a hastily convened meeting, IUCN and WWF decided that all project activities in the Aïr-Ténéré National Nature Reserve—whose creation in 1988 was regarded as a milestone in the battle for the conservation of Africa's natural heritage—should be suspended temporarily. The Aïr-Ténéré project, which had become a conservation model for park planners around the world, became the latest in a long line of conservation casualties resulting from Africa's internal unrest.

After years of tension, conflict between a Tuareg rebel alliance and the central government of Niger and the neighboring country of Mali escalated in 1992. Often referred to as the blue people of the desert, because of their striking indigo-dyed robes, the Tuareg are a fiercely independent and proud people who have roamed the arid land of Niger and other West and North African countries for centuries. In recent years, they have tried to shake off years of domination under colonial rule and have increased their demands for recognition and a more equitable sharing of resources.

The Aïr Mountains in the nature reserve are now a strategic stronghold for dissident Tuareg. As of early 1993, the area was under military control. But some

Tuareg, who helped in the planning and creation of the nature reserve and its companion conservation activities, have committed themselves to help resuscitate and continue the project.

Like the majority of Niger's 7 million inhabitants, the Tuareg depend on the country's limited natural resources. One of the last relatively unspoiled areas is in the Aïr Mountains, or Blue Mountains, of north-central Niger. They contain some of West Africa's last remaining populations of addax (*Addax nasomaculata*), ostrich (*Struthio camelus*), and Dama gazelle (*Gazella dama*). The Aïr Mountains are also home for some 5,000 Tuareg, half of whom are farmers and the other half, herders. The Tuareg herd camels and goats and, where possible, farm small, irrigated gardens for wheat, corn, and tomatoes. Until a few years ago, they regularly undertook caravans to trade garden produce and livestock for the salt and dates of the desert oases, exchanging these for grain and other commodities unavailable in the Aïr. Now the camels are too few and too weak. Drought and desertification have severely reduced the pastoral potential of the area, and gardening is being hard hit by falling water tables. Nevertheless, the people of the Aïr are still very much in equilibrium with their environment, harsh as that may be. Some Tuareg say that they find themselves caught in the heart of a terrible crossfire. The protected area that they helped create and eventually began to assist in managing is in the midst of a conflict, with no immediate end in sight.

The site of the conflict is northern Niger, a harsh, beautiful land. In midsummer, temperatures soar to 50 degrees centigrade; in winter, they can plunge below freezing. Rain, if and when it comes, is sparse and unpredictable, and some areas may not receive rain for years. The fierce, dry heat sucks all the moisture from the earth's surface, creating an enormous water deficit. In order to live, plants and animals must rely on survival strategies fashioned by evolution.

Over the years, the Aïr-Ténéré project—and the protected area it helped to create and manage—evolved as a microcosm, a mirror, of the evolution of conservation philosophy. From its origins as an attempt to save a few species of rare wild animals, it grew into a campaign to protect the habitat in which they lived. It expanded to incorporate invaluable support of and benefits to many local people. In 1991, in recognition of the region's natural and cultural resources, the Aïr-Ténéré National Nature Reserve became a World Heritage site.

The huge (77,000-square-kilometer) Aïr-Ténéré National Nature Reserve, twice the size of Switzerland, lies where the endless sands of the Sahara meet the stony plains of the Sahel. The western third of the reserve is dominated by the Aïr massif, a rugged, eroded mountainous area whose climate and 2,000-meter elevation provide relief from the hot, dry plains below. High up in the Aïr, hidden springs and shady, water-filled potholes provide life-giving moisture to agile Barbary sheep and many species of birds. Small, sheltered plateaus harbor stands of figs and acacias, perennial grasses, and herbs. After even a brief shower, large volumes of water run off the rocky slopes to collect in the shallow *wadis* at the foot of the mountains. Some of the water, however, disappears underground to fill the shallow aquifers used for irrigation by farmers living in the lowlands.

The Aïr contributes much to the region's biodiversity, harboring some of the world's rarest ungulates as well as the cheetah, the hyena, and the shy desert fox, the fennec. The reserve is also a vital area for birds. The migrants, numbering millions of individuals, include all sorts of birds, from waders to warblers, from swallows and swifts to ducks and birds of prey. So far, some eighty species of Palearctic migrants winter in or migrate through the Aïr reserve, roughly half of all species seen. The annual migrations take an enormous toll on bird life, and it is remarkable that minute birds like the chiffchaff, which weigh only 5 to 10 grams, manage the migration at all. This is especially pertinent when one considers that lying between breeding and overwintering grounds is the broad, hostile expanse of the world's largest desert, the Sahara. For many of the species migrating south from Europe, the Aïr is the first sight of green vegetation since the Mediterranean coast.

One area of the reserve of special importance to bird migrants is Adrar Madet, a long, rocky outcrop some 60 kilometers east of the Aïr and completely surrounded by desert. Lying as it does, perpendicular to the prevailing winds, the outcrop provides shelter for the large number of acacia trees that have grown on its protected leeward side. In spite of harsh climatic conditions, the trees are some of the healthiest and least disturbed in the Sahara. When it rains, they put on foliage quickly and soon harbor an astonishing amount of ephemeral insect life. The shade and the insects are, of course, most attractive to travel-worn immigrants, and during September and October the place throbs with life, the trees literally crawling with an abundance of warblers and other insectivores.

In rainless years, it is a different story. Adrar Madet becomes a place of death, and the Sahara becomes a graveyard for thousands of migrants. Without the insects, the warblers are especially hard hit and die in large numbers, literally falling from the sky or from their shaky perches in leafless thorn trees. As night falls, the birds, too tired to fly on, seek shelter behind rocks or tussocks of dry grass. In the morning, their cold corpses litter the ground.

More than fifty plant species also occur in the reserve, including the wild relatives of olive, millet, and sorghum. It does not take much imagination to see that wild plants, able to endure the harsh environment of the Sahel and the Sahara, could genetically improve the vigor of their cultivated relatives. The wild sorghum is just one example, but the Aïr gives refuge to others, too: both wild millets (*Pennisetum* spp.) and olives (*Olea lapperinei*). The wild olive is the only known living ancestor of its cultivated equivalent, being restricted south of the Sahara to a few peripheral high-mountain massifs like the Tibesti, the Ennedi, and the Jebel Marra. As a catastrophic crop disaster in Italy has shown, more drought-resistant strains of olives are needed. Drought resistant the Aïr olives certainly are. Living on only a few of the highest peaks above 1,500 meters, they cling to scree slopes and erosion scars, inveterate witnesses to a more clement past.

While WWF and IUCN were not the first to recognize the richness of the Aïr's flora and fauna, its project executants came to view it at a time in history when it represented something of "nature's last stand" in the Sahel. Certainly there were other areas where pockets of wildlife survived, but in the region as a whole, years of human population growth, overuse of the scarce resources, drought, famine, and civil wars had depleted the larger species to the point of extinction. When the establishment of a protected area was first proposed in 1982, the initiative was primarily motivated by concern for the region's unique and increasingly threatened fauna and flora. Wildlife was under pressure from uncontrolled hunting and tourist harassment, and after several years of drought, woody vegetation was being rapidly destroyed by overuse and abusive cutting. By the time the area was gazetted as a nature reserve, in 1988, it was obvious that the ecological problems facing the Tuareg needed to be addressed before the future of the ecosystem could be secured. Sahelo-Saharan ecosystems are fragile; because of the nature of the soils and the climatic extremes, overexploited ecosystems take a long time to recover. A management system to prevent further degradation in the reserve was badly needed, but it could succeed only with the full support of the Tuareg. A consortium of donors, including the Swiss and Danish governments, channeling funds through IUCN and WWF, provided the necessary support.[2]

In many conservation areas, rules and regulations for restricting use and preventing abuse of natural resources have provoked anger and resentment. In the Aïr-Ténéré, only about 12 percent of the reserve was set aside as a strict wildlife sanctuary to which access was prohibited. This land had been very rarely used by the local population anyway. To a large extent, the legislation covering the reserve reiterates, albeit in a site-specific way, national law and has brought with it no fundamental changes or restrictions to the people's way of life. The same is true of bush meat and a ban on hunting. People used to hunt for food and for meat for the caravan trade,[3] but this is rarely done today: wildlife is too rare and inaccessible to render it profitable. In fact, the general attitude to wildlife is one of benevolence, the Tuareg often stressing its cultural and aesthetic values. As might be expected of a people almost wholly reliant on natural resources for its existence, perception of environmental health is acute, and wildlife is seen as both an indicator and a product of environmental well-being. If wildlife populations are under threat today, it is not from the Tuareg but from drought, desertification, harassment by tourists, and hunting by the armed forces.

Predator control, however, is a bone of contention between the reserve's authorities and the local population. Although the law specifically forbids it, the use of poisons such as strychnine to control jackals (*Canis aureus*) and striped hyenas (*Hyaena hyaena*) is generally condoned by local administrators. The reserve's management recognizes that livestock predation is a problem, but it can hardly be expected to accept the use of such environmentally dangerous poisons. Use of strychnine has killed nontarget species like crows, ravens, and vultures and beneficial carnivores like the fennec (*Fennecus zerda*) and Ruppell's fox (*Vulpes ruppelli*). Attempts to solve this thorny issue might entail granting people living in high-risk areas periodic dispensation to use traditional methods of control. Experiments will also be carried out using nonlethal traps.

Although it is impossible to please all of the people all of the time, the positive aspects of the reserve's creation by far outweigh the disadvantages. Thanks partially to a series of relatively good rainy seasons from 1987 to 1989, results to date have been encouraging, and in spite of the fact that habitat rehabilitation takes a long time, improvements are already discernible. These have been noticed by the local people and have heightened their appreciation of the reserve's value. Some people have argued that the establishment of the reserve had a detrimental effect by depriving people of access to resources or land previously available, but there is little evidence of this. Despite strictly enforced restrictions on tree cutting and hunting in the remainder of the reserve, the project became such a source of pride that as it progressed, many people living outside the reserve asked that the project's activities be enlarged to encompass their communities.

The key to the project's success has been twofold; first, the Tuareg, through a network of voluntary representatives, gradually became involved in the reserve's management. Local support for the project sprang not only from visible improvements in the condition in the rangelands within the protected area but also from the Tuareg's traditional love and respect for wildlife and their concern that it was fast disappearing. Second, experiments to demonstrate improved housing, irrigation and agricultural techniques, energy-saving wood stoves, and recovery and sustainable use of deteriorating pastures were met with widespread interest.[4] All of these demonstrations involved the use of appropriate technology, which meant that local materials and skills could be deployed. For example, the cutting of trees for roofing beams was one of the major causes of deforestation in the area. A prototype building, walled and roofed entirely by adobe (mud) bricks, was constructed for WWF staff members in Iferouâne, at the edge of the reserve. It attracted much attention, and local masons began copying the design. Inspired by the Institute for the Study and Application of Integrated Development (Tapis Vert Project), the system was started in order to replace wood as a principal roof material in traditional building. Well digging and maintenance, capture of runoff water using drystone dikes, and solar drying of vegetables were also demonstrated. Another community-based project involved the training of village and nomadic health workers.

Prior to the present unrest in the area, several thousand tourists visited the protected area annually. Although tourism contributed to the local economy, it soon became evident that controls and checks were needed. Some of the visitors used high-speed desert vehicles to chase addax. They photographed the exhausted animals, roaring after them, checking their speed against speedometers, and often driving them to their death.[5] It is probably fair to say that tourism sometimes poses a greater threat than poaching in the Aïr. But the local people need to benefit from the tourists' presence; thus, before the project was suspended, solutions were sought to develop ecologically friendly tourism that would reap the necessary economic returns for the local nomads. An information center was built, incorporating educational displays as well as a craft shop, and local guides were made available for trekking.

Most local people hope that the Aïr-Ténéré project will soon resume its former activities, ranging from well digging and health training to adult literacy and woodless adobe construction. Although civil war has engulfed the region, the project has not come to an end, and there is new hope. In late 1992, the conflict moved away from the centers of wildlife concentration. Good rains benefited both the Tuareg and the reserve. Overcoming the difficulties of living in a war zone, local people have taken the initiative to continue the project. They expect that the staff of more than forty people, including foresters, wildlife experts, tour guides, tree nursery workers, and park rangers, can get back to work again. The first step the Tuareg have taken toward normalization of activities was to appoint five of their number to enter into negotiations with WWF, IUCN, and the Nigerian government to obtain moral and financial support. In addition, they have formed a Comité Provisoire (Provisional Committee) to oversee watershed management, tree planting, and well maintenance.

The ultimate aim of the project has not been forgotten: to transfer as much responsibility as possible for the reserve's management, law enforcement, and surveillance from the largely "alien" government staff to the land users themselves. The results so far are encouraging. The Aïr Mountains experience has confirmed the role that appropriately designed and run protected areas can play in natural resource management and, by extension, in sustainable rural development. What guarantees are there, however, that the short-term gains and benefits made possible by the reserve's presence can be sustained or that the resources, once restored, will be used correctly? In theory, the solution lies in effective management. In reality, management is unlikely to work unless it is realistic enough to gain popular support.

In other, unmanaged parts of the Sahel, the land can no longer sustain the people's modest needs: pastures are overgrazed; soils are eroded; wildlife has disappeared. As the world's population increases, people are obliged to compete for diminishing returns. Although it is difficult to see how the Sahel and its natural resources can be restored, nurtured, and coaxed back into providing sustenance to growing populations, protected areas can offer considerable potential for innovative management and habitat rehabilitation. In a rapidly changing world, protected areas must change to meet the demands of new situations. It is no longer reasonable to "set aside" large tracts of Africa for the unique benefit of wildlife or privileged visitors. It is equally unwise to throw the baby out with the bathwater and reject the whole concept of protected areas because some parks and reserves are no longer appropriate. On the contrary, the protected areas approach to sustainable development through the conservation and management of land and natural resources, as demonstrated in the Aïr-Ténéré Nature Reserve, is more urgently needed than ever before.

Tourism versus Turtles

Every year, as the summer vacation season approaches in the Mediterranean, two types of travelers begin their annual competition for space on the vast, sandy beaches of Greece: tourists and sea turtles. The turtles, which have been migrating to these nesting grounds for millions of years, are facing stiff competition from a yearly influx of millions of vacationers. Each year some 100 million sun worshippers descend upon the Mediterranean, comprising one-third of the world's tourists who trot the globe annually.

Head-on collisions between the turtles and the mainly British and German tourists are most common on the Greek island of Zakynthos in Laganas Bay, whose beaches are the nesting grounds for the loggerhead sea turtle (*Caretta caretta*), an endangered species within EEC boundaries. The Ionian island of Zakynthos has one of the highest densities of nesting loggerhead turtles in the world.[1] Some 50 percent of the Mediterranean's loggerhead turtles swim ashore to six of the island's beaches to lay their eggs, as they have done for millennia. This instinctive routine is hampered as the females, heavy with the weight of 100 to 150 eggs, crawl up the beach, bumping into lounge chairs, beach umbrellas, inflatable zodiacs, boat motors, garbage cans, refuse, and even Jeeps and cars. Often, unable to plow their way past the debris, the turtles swim away, dropping their eggs in the water.

Swimming to and from shore can also be a life-threatening ordeal for the turtles. The harassed animals must take their chances along with the tourists, as I did in the summer of 1992, and risk being maimed or decapitated by a reckless speedboat driver. "Splash a lot and kick water in the air" is the advice given to swimmers who venture more than a few hundred feet offshore. In 1991, the Sea Turtle Protection Society of Greece (STPS), which has been working on the island since 1982, reported that five sea turtles were killed by the propellers of boats racing through the waters—many of them in violation of a boating ban off the main nesting beaches of Sekania, Dafni, and Gerakas and of speed limits, rarely enforced, off Laganas, Marathonissi, and Kalamaki beaches. Another seven injured turtles were treated by the society and successfully returned to the sea. In the summer of 1992, in Laganas Bay, two sea turtles were killed by propellers; three were killed by some pointed object (which may have been a propeller, a harpoon, a knife, etc.); three were drowned in fishing nets; and one was given medical treatment by the STPS and released.[2]

Despite the fact that the Greek government has passed legislation to protect the sea turtles and their six main nesting beaches on Zakynthos, a handful of landowners flout the law. On our arrival in Zakynthos at the height of the tourist season in August 1992, Georgia Valaoras, director of WWF's office in Greece, and I were met by veteran STPS volunteer Michalis Antypas, who was recovering from injuries he had suffered at the hands of a tour operator while distributing informational leaflets to tourists on Kalamaki Beach. He informed us that a few days earlier an Italian volunteer had also been assaulted on the nearby island of Marathonissi, while monitoring a turtle nesting beach. That afternoon, the Italian and two fellow volunteers were hauled off to the local jail after they refused to remove an STPS research tent from the uninhabited island of Marathonissi. The owner of the island, who had announced plans to build a hotel in the protected turtle zone, looked on from a nearby boat as the volunteers were taken into custody. Her scheme to build the hotel has been met with a wave of protest—the church, all five local communities, the local hoteliers' organization, local boat owners, the area's member of Parliament, the mayor, and the local conservation NGO, the Zakynthian Ecological Movement, all objected to the development of Marathonissi. The owner opposed the presence of the tent on the grounds that the volunteers were camping on the island. Some local hotel owners came to the defense of the volunteers, and by evening they were released. That night they were back at work, carrying out research at their permanent field station on Marathonissi.

Since 1982, trained STPS volunteers—with the support of WWF and the EEC—have been counting the number of turtles that nest on the beaches nightly (and obliterating fresh tracks); marking and, when necessary, fencing the nests; monitoring the nests for the emergence of hatchlings; and noting whether the hatchlings win their race for the sea. Not all of the eggs hatch. The temperature of the sand should be around 28 to 32 degrees centigrade; if the shadow cast by a beach umbrella or a lounge chair causes the temperature to drop below 24 degrees, the eggs will die. Thus, when STPS volunteers find nests on the busier parts of the beach, they try to mark them with protective wire mesh, alerting tourists to avoid shading them, or they move them—with great reluctance and care. In 1992, seven otherwise "doomed" nests were transferred to an STPS beach hatchery with a hatching success of nearly 70 percent, compared with less than 40 percent success in 1991.[3] If the eggs do hatch, the baby turtles sleep below the surface of the sand for as long as three days. Then they have to survive the mad scramble to the shore past a host of predators, including gulls and rats, and must overcome the dangers that await them in the water, primarily the hungry mouths of fish and seabirds. Approximately 1,000 nests are made on Zakynthos each year, yielding an average of around 100,000 hatchlings. One out of 1,000 will survive. Twenty to thirty years later, the females will return—by means of some remarkable memory and navigational instinct—to the very same beach where they hatched.

Thirty years ago, the beaches on Zakynthos were deserted; now most of them have been turned over to tourism, with turtles encountering humans for the first time. In the main resort of Laganas, partying, the roar of mopeds, and deafening music go on all night long—hardly the reception for a weary traveler returning after several decades at sea. Ulysses, whose home was the neighboring island of Ithaca and who loved the monk seals and the other natural wonders of the Mediterranean, would have been heartbroken to return from his odyssey to find the caves of the monk seals deserted and the beaches—once populated by what Homer called "the lovely child of the ocean" and its cousin, the turtle—covered by concrete and a string of bars and hotels.

In order to make the return of the nesting turtles as natural as possible, vacationers and local people are prohibited by law from walking on the turtle nesting beaches at night. The zones are marked, some with well-placed signs, but signs are not present at the entrances to all the beaches. Many have been defaced or pulled down, and they are not always replaced. In 1992, port police never once came to enforce the night curfew on the nesting beach at Laganas. In previous years the police had appeared infrequently, but this year only the STPS volunteers were there to inform tourists about the ban. Starting in 1986, the STPS stepped up its public education program dramatically in an attempt to resolve conflict with and among local developers and to raise awareness among tourists about the need to safeguard the turtles' future.[4]

In Britain, WWF-UK persuaded four major tourism companies to distribute informational brochures to vacationers before their departure for Zakynthos. Locally, leaflets and brochures are circulated in several languages, explaining to tourists why the protected zones have been created and what they can do personally to ensure the turtles' survival. Local hotel owners have also increased the number of STPS slide shows on turtle conservation. More than 200 shows were presented to some 12,000 guests in ten hotels on the island in 1992. An information kiosk in Laganas operated for a sixth year in cooperation with the local town council. A new public education center was also established on private land near Gerakas close to the site of a former information kiosk destroyed in 1990. According to Dimitrios Dimopoulos, director of the STPS in Zakynthos, a third STPS information kiosk was set up in Lithakia, with the endorsement of the local community and church. He estimates that more than 40,000 tourists visited the stations in 1992.[5]

Naturally, when we arrived on the island, the STPS whisked us off to an ecologically friendly hotel, where the manager greeted us warmly. At the hotel's reception desk, a prominently displayed poster announced slide presentations on sea turtles in several languages. The manager apologized for the events of the past few days and assured us that he was among a growing number of community members, tour operators, and hoteliers—including the Hotel Owners Association of Zakynthos, the Local Union of Municipalities and Communities of Zakynthos, and the Zakynthian Ecological Movement—who are in favor of establishing a national park in Zakynthos like the one created in the Sporades Islands in June 1992. As of 1992, 25,000 signatures had been collected by the STPS on a petition urging the government to proceed immediately with establishment of the park.

The National Marine Park of Alonnisos and the Northern Sporades, Greece's eleventh national park, encompasses seven Aegean islands and is divided into varying protection zones. Boats may not approach within 4.8 kilometers of the core zone, where the deserted island of Piperi gives refuge to Europe's most endangered mammal, the Mediterranean monk seal. The seal has been classified by IUCN (the World Conservation Union) as one of the world's twelve most endangered species. Boats are not allowed to come within 366 meters of the other six islands in the archipelago, several of which are uninhabited. Fortunately for the seals and turtles of the Sporades, Prince Sadruddin Aga Khan, internationally renowned humanitarian and statesman and founder and president of the Geneva-based Bellerive Foundation, has mounted a $500,000 drive to build a monk seal rescue and research center in the park. Most important of all, the local communities, particularly the fishermen's cooperative on the nearby island of Alonnisos, back the marine park and have taken the last twenty-five monk seals and other endangered wildlife in the area under their protection. The present estimate for the number of Mediterranean monk seals, based on available data, is around 400 individuals. There are no accurate estimates from previous years.[6]

Recognizing the essential ingredient in any conservation program—local support—environmentalists throughout Greece are stepping up their public awareness activities, especially among local residents. On the Ionian island of Kefalonia, WWF project leader and monk seal scientist Aliki Panou began her initial research not only with the seals but also with the fishermen and villagers. Every day, she interviews fishermen, discussing the type of gear used, the amount of fish caught, damage to fish and gear, and seal sightings. Her zeal and dedication are paying off. Communities are approaching her for help in establishing protected areas to save the island's last nine to ten monk seals and some 250 loggerhead nests on the southern coast of Kefalonia.[7]

Thanks to the pioneering work of such conservationists as Professor Michael Scoullous, president of Elliniki Eteria and principal coordinator of monk seal conservation for Greece, and German documentary filmmaker Thomas Schultze-Westrum, who has for thirty years publicized the plight of the monk seal and other endangered Greek species and habitats, the conservation ethic is spreading throughout the Greek isles. On Zakynthos, about an hour's ferryboat ride from Kefalonia, WWF biologist Ada Vlachoutsikou is working closely with villagers, especially fishermen, in conserving a population of about twenty-six monk seals, comparable in size to the group in the National Marine Park of Alonnisos and the Northern Sporades. Although the population appears to be biologically stable, the seals are in danger, mainly because of the deliberate killing of the animals by certain fishermen. Reacting angrily to damage to nets caused by seals searching for food in overfished seas, the fishermen sometimes shoot, harpoon, or dynamite the hungry and defenseless seals. But the fishermen also have mouths to feed, and both Panou and Vlachoutsikou strongly recommend that fishermen be compensated for lost fish and damaged gear. Nearly 16 percent of all fishing trips off the western coasts of Zakynthos result in net damage caused by seals.[8]

"The monthly loss of income to fishermen may be equal to anywhere from a day's to a month's wages, especially if an entire net is destroyed," says Panou. Loss of time in repairing nets, she emphasizes, can cause loss of secondary earnings from such activities as small-scale agriculture. Panou believes that this loss of income could be compensated by paying fishermen to work as guards or participate in fishery research or by reducing regular expenses, such as the cost of fuel and gear. Above all, overfishing and illegal fishing have to be controlled and existing regulations enforced to minimize the conflict between seals and fishermen.[9]

Like the turtles, the monk seals' nesting season coincides with the height of the tourist season. While the monk seals are giving birth, usually from May to November, tourists are disturbing their nesting sites, the dark, shallow caves that line the steep cliffs of the islands, with increasing frequency. Over the years, the seals have retreated as deeply as they can into these caverns to nurse and feed their young beyond the reach of man. Seal pups, which take four months to wean, remain with their mothers for three years, until they can fish for themselves. But fish stocks are crashing, resulting in competition between seals and fishermen for food, and pollution and boat traffic are increasing. In the Sporades marine park, a rescue and research center for injured and orphaned seals has been established by the Hellenic Society for the Study and Protection of the Monk Seal (HSSPMS) and the Seal Rehabilitation and Research Center (SRRC) of Pieterburen in Holland. When it is expanded, the center is expected to shelter an average of twenty orphaned and wounded seals per year.[10]

Since prevention is the best cure, additional measures for marine conservation in the Mediterranean have been recommended. The turtles and monk seals, important among the Greeks for centuries, have become the symbols for conservation programs throughout the Mediterranean. Greek biologists, including Panou and Vlachoutsikou, and international conservation organizations, including WWF and IUCN's Species Survival Commission, are calling for a network of marine reserves in the Ionian and Aegean seas. Protected zones, based on sound management plans, need to be established off the islands of Kefalonia and, particularly, Zakynthos, where the highest concentration of monk seals outside the Sporades marine park lives. A patrol boat, like the HSSPMS patrol boat used in guarding the Sporades park, is needed for the proposed protected zones off the southwestern coast of Zakynthos, and another is needed for Argostoli, off Kefalonia. According to Panou, such boats can be used not only for monitoring seals, but also for controlling and monitoring illegal fishing, drift netting, and oil spills.[11]

Some conservationists are trying to steer EEC funding toward ecologically sound development projects. In the past, EEC money in Greece was frequently used for road building, mainly through uninhabited landscapes down to coastlines. This literally paved the way for invasive touristic development in critical nesting sites of turtles and monk seals, Europe's rarest marine species.

For example, the turtles of Zakynthos must contend with an airstrip located about 1.8 kilometers from the turtle nesting beach of East Laganas. In 1990, 109 night flights were recorded there. Turtle hatchlings, which burrow 50 centimeters through the sand to reach the surface, seek the light of the moon to lead them toward the sea. If they cannot find the moon, they search for starlight reflected on the waves and instinctively head toward it, as their species has done for 90 million years. Twenty percent of the hatchlings on East Laganas Beach go straight toward the airport, attracted by the bright night beams. The Civil Aviation Authority seems willing to modify the light system, but the tavernas will not shut down, nor will the municipal street lights be shut off on half of the 8-kilometer stretch that was for millennia the nesting and hatching ground of the turtles, a species whose symbol was minted on some of the first Greek coins about 4,000 years ago.[12]

But far from the bustle of Laganas, on the deserted beach of Sekania, where half of all nesting loggerheads in the Mediterranean lay their eggs every summer, the turtles have been granted a reprieve. With the help of the EEC, WWF is trying to purchase Sekania Beach, the most important loggerhead nesting site in the Mediterranean. WWF hopes that starting in 1993, the property will be fenced and access restricted to researchers during daylight hours, enforced by a warden on duty around the clock at the site. A field station would also be constructed on the upper part of the property.

Although some residents of Zakynthos are somewhat divided over the sea turtle issue, the majority of local people back the turtles' survival. Those who were unable to get in on the building boom before protected zones were created are resentful, and conservationists believe that like the fishermen with damaged nets, their loss also must be compensated in some way.

"The tide in Zakynthos is slowly but steadily turning for the turtles—the symbol of integrated conservation for the area," said the STPS's Dimitrios Dimopoulos at the end of the 1992 nesting season. "The continuing cooperation between the local communities, the hotel owners, and environmental organizations has borne fruit: all are dedicated to establishing a marine park on Zakynthos as part of a wide network of marine reserves."

In ancient times, Greek poets celebrated dolphins, turtles, and monk seals; the sea, *thalassa,* was the source of life, as it is in many creation myths. Both Apollo, god of the sun (who turned into a giant dolphin), and Poseidon, god of the sea, protected the monk seals and other sea creatures. Now, say Greek conservationists, it is up to us mortals to come up with down-to-earth solutions like conservation management plans, which not only protect our mythical symbols but also benefit the modern-day people on whom their survival depends.

PART FOUR

Creative Communities

Creative Communities
Planning and Comanaging Protected Areas

The highland Phoka people of northern Malawi were moved from their traditional homelands during the 1970s to make way for the creation of Nyika National Park. When the government resettled them in lowland areas elsewhere, they were decimated by malaria, a disease to which they had no natural immunity. Those who survived had lost not only their homes but also their livelihoods. Ancestral apiary grounds had to be abandoned when the government banned the use of trees to make traditional bark and log hives and made it illegal to hang beehives in protected areas.

It was the unacceptable face of conservation—a blatant disregard for people that would be unthinkable today. Twenty years later, rural villagers are being allowed back into those same conservation areas in Malawi—albeit on a restricted basis— to tend and harvest beehives, as described in the chapter titled "Honey for Sale." More than 700 rural people living on the fringes of Nyika National Park have established commercial beekeeping clubs to market honey that meets European Community standards. Using new, environmentally sound production methods, they can produce higher yields and better-quality honey than they did using traditional methods. As a result, relations have improved between villagers and the Department of National Parks, Wildlife and Tourism, and poaching has declined. In some areas, beekeeping club members assist park staff by protecting their apiary sites from trespassers.

Two decades have elapsed since the Phoka people were disinherited. Over that period, the thinking about protected areas has progressed considerably. Today it is accepted that local communities must be taken on board from the very beginning when a protected area is being planned. When they are not consulted, a clash of interests can lead to open conflict. As detailed in part three, on the Greek island of Zakynthos, local opposition has thwarted efforts to protect Europe's most important nesting site for the endangered loggerhead sea turtle. Restrictions on boat operators and the failure to compensate affected landowners have resulted in open conflict with conservationists—some of whom have been attacked.

Local communities and indigenous people are now increasingly consulted about plans for protected areas and involved in the drafting of management plans. In this part, Evelyn Wilcox reports on how, in Haiti, local fishing communities and hotel owners are helping government departments and environmentalists draw up plans for Les Arcadins National Marine Park, which is being established to protect off-shore coral reefs and fisheries. The local fishermen traditionally use simple fish traps and gill nets to harvest fish in shallow waters. But if they were to extend their fishing grounds into deeper waters, they might be able to relieve pressure on the reef fish populations. WWF is working with local fishermen to research catch size in deeper waters and to test cheaper alternatives to costly deep-sea fishing gear. WWF has also put forward the idea of a fish breeding reserve within the proposed marine park to help build up fish stocks.

Elsewhere, in Isabella Bay (Igalirtuuq) in northern Canada, local Inuit people are working with WWF on plans to establish a whale sanctuary to protect the endangered bowhead whale, as outlined in "Inuit Create a Whale Sanctuary" by Arlin Hackman of WWF-Canada. And in the Sumava region of the newly created Czech Republic, more than twenty local mayors sent a formal petition to the government of the former Czech and Slovak Federal Republic announcing public support for a locally produced management plan for Sumava National Park—a former military-controlled border zone from which tens of thousands of people had been removed in the 1940s (see "The Green Roof of Central Europe").

Implicit in the need to gain the active support of local communities and involve them in planning a protected area is the need to ensure that people actually benefit in some way. Wherever possible, this will involve ensuring that community use of natural resources—hunting, fishing, or agricultural production—is allowed to continue on a sustainable basis. In Isabella Bay, for example, it has been agreed in principle that the Inuit may eventually be allowed to resume whale hunting on a sustainable basis, provided the whale population recovers sufficiently. Elsewhere, the need to provide community benefits may involve the development of new sources of income—from ecotourism or craft marketing—as a trade-off for restricted access to a protected area. Other benefits may also include the establishment of community services, such as health centers, latrines, schools, roads, or bridges.

In the Luangwa Valley in Zambia, revenues from controlled safari hunting have been used to build a rural health center for local communities. For WWF, this is one of the success stories from a determined attempt to involve local people and give them not only a stake in nature conservation but also a financial return from it. The result has been a shifting of the boundaries of conservation work, involving WWF in many rural development projects as well.

The Luangwa Valley contains five national parks and seven game management areas. It is one of the most magnificent wilderness areas in Africa, with rich vegetation and a wealth of wildlife, including elephants, rhinos, buffaloes, hippos, and crocodiles. But the people who live there scrape together a living by subsistence farming and have few social services such as schools or health centers. Until recently, the country's thirty-two game management areas were managed mainly for the benefit of safari hunters and city dwellers, with no benefits for the rural poor, who have always lived there. With no vested interest in wildlife conservation, these rural communities actively encouraged poachers—provided they agreed to share the proceeds.

In 1984, the Zambian National Parks and Wildlife Service launched the Lupande Development Project, an experiment in involving local communities in wildlife management. Funding has been provided by WWF and the USAID program. The results have been impressive. Within the first three years, poaching of elephants and black rhinos had decreased tenfold. Meanwhile, 40 percent of the revenues from controlled safari hunting were allocated to local community leaders, and they chose to spend it first on building a health center. The success of this project inspired the setting up of the Luangwa Integrated Resource Development Program and the launch of ADMADE (Administrative Management Design for Game Management Areas), a national program that involves local people in the management of wildlife and ensures that they benefit directly from it.

This dual approach of community development and sustainable resource use is already paying off elsewhere. In the Dzanga-Sangha Dense Forest Special Reserve in the Central African Republic, a local community association has been established to manage the "conservation dividend"—the community's share of the revenue from tourism and safari hunting fees, (see "Banking on a Nature Reserve"). Special interest groups such as fishermen, bakers, and gardeners have formed their own subassociations, and twenty of these are now represented by an elected delegation. Delegates meet twice a month to consider requests for financing small-scale economic alternatives to logging and poaching and to represent the local community in helping WWF project staff members make decisions about the conservation and use of natural resources.

In their chapter on community involvement in Dzanga-Sangha, Fidele Ngambesso and Philip Hunsicker point out that WWF is no longer viewed as a conservation watchdog interested only in the protection of wildlife and habitats. "We are now offering economic alternatives as well as educating the local population about conservation and the need to preserve natural resources in a sustainable fashion," they say. "Our common future depends on it."

In Saint Lucia, Yves Renard of the Caribbean Natural Resources Institute (CANARI) worked closely with the local community during the early 1980s to identify common goals for conservation and development. With support from CANARI and WWF, the local community developed ways of making fishing more profitable through better storage and marketing facilities, established fuelwood plantations to produce charcoal without stripping mangroves, and put sea moss production on a commercial footing. Meanwhile, carefully controlled tourist visits to the Maria Islands Nature Reserve provide jobs and benefits to the local economy. At the same time, protecting the islands helps ensure the recovery of depleted fish stocks in adjacent waters.

In Korup National Park in Cameroon—which contains the largest number of plant species of any African rain forest—WWF financed the construction of two bridges to give all-weather access to the park. Rural training centers have been established to teach building and rural sanitation. Villagers have been advised on the importance of clean drinking water and shown how to use oral rehydration therapy for diarrhea—one of the major causes of infant death in Africa—and rural health workers have been trained in hygiene and sanitation. Tree nurseries have been established; trees are sold at a discount to farmers and distributed free to local schools and church organizations. One result has been a decline in hunting among villagers in the northern part of the park and a request for commercial and nonindigenous hunters to leave the park. Meanwhile, three villages situated near the park research station have voluntarily agreed to be resettled outside the park.

John Newby, who heads WWF International's Africa Program, says that local community involvement is crucial for the success of conservation efforts. "We believe that if people are allowed to participate in and benefit financially from the use of natural resources, they will have a vested interest in taking good care of them and ensuring that they don't become depleted," he explains. "What has taken place is a major shift away from centralized management toward community-based conservation and management of resources. We are now working at the grass-roots level in an effort to ensure that people have both a voice and a stake in nature conservation."

In some cases, local communities have been encouraged to take this a step further and become comanagers of protected areas. This may vary from day-to-day management of the park (with local people being employed as park rangers) to formal or informal representation in park policy and planning matters (via a board of management) or it may be a combination of both. There are no blueprints for comanagement schemes. Each scheme will vary according to the kind of protected area being managed and the aspirations and needs of the local people.

In northern Australia, two national parks—Cobourg (or Gurig) and Kakadu—are run on a comanagement basis with local aboriginals who own the land. They represent two different models of comanagement; so far, neither experiment has proved an unqualified success. Cobourg, a small, isolated park with a scenic coastline, was established in 1981 with an eight-member board of management—four aboriginals, including the chairman, and four representatives of regional government. On a day-to-day basis, the park was originally managed by a staff of eight, which included three aboriginal rangers and an aboriginal laborer. On the face of it, the scheme was a model of equal power sharing. But on the ground, the reality was very different. Sally Weaver, professor of political anthropology at Waterloo University in Canada, who carried out fieldwork in both parks during 1984 and 1985, found that the aboriginals could not exercise their power as comanagers because they lacked the basic educational, cultural, and political skills required. "Only some of the younger generation—teenagers and those in their twenties—had English literacy and numeric skills, and none had political or bureaucratic skills that would enable them to play a role equal to [that of] the other members on the board," she said.[1]

Kakadu is a larger, more developed park, with aboriginal rock sites and wetlands teeming with bird life. It was established in 1979 and listed as a World Heritage site two years later. From the outset, the Australian National Parks and Wildlife Service (ANPWS) employed three aboriginal cultural advisors, who were regularly consulted by the park staff on a wide range of issues. In addition, twelve aboriginals were trained as park rangers, and eight of them were subsequently employed. Unlike the situation at Cobourg, no formal representation existed for the aboriginal landowners in the policy, planning, or overall management of the park. But Sally Weaver found that the aboriginals were, in fact, consulted on a daily basis and that their wishes were taken into account by the park staff.

In neither park was there any real power sharing. Both models failed to involve the aboriginal landowners in the joint policy and planning role that they sought. The formal authority that the aboriginals were given in Cobourg turned out to be an empty shell in practice because no prior investment had been made in educating or training them for that role. But these two ground-breaking park management schemes formed part of an evolutionary trend toward formal power-sharing agreements in Australia. As a result, there has been a shift from informal consultation to genuine involvement in the policy, planning, and overall management of parks. In 1986, a management plan for Uluru (Ayers Rock–Mount Olga) National Park ensured that the aboriginal landowners formed a majority on the park management board and—a key element of the plan—recommended that they be trained in the skills needed to fulfill that role.

In Central America, the Kuna Indians have managed their coastal reserve, Kuna Yala, in Panama for more than a decade. In the first part of this book, Guillermo Archibold, Kuna representative at the IUCN parks congress, recalls how the Kuna people were involved in mapping out the original plans for PEMASKY, the Management Project for the Forested Areas of Kuna Yala, and were determined to run the reserve from the outset. Today this project is under threat as cultural ties are loosened, people emigrate, and natural resources are depleted by bad agricultural and fishing practices. As once-abundant sources of funding dry up, PEMASKY needs to adapt in order to survive.

Elsewhere, new comanagement schemes are being established. Along Nicaragua's Miskito Coast, a newly created marine reserve—the largest protected coastal area in Latin America—is to be managed by local Miskito communities in close collaboration with the local conservation organization Mikupia (Miskito heart) and national and local government authorities (see "Heart of the Miskito"). And on the northwestern Caribbean coast of Venezuela, local fishing communities are cooperating with the country's leading conservation organization, FUDENA, in the management of the Cuare Wildlife Refuge. A successful project involving the cultivation of oysters to restock swamp canals decimated by overfishing proved to be a major breakthrough in community involvement. "There can be no successful management without community participation," maintains Cecilia de Blohm, a director of FUDENA. "Local people must be allowed to manage their own development."

Some of the examples of creative communities discussed here are described in greater detail in the chapters that follow. Others can be found elsewhere in the book, where they are used to highlight other aspects of the relationship between people and protected areas. Meanwhile, a number of guidelines have emerged from the experience of successful and less successful attempts at involving local communities in the establishment and management of protected areas.[2] They include the following:

- It is essential to involve local people right from the start in order to avoid unnecessary conflict and confrontation.

- Social impact assessments could be carried out to determine what effect a new protected area is likely to have on the lives of local people. The aim is to avoid unforeseen consequences that will have an adverse effect on local communities.

- Wherever possible, territorial rights should be respected. Local communities should be allowed to remain inside protected areas and make use of natural resources on a sustainable yield basis. Displacement can lead to social disruption and resentment of protected areas.

- If people need to be relocated outside a protected area, they have a right to be protected from diseases to which they have no natural immunity. Wherever possible, they should be allowed continued—albeit limited—access to a protected area to make sustainable use of its natural resources.

- Cultural preservation may be important for some communities, especially indigenous people, but communities should have the right to choose to what extent they need to develop and—crucially—at what pace. Self-determination must be the guiding principle. But equally, people must not be held back by romantic ideas about primitive people.

- Rural development strategies should adapt a "bottom-up approach," involving local people in the planning and implementation of rural development projects. But rural development schemes must not be imposed on a community against its wishes.

- Provision should be made for conservation-oriented education and public awareness campaigns to ensure that local communities understand why a protected area is being established.

The recognition that local communities should be directly involved in the management of protected areas has led to an increasing number of comanagement agreements. These vary both in the theoretical degree of power sharing and in the management scheme's success on the ground. But a number of general guidelines have been drawn up by the Planning and Conservation Service of the Northern British Columbia Regional Government in Canada. They include the following:

- There is no blueprint for a comanagement agreement. Each agreement should respond to the needs and aspirations of the local community. This may vary from involvement of local people in the day-to-day running of a park as park rangers to formal or informal power-sharing agreements or a combination of these. Elsewhere, instead of comanagement, a community may simply want the right to manage a natural resource, such as fisheries.

- If the local community is to act as an equal partner in managing a protected area, its elected representatives must be trained in the management skills required for them to fulfill that role.

- Comanagement agreements must be written in clear, unambiguous language in order to avoid future misunderstandings and unnecessary conflict.

- Consensus decision making should be the rule, both in drawing up and in carrying out the joint agreement. Majority voting systems can result in polarization of co-management groups.

- Provision should be made for a genuine sharing of scientific and traditional knowledge and for collaborative research.

- The comanagement agreement should be continually updated and refined. There should be an annual review of problems and progress, and cooperative research should be taken into account.

- In addition to the formal comanagement agreement, there should be regular, informal contact with the local community as a whole to share information and ensure smooth working relationships.

In a joint paper presented at IUCN's Fourth World Congress on National Parks and Protected Areas in 1992, Yves Renard and Leslie Hudson of CANARI outlined the preconditions for successful comanagement schemes. They must be based, they said, on meaningful relationships in which the rights, aspirations, knowledge, skills, and resources of communities are fully respected and enhanced.

"The challenge before us is the challenge of human development," they told delegates. "Parks and protected areas can play a critical role in meeting that challenge, and the future of parks lies in their ability to forge constructive relationships with people and their institutions."

Heart of the Miskito

On a sweltering night in February 1991, nearly 800 people packed the Catholic church in Sandy Bay on Nicaragua's Miskito Coast. Kids hung from the balcony, adults crammed the pews and aisles, and all eyes were riveted on the white wall near the altar as, after each click and whir, it filled with a bright color image of their own watery backyard.

Charlie Luthin, until recently the director of programs for the Caribbean Conservation Corporation (CCC), was giving a slide show to a rapt audience of Miskitos, the indigenous people who live along the coast of Nicaragua and Honduras. The slide show illustrated why the CCC supported the creation of a Miskito Coast protected area, particularly since the reserve was initiated by twenty-three coastal communities. Slide after slide dramatically illustrated how the original wealth of coastal resources had been exploited during the past twenty-five years by outsiders—both Nicaraguans and non-Nicaraguans. Foreign drug traffickers use the waterway as a transshipment route and refueling stop, while ships from a dozen countries net and trap huge quantities of lobster and shrimp in the rich fishing grounds.

"The slides were more effective than anything we had said up to then," Luthin says. "After each slide, you could hear murmurs of appreciation and recognition as people saw scenes of places they knew and visited every day. It was probably the first time most of them had ever seen a slide show, and it had an amazing impact."

Luthin, along with Armstrong Wiggins, a Miskito with the Washington, DC–based Indian Law Resources Center, and Bernard Nietschmann, a geographer with the University of California, had been invited by the communities of Sandy Bay to make the presentation and discuss the natural resource problems the Miskito people are trying to tackle. For Nietschmann, a leading authority on the Miskitos, the discussion on that hot February night was another small but important step in his fifteen-year effort to help the Miskito people secure their coastal homeland.

With mangrove forests, lagoons, estuaries, coral reefs, and seagrass pastures, the Miskito Coast of Nicaragua may be the most biologically diverse of any coastal area in tropical America. The coast's continental shelf is the most extensive in the Caribbean and accommodates the world's largest populations of green sea turtles and hawksbill turtles, as well as the most productive fishing grounds for spiny lobster and many shrimp species.

The huge coastal lagoons teem with fish and host one of the largest populations of manatees in Central America and the Caribbean. Caimans and crocodiles cruise the interconnecting waterways, and thousands of resident and migratory waterfowl mob the vast wetlands.

In the 1960s, Dr. Archie Carr, famed biologist and founder of the Caribbean Conservation Corporation, discovered that a large percentage of the female green sea turtles he tagged at Tortuguero National Park on Costa Rica's northern Caribbean coast migrated north to the Miskito Coast to graze in the fields of seagrass. To save sea turtles, he found, it was not enough to secure the turtles' nesting site; their feeding grounds needed protection as well.

The Miskito Coast communities had long sought protection of their territorial fishing and turtling grounds from exploitation by foreign fishing fleets, but they received no support from President Anastasio Somoza's regime. In fact, Somoza's gang ruthlessly logged the coastal pinelands and had its own sea turtle slaughterhouse.

In an eventually successful effort to get Somoza's support, Carr, Nietschmann, and Nicaraguan conservationist Jaime Incer met with Somoza and his wife in 1976 to urge protection for the coastal area. Four years later, the government proposed a Miskito Cays National Park. A grass-roots indigenous organization drew up plans to use wisely and protect the coastal resources.

But then war intervened.

"The Sandinistas attempted to invade, occupy, and take over Miskito territory, resources, society, economy, culture, and local institutions," says Nietschmann. Many of the Miskitos were active resistance fighters during the violent civil war.

In February 1990, President Violeta Barrios de Chamorro was elected to replace Sandinista president Daniel Ortega, and the war fizzled. Six months later, Jaime Incer, who had just been appointed head of IRENA, the natural resources agency, led an expedition to the Miskito Cays to talk with community representatives. Incer's pilgrimage included Luthin, Stephen Cornelius of the WWF-US, Archie Carr III of Wildlife Conservation International, and Kenneth Bushy, Rony Pont, and other Miskito leaders. Their goal was to gain government recognition of the protected area and offer technical assistance to the Miskito people, who would continue to manage the area themselves. After a flight from Managua to the coastal town of Puerto Cabezas, the expedition boarded a work-worn lobster-fishing vessel and set sail for the cays.

"It was the first time in memory that a minister from the central government had come to the Miskito Coast, and probably the first time ever that the government had asked the Miskitos to take an active role in designing their own future," remembers Nietschmann. There was little reason for the indigenous people—about 15,000 live along the coast—to trust what might be yet another government hustle.

But the Miskitos understood that they did need outside help. "With the increasing outside pressure on Miskito land and sea environments and resources," says Nietschmann, "many leaders and community people recognized the need to formalize Miskito environmentalism as an integral part of the Miskitos' long struggle for self-determination and autonomy."

So, under a full Caribbean moon, about forty leaders of the Miskito nation climbed over the rails of the lobster boat and stood warily on deck. Incer stepped forward and, with the help of Nietschmann, known to the Miskitos as a trustworthy ambassador to the outside world, outlined the plan for a reserve where fishing would be scientifically managed, so that the Miskitos could continue harvesting the sea's bounty indefinitely and begin to profit from the export of shrimp and lobster.

Slowly at first, then with more confidence that they were really being heard, the Miskitos outlined their concerns. At the conclusion of the following day's discussion on the deck of the gently rocking lobster boat, everyone shook hands. Four months later, Nietschmann, Luthin, and Wiggins were at Sandy Bay, equipped with a slide projector, a videocassette recorder, and ready answers to the many questions.

The days will soon be gone when government agencies, conservation groups, or businesses dare to march into a protected area or buffer zone and set up a project without involving those who live nearby. Whether it is a reforestation project, an antipoaching campaign, or a visitors' center, a project will have little success unless it has the support of the local community. This seems obvious, but it is not a lesson easily learned.

Many park managers and NGOs understand the importance of communicating with local communities. But there are no clear rules for *how* to communicate. Town meetings often work well, but efforts must be made to attract to the gathering as large a cross section of the community as possible—not every town will respond as enthusiastically to an announced gathering as did the villagers of Sandy Bay, Nic-aragua. And the message must be delivered without jargon and with plenty of time devoted to answering questions.

The traditional NGO tools used to describe conservation projects are brochures, fact sheets, and other written handouts. But the written word is not always the best technique for communicating with rural residents, especially in an area like the Miskito Coast.

"Meetings are the customary way of communicating on the Miskito Coast," says Luthin. "There is truly an oral tradition in these communities. Nothing is written down."

WWF-US provided IRENA with funds to hold presentations like the one in Sandy Bay. But seminar leaders Luthin, Nietschmann, and Wiggins wanted to do more than talk—they wanted to leave a lasting impression.

"So we hauled down $10,000 worth of audiovisual equipment, a truck battery, and an AC-DC converter," Luthin explains. "With the VCR's auto-feedback, we could tape the seminar and immediately show it to people. That was a big hit. Everyone likes to see himself on camera."

After the Sandy Bay show, Luthin, Nietschmann, and Wiggins loaded their audiovisual equipment and generator into a small launch and set sail south, to the town of Karata. "We were almost swamped in high waves," Luthin remembers with a shudder. "No one could bear to think of losing all that equipment if we sank."

WWF also funded a series of community workshops attended by representatives selected by each of the twenty-three Miskito coastal communities. Topics of the sessions for the seventy or so seminar participants were the biology and ecology of key species and environments in the coastal area; why resources are vulnerable to overharvesting and environmental damage; how protected areas have been created and how they are managed; and an overview of protected areas and indigenous peoples in the Americas. Maps and photographs were an important part of all discussions, and each participant received a T-shirt and hat, a visual recognition that they were part of an important effort.

"We learned as much from them as they did from us," Luthin emphasizes. "At one point, I showed a slide of a jabaru stork and mentioned that it was very rare. Afterward, a man came up to me and said, 'I know where you can see a lot of those birds. I'll take you there.'"

After a discussion on the value of mangrove swamps, Luthin recalls, "An old-timer stood up and said 'T'ankee, t'ankee.'" Apparently, a U.S. company had offered to buy a mangrove swamp in the village of Tuapi, and the community had been considering the offer. "Now we know not to sell," the Tuapi villager told Luthin.

Wiggins adds that the slide show especially impressed the women of Sandy Bay. "Afterward, many women came up to me crying," he says. "Every morning, they had seen their husbands go off fishing, but they had never seen where they went. Before those slides, they had never seen the Miskito Cays."

The seminar participants overwhelmingly supported creation of an official protected area, one that they would manage and defend. With support from WWF and Cultural Survival, a Boston-based human rights organization, they created a conservation organization called Mikupia, an acronym meaning "Miskito heart."

And in November 1991, President Chamorro created the Miskito Cays Protected Area—at 1.3 million hectares of coastline, lagoons, bays, and cays, it is the largest coastal protected area in Latin America.

Luthin has left the CCC but hopes that audiovisual equipment will have a starring role in phase two of the CCC's community communication work on the Miskito Coast, with audiovisual units and a series of slide shows on such topics as health, natural history, fish management, and small-scale agriculture.

Meanwhile, Nietschmann and the CCC's Bill Alevizon have held another workshop on the Miskito Coast, this one in response to a serious side effect of resource exploitation. Foreign fishing fleets, mainly from Honduras and Colombia, illegally pull lobsters from the bay's waters. They hire the experts at lobster hunting—the Miskitos—outfitting them with scuba gear but providing little instruction. As a result, many have suffered serious and permanent injuries from diving too long, too often, and too deep.

So the latest seminar was on scuba diving safety. "To the community, this was the first meaningful result from the protected area project," says Nietschmann.

Scuba diving instruction may seem to have little to do with resource conservation, but NGOs have learned that meeting a community's immediate and urgent needs is a necessary first step in a long-term management plan.

Wiggins agrees, stressing that follow-up to the initial NGO work on the Miskito Coast is paramount. "Too many times, NGOs come into an area with funds, very excited. Then the money runs out and they disappear, leaving disappointed and frustrated people."

He also points out that the environmental education process along the Miskito Coast is a two-way street, with the NGOs learning as much from the Miskito people as the residents do from the conservationists. "We Miskitos have been hunting turtles for centuries. We have a lot of information for conservationists. But they have to learn to understand beyond the science, to real-life experience. They must be more sensitive to the social side of conservation."

Thus, the newly created marine reserve will be managed by residents from the Miskito communities in close collaboration with Mikupia, the local conservation NGO, and national and local government authorities. In late 1991, a commission was established to help develop a management plan for the protected area. Under this plan, local people living in the area will probably restrict human activity in a core zone, but they propose to harvest, on a sustainable basis, the rich waters in limited use zones. The plan will also address the fears and hopes of the local people: the fear of losing fishing rights or being unable to defend themselves against pirates and drug traffickers and the hope that the protected area will create jobs in the long run and increase lobster and shrimp catches.

Meanwhile, the CCC is coordinating the scientific research on this vast, virtually unstudied area (biological inventories, mapping of habitats and wildlife concentrations, reef-seagrass-mangrove interactions) and trying to ascertain sustainable use levels for the area's natural resources.

Backing for the protected area is gaining momentum. As a Miskito fisherman said during one of the planning sessions: "If we had a protected area, we would guard it twenty-four hours a day!"

Inuit Create
a Whale Sanctuary

In late summer, the arctic ice briefly departs from Isabella Bay, and its dark waters come alive as dozens of endangered bowhead whales temporarily gather to feed on tiny copepods in deep glacial troughs, to socialize, and to escape killer whale predation. While our twin Otter airplane crisscrosses the bay at 150 meters, we lie pointing our cameras through a port on the floor, hoping to learn something of the life of these massive creatures and perhaps aid in their recovery. It seems impossible. Our gadgets and crude observations seem such feeble tools to take the measure of this vast, silent territory and the forces both sustaining and stressing the 200 to 300 eastern Arctic bowheads, which hang on a century after the devastating assault of European whaling caused their numbers to drop from 11,000.

One hundred kilometers up the eastern coast of Baffin Island, Elizabeth Agnew and I joined in a meeting of the Clyde River Hunters and Trappers Association (HTA) for an equally humbling encounter. Here we tried to discuss a range of options for protecting the bowheads and their habitat at Isabella Bay, an area that is uninhabited but is traditionally used by the people of Clyde River. Struggling to span the gulf between English and Inuktitut, we searched for a common understanding of the real-world consequences associated with choosing one paper scenario over another.

Fortunately, our success did not depend on this one meeting. Concern for the future of the bowhead was already well rooted in the community. In 1983, it was a local hunter, Apak Qaqqasiq, who first informed a WWF-sponsored biologist, Kerry Finley, of the annual gathering of bowheads in Isabella Bay (Igalirtuuq). And in 1987, after four seasons of mutual learning through Finley's fieldwork, it was the

HTA—representing the hunters and trappers themselves—that wrote to outside agencies, seeking ways to protect the whales in Igalirtuuq and the surrounding region.

Here was a rare invitation, and it drew us quickly to Clyde River. Since then, though tested by our physical and cultural distance, crosscurrents in regional politics, and frail leadership, this local concern has persisted. It remains the key to future prospects for the whale sanctuary and biosphere reserve proposal that the community presented to the government of Canada on February 1, 1990.

When we first exchanged cigarettes across the HTA table, a kind of meeting icebreaker, we had little more than good intentions to work with. Neither WWF nor Clyde River had much firsthand experience in community-based conservation planning. Joe Tigullaraq, a local wildlife officer who played a major role in preparing the HTA's letter, left for college shortly thereafter. It could be said that we were free to "learn by doing."

There were, of course, a few guiding realities. Although many gaps remain in our knowledge of bowhead biology and arctic migration, the whales' potential recovery appears to be limited by a slow rate of reproduction as well as by killer whale predation on bowhead calves. Not much can be done about this, and with bowhead hunting prohibited under federal fisheries legislation, the main conservation action available is to protect the bowheads' known critical habitat. Isabella Bay is surely the best place to start.

We also realized that now, in the early 1990s, was the best time to start. Although industrial pressure remains low in the region, the settlement of Inuit "land claims," as well as first steps in land use planning, are starting to pattern the legal landscape. Recent tourism proposals, such as construction of an airstrip at Isabella Bay, would also disadvantage Clyde River and impede bowhead conservation.

Pressure has also been building among the Inuit for a resumption of bowhead hunting, which is allowed in the western Arctic, where bowhead numbers are much higher. If this desire is to be satisfied, preferably from a secure and growing bowhead population, every effort must be made to minimize other stresses on the whales. Further sensitizing this issue, Clyde River is one of the communities hardest hit by the European boycott of seal products, an overnight blow to its remarkably adaptive mode of subsistence production. This made it imperative for the community both to "own" the process of developing a bowhead conservation plan and to secure management authority and other benefits related to its implementation.

In hindsight, it is clear that we followed a four-pronged strategy:

1. Helping Clyde River to develop its own conservation goals and management policies for Isabella Bay, linking self-determination for local residents with better protection for the bowhead.

2. Establishing liaison with a wide range of agencies and experts to ensure that the best information was available to Clyde River and that its proposals were feasible.

3. Challenging land use proposals that might preempt the community while under development, while being careful not to overstep community consensus.

4. Promoting the community's proposals within government, recruiting support from other parties as needed.

With the HTA's letter in hand, we flew 3,000 kilometers north from Toronto to Clyde River in the fall of 1987. In many respects a "modern" community of 500 mostly Inuit residents, Clyde River is served by commercial aircraft, satellite communications, a nursing station, a public school, a small hotel, and a Hudson's Bay Company store selling everything from videocassette machines to kiwi fruit. But looks are deceiving. Although only two families live year-round on the land, away from town the community still depends heavily on traditional subsistence use of the land and wildlife and receives few visitors. Summer and winter camps for hunting, fishing, and trapping are set up throughout the region every year, harvesting ringed seal, arctic char, walrus, narwhal, polar bear, and caribou. Incorporated in 1973, the HTA supports this economy, helping its 100 members to secure supplies and equipment as well as to deal with government policies and programs.

Wary of conservation organizations, the HTA and other community members welcomed WWF's arrival because of the good work of Kerry Finley. We were invited to stay in the home of one of the HTA's directors, Joelie Sanguya, and in a few short days we were able to meet with the Hamlet Council and the HTA, host a phone-in show on the community's radio station, and award prizes at a bowhead drawing contest in the school. Finley's tape of bowhead "songs" fascinated all.

It appeared that no other agency had responded to the HTA's letter, and our meetings seemed to convey approval for WWF to provide further advice on conservation options for Isabella Bay. Although we did not receive specific guidance in terms of the community's objectives, there was clear support for some type of special protection for the bowheads and their critical habitat, an interest in community involvement and benefits from this action, and divided opinion as to whether or not tourism based on bowhead viewing would be a good thing for Clyde River. We departed, promising to return the following spring, in 1988, with protection options.

Stopping in Iqaluit, the regional center serving Baffin Island communities, we met with a range of federal and territorial government officials as well as the staff of the Baffin Region Inuit Association and Arctic College, which has a number of training programs in resource management and tourism. Everyone seemed happy with Clyde River's initiative and wished WWF well in supporting it.

Back home in Toronto, at WWF-Canada's headquarters, we faced two challenges. First, there was so little data on Isabella Bay that it was hard to develop options in the kind of detail we believe is needed to get government action. So we set up an informal working group in Ottawa, the Canadian capital, with people from federal and territorial governments, as well as Inuit political organizations, which are likely to be implicated by any proposal. We expected that whatever management plan this group developed would stand a good chance of success.

Meanwhile, we stayed in regular telephone contact with several English-speaking community members in Isabella Bay during the winter of 1987–1988, but we made little headway in defining community goals for Isabella Bay and WWF's work. It soon became clear that project staff support was needed in Clyde River. Telephones and fax machines were not enough to maintain the much-needed communications link.

Fortunately, Heather Myers, a land use planner working in the region, became available just as we were planning to return to Clyde River. Temporarily released from her duties with the territorial government in order to work with WWF, she took up residence in Clyde River for the summer. Together with Kerry Finley, who had mapped bowhead habitat, she offered to assist a newly formed Special Committee on Igalirtuuq, using options we brought with us to start our initial discussions in 1987.

Creation of the Special Committee, representing the Hamlet Council, the HTA, community elders, and young people, was a major step forward by the community. Chaired by Sanguya, an energetic young schoolteacher and hunter, the committee recommended specific management policies to protect Igalirtuuq that reflect local values and needs.

One of the committee's first tasks was to visit Igalirtuuq for several days; there, members were able to relate their firsthand observations of the whales, along with traditional knowledge, to Finley's maps. Still an arduous journey despite the relative safety of the HTA's 12-meter-long boat, the *Uncle John,* this trip was a great opportunity to discuss the good and bad points of potential tourism. Committee members also visited a former whalers' harbor where old bowhead bones are being taken for carving. They came upon whalers' graves and, farther along, an old Inuit camp with copper doorknobs and pottery shards, a legacy of Inuit participation in the whalers' hunt. As Myers observes, "Now here we were, descendants of those Inuit and whalers, cooperating in protecting and potentially increasing the numbers of whales."

Back in Clyde River, elders were interviewed, the committee reported on the radio, an open house was held, and a permanent display was mounted in the school, all leading up to a community meeting at which the committee presented its recommendations. In brief, the committee sought to prohibit hydrocarbon and mineral development as well as to impose strict control over shipping and local boat traffic, thereby also minimizing the potential for water pollution. It also opted to discourage hunting of marine mammals during the time when bowheads are present. Carefully controlled tourism was also supported, preferably land based, relying on Clyde River outfitters, and starting at a very low level, with regular monitoring of impacts. Continuing scientific research was also seen as important for conservation and community training purposes, so long as there is local involvement and the whales are not harassed. And again, though no one alive today in Clyde River has hunted bowheads, one reason for proposing all of this is an interest in resuming "traditional" bowhead hunting if and when the whale population ever becomes large enough to support it.

One of the four basic options prepared earlier by WWF was chosen as a framework to accomplish all of this—a combination of whale sanctuary, biosphere reserve, and protection for archaeological sites. A national or territorial park was not favored because of the potential influx of tourists and possible constraints on community activities that might be involved. On the other hand, another option, mere designation of the area as some kind of special conservation zone in the regional land use plan, was not seen to guarantee enough protection.

Overall, the committee did a fine job, and on October 13, 1988, its recommendations received unanimous endorsement from an unusually large crowd at a community meeting. WWF then assembled the recommendations, background information, and initial action steps in a printed proposal, which the Special Committee approved and submitted to the federal and territorial governments. The federal Department of Fisheries and Oceans was called on to set up a steering committee of relevant agencies to implement the plan, with major involvement by Clyde River.

The government of the Northwest Territories, the Canadian Coast Guard, and

Canada's Man and Biosphere Committee, three key players in implementing the plan, were immediately enthusiastic. The Lancaster Sound Regional Land Use Plan, signed by the federal and territorial governments and to be implemented by the Nunavut Planning Commission, also lent official support. Endorsements also rolled in from other groups and individuals consulted. The community's initiative was widely reported in regional media, and the project was showcased in various conferences as a model of community-based planning.

Everyone was enthusiastic, it seemed, except for the Department of Fisheries and Oceans, which was preoccupied with commercial fishing issues in the south and traditionally weak in community relations—and, apparently, unable to recognize good news when it happens. However, external support had its effect, and on November 5, 1990, the fisheries minister notified the Igalirtuuq Special Committee that he had appointed a senior official to establish immediately and chair an interagency steering committee, as called for in the proposal.

Just as this milestone was achieved, questions emerged from an unexpected quarter. A number of Inuit organizations raised concerns about the depth of understanding and support for the proposal within Clyde River and about the proposal's implications for Inuit hunting and access rights as provided for in the comprehensive land claims agreement finalized by then for Nunavut, their vast homeland in the eastern Arctic. (See "Boundaries and Bloodlines," the introductory chapter for part two.)

While the origin of these concerns was unclear, we sensed a few contributing factors: the Inuktitut translation of the Igalirtuuq proposal contained errors, one saying that Inuit would have to use sailboats at Isabella Bay; new restrictions on beluga whale hunting off Baffin Island's southeastern coast raised a furor in Iqaluit; and the final stages of land claims negotiations made for a highly charged political environment all around.

Whatever the case, the issues raised were serious and sensitive, triggering a new round of discussions among Clyde River, other Baffin Island communities, the Baffin Region Hunters and Trappers Committee, the Nunavut Wildlife Management Advisory Board, and national Inuit leadership. This discussion continued as of September 1992, with WWF awaiting the outcome before taking any further action.

Despite some gains made in recent years by indigenous peoples in regard to protected areas, a veritable flood of government policies and strategies for sustainable development has delivered little evidence of practical results across Canada.

Many protected area proposals, for example, drag on year after year in seemingly interminable conflict over resource access or jurisdiction.

The Igalirtuuq proposal emerged from an opportunity that WWF recognized for community-led planning in an environment relatively free of contention, where a cooperative, win-win approach seemed to be possible. Its model approach, if successful, should help to establish a favorable climate for protected area proposals elsewhere, as well as further steps to conserve the eastern Arctic bowheads. But will it succeed?

Given widespread support for bowhead conservation and recognition of the Special Committee's leadership, some form of protected status will probably be achieved for Igalirtuuq. But when, and what this will amount to, depends, as it should, on how Clyde River pursues the proposal through the new institutions of governance for Nunavut. As of early 1993, this was still unclear.

What is clear is that mere passage of federal government regulations drawing a line on the map would accomplish little for the bowhead. To work, the sanctuary must embody a conservation ethic and reinforce a sense of self-determination among local people. It must also provide a common reference point, a meeting place for cross-cultural exchange of knowledge and ideas during a period of rapid social and environmental change in the North. The Igalirtuuq proposal holds out this promise. Let's take it.

ELIZABETH KEMF

The Green Roof of Central Europe

When Europe's Iron Curtain fell in 1990, it unveiled tragic ecological disasters and human suffering. In Poland, where 65 percent of the river water has been found to be unfit for industrial use, let alone drinking, children are bused out of the polluted cities for clean-air vacations, and in Hungary, entire villages truck in bottled drinking water because local water has been contaminated by agricultural drainage from poisonous chemicals, banned for years in Western Europe.[1]

Despite the horrific environmental damage, discovered on a daily basis, some surprisingly pristine ecological havens have been uncovered, many of them along the treacherous path of the Iron Curtain itself. These cold war border zones, which separated countries with barbed wire, armored tanks, and miles of sentry towers and listening posts, have harbored untold biological wealth, prompting some eighteen nations across Eastern and central Europe to consider declaration or strengthening of protected areas in these former no-go zones.

One of the most remarkable of these "ecological bricks,"[2] or transfrontier reserves, is the Czech Republic's Sumava National Park and Germany's Bavarian Forest National Park, which straddle remnants of the old Iron Curtain that separated the two countries for nearly fifty years. Adolf Hitler annexed the area in 1938, but after his defeat in 1945, the Czechs promptly expelled German-speaking peoples. When the Iron Curtain was constructed, tens of thousands of people were removed from the border zone, and the population was reduced from around 150,000 to around 60,000 people today. What remained was a sparsely populated, heavily forested stretch of land, commonly called the Green Roof of Central Europe. For decades, the military-patrolled zone on the eastern side of the Iron Curtain in Bohemia was used as a favored hunting ground for the Communist elite, or Nomenclatura.

Plans for a transfrontier protected area bridging forests between Bavaria and Bohemia have been around since the nineteenth century. Before the Soviet invasion of Czechoslovakia in 1968, German and Czech environmentalists discussed ways in which they could jointly manage an international forest park in the heart of Europe. It would have been called Intersilva.[3]

Conservationists in Germany, who declared a forest park on their side of the border in 1970, welcomed the creation of the Sumava National Park in 1991. Sumava National Park, five times larger than the German park, is central Europe's largest unspoiled space.

Creating a protected area of this size in an economically depressed area of a country that was shaking off the shackles of a regime that had little regard for the environmental and health effects of poorly designed development schemes required full participation of local communities, forestry officials, military officers, and the federal government. Insightful NGOs such as the Green Circle in Prague and the Ekoing in Sušice, not far from the park, recognized early on that the most important key to the park's success would be involvement of the local people. Realizing this, they and a handful of conservationists who had been trying for twenty years to create Sumava National Park, including Pavel Trpak, deputy minister for the environment of the Czech Republic (and former WWF project leader for Sumava National Park), approached WWF International to help it develop a management plan and to support its efforts in finding a peaceful resolution among the somewhat conflicting interests of the involved groups.

Jan Habrovsky, WWF International's program officer for Eastern Europe, traveled to the region several times to meet with local groups. In 1992, these discussions with government officials and local NGOs culminated in a ground-breaking workshop convened by the Czech Ministry of the Environment in Srni, one of four remaining residential centers inside the park.

At that meeting, for the first time in history the mayors of the Sumava region in southern Czechoslovakia—where the voice of democracy had been silent for more than forty years—made a public appeal to protect the Bohemian forest, the largest unspoiled tract of woodland in central Europe.[4]

In a formal petition issued to Petr Pithart, prime minister of the Czech government, twenty-one mayors representing the citizens of the entire Sumava Biosphere

Reserve announced their support for a locally produced management plan for Sumava National Park.

"We were delighted to take part in the discussion on the future of our region, a pleasure which has not been granted to us before," stated the mayors in their formal petition to the federal government. Formerly, emphasized the mayors, they had "always been bypassed and forgotten . . . access at last [to our forests] has been restored. Our question is, how can this be utilized to the economic advantage of our people? How can we economically advance without destroying our national endowment?"

The management plan, developed with support from WWF, is a benchmark scheme that addresses these questions by giving varying degrees of protection to the 70,000-hectare Sumava National Park, an integral part of the 162,000-hectare biosphere reserve. A strict nature reserve of around 3,000 hectares would also be established.

In 1991, the citizens of the Sumava tore down miles of barbed wire fences and left the region to the lynxes, wild boars, roe deer, and red deer that have made the forest their home for centuries. In winter, tourists explore the inner reaches of the park on cross-country skis, gliding among the snow-covered pine and birch trees.

Otters and freshwater pearl mussels are still found in the rivers, while the forest harbors approximately ten pairs of eagle owls, black storks, and black grouse, as well as the capercaillie.

In former no-entry zones, these first tourists are also discovering the park's primeval forest, where there are trees 30 meters tall and more than 400 years old. They also encounter glacial relics, including the crowberry, the dwarf arctic birch, and the dwarf pine, species that have survived since the Ice Age, 10,000 years ago.

Unwelcome discoveries also occur: some of the trees have been affected by air pollution, although favorable winds have spared the Bohemian forest from serious damage in this country, where leaf and needle damage was measured in 1991 at 35.5 percent, among the highest in all of Europe. In northern Bohemia, less fortunate residents are reported to die younger than elsewhere in the country because of high pollution levels. They are compensated for their shortened life span with "burial money" payments.[5]

In the relatively pollution-free Sumava National Park, large tracts of gouged land, cleared of forests—where the Czechoslovak army played war games with Russian-made tanks and other weapons—mar the landscape. And the sound of gasoline-powered chain saws still breaks the stillness in the Core Zone, where the military is reluctantly giving up its right to log. Local villagers, whose economy has been depressed for years and whose situation has worsened, are still being hired to cut trees in the Protected Zone. Park authorities are patrolling the territory and informing the Ministry of Defense that this cutting must stop.

WWF has funded an economic cost-benefit analysis that compares the amount of revenue to be gained from forestry activities in the region with the revenues gained from ecotourism, or "soft" tourism. This study should provide a convincing argument in favor of developing well-managed ecotourism.

"Up until 1989, it was forbidden for anyone but the military to enter a 10-kilometer zone from inside the forest up until the border itself," explained Jiri Kec, director of Sumava National Park. "Now 600 people will live inside the protected area in what we define in our management plan as a Traditional Use Zone. The core area and the Traditional Use Zone should represent nearly 70 percent of the park."

WWF project leaders and chief architects of the WWF-supported management plan Frantisek Krejci and Vaclav Franek readily point out that their concept for this national park is a slight departure from the strictly traditional IUCN definition of a category II park. Four inhabited villages will remain in the park, and several abandoned enclaves of cultural value will become park centers.

"This concept employs a new philosophy," says Franek, head of the Nature Protection Office. "We need people to continue living here in the Bohemian Forest. We want to create conditions for people to live near the park, in harmony with the park."

Franek also points out the need to reduce dramatically the heavy traffic passing through the heart of the park on two major roads linking the two countries, the Philippsreuth (which bisects the park) and the Bayerisch Eisenstein. He recommends using a railway in the southern part of the park to transport tourists and goods, thus cutting the rising air pollution caused by a surge of motor vehicles that are using the park as a shortcut for quick border crossings. The park's proximity to major population centers—only 125 kilometers from Prague, 180 kilometers from Munich, and 230 kilometers from Vienna—makes it an attractive tourist spot. In the summer, every month an average of 3,000 trucks, 1,500 buses, and 32,000 cars drive through the center of the protected area.

Obviously, compromise will be the key to the success of Sumava National Park. The Ministries of Defense, Agriculture, and the Environment have hammered out various agreements, including one regarding the size of the park's Core Zone. As could be expected, the Ministry of the Environment wanted the Core Zone of the park—where hunting, forestry, and agriculture would be strictly prohibited—to be as large as possible. The core area will be approximately 20,000 hectares, while the Recuperation Zone, encompassing the main areas of former military presence, will be around 5,000 hectares. Limited use for monitoring, removal of roads, and electric power lines would also be permitted in this zone.

In the Traditional Use Zone, tree nurseries are being established, replanting is being encouraged, and logging is being phased out over a forty-year period. The latter is being done slowly in order to avoid economic hardship and to allow time for sustainable development of alternative industries. It has been proposed that meadows in this area be cut but not grazed. Traditional agricultural practices that do not diminish biological diversity would also continue.

The Public Use Zone would encourage environmental education and ecotourism use. Nonmotorized boating, hiking, and camping would be further developed, but access by visitors would be confined to nature trails.[6]

According to Pavel Trpak, agricultural development is the biggest threat to the park, and the zoning must be carefully planned. But he points out that the local people have had only a short time (since the change of government in 1989) "for this new doctrine of nature protection and sustainable development to get into the blood."

Trpak, whose roots are in Bohemia, is one of a handful of dedicated environmentalists who have kept the idea of the park alive for years. He lives in Prague now, near the Ministry of the Environment. But like a growing number of his former neighbors, he says, "I am happy that the dream of my youth has been realized and that the dream of my friends and colleagues, like Ladislav Vodak, who has been working for decades to protect the Bohemian forest and who is now over seventy years old, has also come true."

PETER PROKOSCH

Siberia's Keepers of the Tundra

In the old fisherman's cabin, a fire roared in the simple stove, which had been knocked together from bits of scrap metal. Firewood was stacked outside in interminable piles. Here, on the Tumatskaya branch of the lower reaches of the river Lena, just 20 kilometers from Siberia's northern coast on the Arctic Ocean, gigantic logjams made up of tree trunks clog the waterways. They originate from all over eastern Siberia, having come adrift from log rafts floating downstream or from trees that have been uprooted naturally and have plunged down the steep banks of the mighty, 4,300-kilometer-long river straight into its raging spring spates as it sweeps along its dynamic course through the Yakutsk and Irkutsk regions. Even some of the Lena's tributatries have more energy and more unbridled dynamic power than the largest rivers of central Europe.

It was near one such tributary, the Aldan, that Valeri Michaelovich Dormidontov was born in 1957. Today, he is an inspector in the Ust-Lenski-Sapovednik, the Lena Delta Nature Reserve. In 1992, he spent many days in his small boat guiding a team of German, Dutch, and British biologists safely down the Tumatskaya to their research areas. Valeri Michaelovich belongs to the small Ewenk ethnic group, which originated in the Baikal region as early as the Stone Age. The Ewenk are still herders of the largest reindeer, which they ride high on the shoulder. From the animals they obtain fur, meat, and even milk.

It is estimated that in the nineteenth century the tribe numbered some 40,000 people. Most have lost their original language, first to the Yakut, Siberia's largest ethnic group, and then to the Russians. Valeri estimates that today the Ewenk number only about 1,500 people. For the most part, they are scattered throughout the Yakutsk region, with about 100 of them—mostly fishermen and hunters—

living directly in the area of the Lena Delta. Originally, however, Valeri does not hail from here. One evening, when we were warming ourselves around the stove after a long, cold day of footslogging through the tundra, he told us how he came to join the *sapovednik* (nature reserve) service.[1]

Valeri was born in the small village of Kutana in the Aldanskoye highlands, some 500 miles west of the Sea of Okhotsk and 500 miles northeast of the northernmost part of China. He was raised there until his family moved to the neighboring village so that he could attend high school. Two years in the Soviet army brought him to the vicinity of Irkutsk. After that, back in the village of Kutana, where his parents lived, his most ardent wish started to take shape: he wanted to learn a trade that had to do with nature. His introduction to this world took the form of two years as an apprentice in a technical school and a management course dealing with furbearing animals. He left Kutana qualified as a specialized gamekeeper. Then, in 1980, he moved to the Lena Delta. In the village of Taymyrlyr on the Olenjok, the western branch of the Lena Delta, he worked in a *sovjose,* a collective farm for reindeer raising and husbandry. After a couple of years, he was appointed head of the arctic fox hunting group on Kotel'nyy, the largest of the Novosibirskiye Islands. Under the most extreme arctic conditions, he saw how nature still appears in its purest form in these remote parts, where still only very few (seasoned) people manage to eke out an existence.

In Valeri's view, the Novosibirskiye Islands, which, together with the Lena Delta, are administratively attached to the Rajon Bolunski District, are worth conserving. The islands—more or less surrounded all year long by ice from the Laptev and East Siberian seas in the continental shelf area of the Arctic Ocean—consist partly of ice cores overlaid by a thin covering of tundra. The region is the habitat of polar bears, reindeer, white whales (belugas) and narwhals, wading birds, and geese. This is where the world's largest mammoth graveyard is to be found. In addition, skeletons of giraffes and rhinoceroses from earlier periods in the earth's history have been discovered here, as have petrified trees.

In 1984, Valeri returned again for two years to the reindeer breeding farm at Taymyrlyr in the Lena Delta. But his enthusiasm for nature protection led him inevitably toward the study of biology at the university in the regional capital of Yakutsk. Unfortunately, a sudden illness caused him to interrupt his studies once again. Meanwhile, the management plan for the western part of the Lena Delta Nature Reserve was being prepared under the supervision of Professor Nikita Gavrilovich Solomonov, director of the Institute of Biology at Yakutsk University. Valeri got to know Vassili Vinokurov, who later became the first director of the reserve. One day, Valeri called him up and asked for a job. And he got it, just as the reserve was opened, in 1986.

In the summer of 1992, pointing to a map, Valeri proudly showed our team the location of the second largest nature reserve in Russia (as well as in what was formerly the Soviet Union), the Lena Delta Nature Reserve. The largest protected area in the Russian Arctic, the Great Arctic Reserve in the Taymyr Peninsula in the northernmost part of the Eurasian continent, was established in 1993 with the help of WWF. It covers 5.1 million hectares, while the Lena Delta Nature Reserve encompasses almost 2.8 million hectares. Officially declared a nature reserve in 1986, the protected area of the Lena Delta is split into two parts, the central area (1.4 million hectares)—a traditional Russian *sapovednik*, that is, a reserve that is totally protected and in which nothing can be tampered with—and a buffer zone, the Ohrannaya Zona (1.3 million hectares). In the transitional zone, in the unprotected eastern half of the delta, a handful of indigenous fishermen and hunters are permitted to practice traditional hunting and fishing methods in compliance with specific regulations. They may catch sturgeon (which supplies them with high-priced caviar) and salmon for their own survival and subsistence. Mainly, the Ewenk exchange the fish and caviar for vegetables and other food items not available in the Lena Delta. They may also hunt arctic fox and reindeer. Most of the few remaining small settlements and fishermen's cabins are situated on the major branches of the ramified, treelike delta, mainly to the north and east.

The branches of the Lena, up to 2 kilometers wide in places (before it branches into the delta, the river measures an impressive 4 kilometers across), are the main transportation thoroughfares for the local people. Throughout the long winter months, sleds and vehicles glide over the frozen river. Not until June, when the ice finally breaks, does the Lena rise, by 8 to 10 meters. As a result, nearly all of the delta is under water, and even those who know the area best have trouble identifying the vast landscape. In the summer, from July to September, the fishermen rely on a storehouse of local lore and knowledge to find their way by boat in the interminably ramifying and intertwined river network and to negotiate the meanders with the skill required to keep them from running aground in the shallows. On several occasions, Valeri showed our team proof of such specialized knowledge. There are many days, however, when the wind and waves do not permit venturing out in small craft.

The eastern part of the delta—the central area of the reserve—is much more homogeneously covered by a gigantic network of diversified tundra, with innumerable scattered lakes and ponds of every shape and size. The regular configuration of these four-, five-, and six-sided ponds is a fascinating sight. Their edges are formed by underground ring-shaped ice "wedges" that throw up material from below ground. Cracks in the permafrost layer, the surface of which thaws during the summer, are filled with melted ice. Then, with every new freeze, ever-expanding ice "wedges" are once more formed. As a result of the disintegrating steep banks of the rivers, the vertical structure of these outgrowths, with their pure ice rings in the shape of wedges, can also be studied.

The natural configuration of the landscape of Eurasia's largest arctic river delta, still largely untouched, is worth preserving in its own right. Here in the Russian Arctic, over many decades track-type vehicles, commonly used not only by the military but also by local hunters, have marred the sensitive tundra. It is one of Valeri's tasks to prevent such transgressions from occurring today in the core of the reserve. His duties also include enforcing regulation of the Lena Delta's rich fish stocks. The delta has a particularly rich fish fauna, including several rare species of salmon as well as the Lena sturgeon, which is found only in the delta. Thus, it is in the direct interests of the indigenous hunters and fishermen to maintain spawning grounds for fish and, in other areas, to observe the fishing regulations, which are designed to guarantee sustainable use of the resources and ensure a basic subsistence for the Ewenk and other inhabitants.

In addition to 26 species of fish, the tundra and freshwater areas of the Lena Delta Nature Reserve contain 523 species of flowering plant, 138 species of moss, 182 lichens, and 290 different freshwater algae. So far, 32 species of mammals and 91 birds have also been recorded.[2] Although species numbers are low, their quantities are high. For example, the population of the little stint, a small wader and one of the most common birds, probably numbers some 10 million.

In July 1992, our team of biologists took on the task of recording the wading birds and waterfowl found in sixteen research areas scattered evenly from north to south throughout the delta. The species recorded include the red-necked phalarope (*Phalaropus lobatus*), the dunlin (*Calidris alpina*), the pectoral sandpiper (*Calidris melanotus*), the little stint (*Calidris minuta*), the red-necked sandpiper (*Calidris ruticolis*), and Pacific plovers (*Pluvialis fulva*), which build their nests here in large numbers in the tundra vegetation. Immediately after the short arctic summer, they usually migrate to the shores of the Pacific Ocean, as far away as Indonesia and

Australia. We came across a very few species that also use the east Atlantic migration route to reach their winter quarters in western Europe and Africa.

The grey plover (*Pluvialis squatarola*), which occurs here, there, and everywhere in the tundra, may be one such species. There are also species such as the long-billed dowitcher (*Limnodromus scolopaeus*), which is more associated with the avifauna of the Americas. In the vast marshlands, Sabine's gulls (*Larus sabini*) breed in colonies on islands. And even the pink gull (*Larus roseus*), which is very rare elsewhere, occurs at various sites. Members of the duck family, which tend to breed more on larger bodies of water, include Bewick's swans (*Cygnus bewickii*), white-fronted geese (*Anser albifrons*), king eiders (*Somateria spectabilis*), and Steller's eiders (*Polysticta stelleri*). The Pacific brent goose (*Branta bernicia nigricans*), which still breeds only in small colonies along the coast, would appear to be an endangered species. Unlike the populations of dark-breasted brent geese (*Branta bernicia bernicia*) that occur in westerly parts of northern Siberia, which are well protected during their migration to the mud flats of Europe and thus are able to breed and thrive there, Lena brent geese, which migrate eastward, are still openly and intensively hunted in various countries.

The day-long treks made by our team of western Europeans and Russians through the half-water, half-tundra landscape, which is often very hard going, were helped by the cool July temperatures. We got to know more about this untouched natural area as well as the living conditions of the few people living there. And at the request of the reserve's administration in Tiksi, we also undertook the first comprehensive inventory of the delta's rich avifauna. The results of the inventory produced new arguments for increased protection and expansion of the protected area.

One Russian scientist who has been leading the drive for increased support for the protected area is Sergei Larionov, director of the Lena Delta Nature Reserve. The Ministry of the Environment in Moscow regards him as one of the most competent nature reserve heads in all of Russia. In order to raise support for the reserve among the national and international communities, he invited our team to have discussions with representatives of the Yakut administration in Yakutsk and of the Rajon Bolunski in Tiksi. Larionov proposes to incorporate the existing nature reserve in a biosphere reserve covering some 10 million hectares, which would include the Novosibirskiye Islands and large areas of the continental shelf of the Laptev and East Siberian seas. According to Larionov, this form of conservation and protection makes it possible to begin as soon as possible to integrate traditional forms of utilization by the indigenous population while safeguarding the area from far-reaching rural alterations and intensive interference and encroachment. The overall area would then develop into one of the most important protected zones in the circumpolar chain of arctic reserves.

These plans had scarcely been understood and endorsed in Bolunski in 1992 when the administration of the Yakut Republic put its full backing behind the scheme. The Yakut minister of the environment, Igor Nikolaivewitsch Chemezov, subsequently requested that WWF support the proposal. Even the Yakut president personally took part in an expedition to the Novosibirskiye Islands in order to gain his own impressions about the development plans for the proposed biosphere reserve. However, it still remains to be seen whether expectations can be realized through international cooperation. But who will act most quickly? United States oil companies, clamoring for prospecting rights? The Japanese, who are sounding out possibilities in Tiksi concerning the large-scale acquisition of the velvet from reindeer horns for alleged potency-increasing products? Polish fishery representatives, who are keen to industrialize fishing methods? Or, last but not least, conservation groups, which would like to set aside extremely precious sectors of the arctic wilderness for future generations?

Since our first visit to Siberia in 1989, in the wake of *glasnost* and *perestroika*, a solid partnership has begun to flourish among our group, local scientists, and some of the decision makers we have met. So far, we have not met many people in Russia who exude a great deal of optimism about the future, which early in 1993 was still uncertain, if not gloomy. But we worked with a few people who had visions for a bright tomorrow. Valeri Dormidontov was one of them. Today, Valeri feels more freedom than he did some years ago; he is overjoyed that the Ewenk people stand a chance of regaining the right to manage or control their own territories; and he is a thoroughly convinced champion of the concept of the new biosphere reserve, for which he says he would like to work.

A. S. M. BANDA & HILARY DE BOERR

Honey for Sale

Malawi has a problem with space. Almost a quarter of the country is lake; another 21 percent is set aside for conservation areas. Its 8.2 million people live on what is left, making Malawi one of the most densely populated countries in Africa.

Such restrictions are problematic for both conservation and development. There is pressure on the government to open its protected areas to agriculture and other uses. Poaching occurs in conservation areas, often for subsistence reasons. But because wildlife is not abundant—even in protected areas—rural people cannot supplement their incomes by approved schemes such as safari hunting, as in other African countries. An answer, it seems, may lie in another exploitable resource—bees!

Apiculture is a traditional practice in Malawi; between 1893 and 1961, more than 60,000 kilograms of beeswax was exported. However, increasing human numbers, rapidly disappearing forests, and the spread of farmland have reduced honey and beeswax production. In the 1970s and 1980s, rural dwellers like the Phuka (Phoka), traditionally a beekeeping people in the north of the country, were moved from their traditional homelands to make way for national parks. Ancestral apiary grounds had to be abandoned. The government prohibited the making of traditional log and bark hives using trees from protected areas and made it illegal to hang hives in conservation sites. A way of life seemed threatened.

Today, villagers are being allowed back into conservation areas on a restricted basis to tend and harvest beehives. By 1992, more than 700 rural people living around Nyika National Park in the north had set up seventy-one commercial beekeeping clubs in an experimental program aimed at sustainable development. The enterprise looks promising.

Honey consumption in Malawi is high. Honey supplements the diet of an ever-growing population and has medicinal properties and marketable by-products, such as wax. Beekeeping increases crop production through pollination and can bring in much-needed foreign exchange through the export of hive products. Studies show that Malawi could satisfy its domestic demand for honey, yet 80 percent of the honey consumed is imported—as is 95 percent of the beeswax on the market.

The Malawi-German Beekeeping Development Project (MGBDP), started in 1989, is taking advantage of the country's prime conditions for apiculture. It aims to develop beekeeping as a viable alternative source of income for people living in rural areas; to reduce the price of honey so that the average Malawian can afford it; and to foster a conservation culture among rural people.

The eight-year project is supported financially by the German government through the German Agency for Technical Cooperation. It is implemented by Malawi's Department of National Parks, Wildlife and Tourism and by the Save the Children Federation in the United States. The goal is a countrywide, privately run beekeeping industry by 1997.

The project is based on beekeeping clubs, with as many as ten members each, formed in rural communities. Each club is run by a committee consisting of a chairman, a secretary, and a treasurer, who receive training in club management, accounting, and financial management. All club members are taught apiary siting, colony management, and techniques for harvesting honey and wax. Training is undertaken by MGBDP field staff members.

Whereas rural people used to construct small hives from log and bark, they now increasingly use the Malawi Standard Hive, a topbar hive that local craftsmen are being taught to make. Instead of just going to the hive when they feel that the honey may be ready for harvesting, beekeeping club members now actively manage hives. The once-unusual sight of "astronauts" strolling through the forests in protective white beekeeping suits is increasingly common.

Not only do the beekeeping clubs produce more honey than was harvested with the traditional approach, but also what they do produce is of a better quality. In fact, they market only honey of European Community standards. Their new methods are also better for the environment. Fewer of the country's brachystegia trees are stripped of their bark to make hives because only one-third of the hives are now made in the traditional way. Harvesting practices, meanwhile, no longer involve burning the hives to reach the honey, a method that kills the bees and destroys surrounding vegetation.

An additional benefit is a reduction in poaching incidents in protected areas such as national parks and forest reserves. Relations have improved between villagers and the parks department as villagers are allowed back into protected areas—the lands of their ancestors—on a controlled basis. In some cases, beekeeping club members now even provide additional security in protected areas. By making their apiary sites prohibited areas to other villagers, they guard against trespassers and aid the park staff.

The project's catch phrases, "Without trees—no bees" and "Make money from honey," have come to have real meaning for rural people—so much so that in 1992, requests from village headmen to form beekeeping clubs in their areas were having to be turned down. Demand was simply too great for available resources.

The earning potential of beekeeping is such that by the third year of beehive operation, a beekeeper can earn the equivalent of $5.70 a day, approximately ten times the country's minimum daily wage. Labor requirements are not constant, however. The total annual labor requirement for twenty Malawi Standard Hives is estimated at about 108 person-days by the third year, with the highest input needed between April and June and between October and December, for swarm prevention and harvesting.

Beekeeping clubs succeed because of financial and administrative assistance in their formative years. Once a club receives official status, it is given a loan by the project operators in the form of hives, beekeeping suits, and smokers. The loans are for a period of three years—with no repayments due in the first year—at an annual interest rate of 16 percent. Repayment of a loan is guaranteed by the sale of honey and beeswax, which is channeled through the project operators.

The project is proving to be a reliable source of income. In 1991, the seventy-one clubs in the Nyika area—eight of which are women-only clubs—produced almost 4 metric tons of honey. One year later, the harvest was nearly 6 metric tons, worth more than $10,825 to local communities. Local craftsmen are also beneficiaries of the beekeeping project. They are being taught to construct not only beehives but also protective clothing and smokers.

The project also appears to be moving in the right direction when it comes to making honey affordable to the average Malawian. In 1989, a kilogram of honey cost $2.50. By 1992, the price had fallen to $1.70. However, it still needs to be halved, to $.85, the price on the world market, if honey is not to remain largely the preserve of wealthy Malawians and expatriates.

The total domestic market for honey is projected at about 30 metric tons per year if the price falls enough to make it competitive with products like jams and marmalades. Higher hive occupation rates and lower—but still comparatively advantageous—beekeeping wages are seen as ways of achieving lower honey prices.

Beeswax, meanwhile, already competes effectively with imports. At $1.84 per kilogram, its cost is only about 79 percent of world market prices.

The beekeeping project's success in the north is to be followed by further club launches in Malawi's central and southern regions until mid-1999. The newer clubs will benefit from lessons learned in the early years.

The main teething problems have been in the areas of training and marketing. There is a dearth of trained beekeepers in Malawi, a problem that is restricting the country's beekeeping potential. Trained field staff members are expected to visit the beekeeping clubs at least once a month to supervise training and management, but there is not enough manpower. A formal training course is seen as compulsory. Also, more female field staff members need to be recruited to allow the women-only beekeeping clubs to realize their full potential.

Marketing has been problematic without formal channels for collection and purchase of the clubs' honey and wax. The project organizers have filled the void in the absence of buying agents, but a reliable marketing system is crucial to the project's ultimate success. Such a system would set and enforce quality standards; establish a collection network; process and store honey; and find and maintain a reliable customer base.

When the MGBDP winds up in June 1997, its responsibilities will transfer to the nascent Beekeepers' Association of Malawi, which ultimately will operate as an independent enterprise. The vision is that as honey quantities increase and prices decrease, the country's beekeeping industry will eventually be able to compete in export markets as well as domestically. When this happens, the success of the beekeeping clubs will be very sweet.

PHILIP M. HUNSICKER & FIDELE NGAMBESSO

Banking on a Nature Reserve

What has forty legs; eats duikers and monkeys as well as fish and fruit; is a very social creature; emits a wide range of vocalizations, from deep groans and growls to high, piercing laughter; has many tales; and is an important link in the tenuous food chain of the African rain forest? If you think it is a new species recently discovered in the Central African Republic, you are partially correct. It is a community association of twenty elected individuals whose objectives are to promote conservation, to stimulate small business enterprise, to encourage rational rural development while safeguarding the region's rich natural heritage, and to act as a community forum for open discussion of natural resource management and other issues relating to the newly established Dzanga-Sangha Dense Forest Special Reserve and Dzanga-Ndoki National Park.

The Association Communautaire de Yobe-Sangha (ACYS) was created to encourage local participation in local conservation issues for the mutual benefit of both the community and the WWF-supported Dzanga-Sangha project. Unfortunately, there is a long, dubious history of conservation endeavors that have started with enormous funding and lofty ambitions only to fail because social programs were not considered and local concerns were not addressed. Local populations can play a major supportive role in conservation and rural development if it is in their best interest to do so, through incentives such as better health care, more money in their pockets, more food on their tables, or an invigorating sense of empowerment. When ignored, a local population will inhibit all efforts at conservation and will surely bring about a project's downfall. That is why in all projects dealing with the management of natural resources, it is absolutely necessary to gain the support of the local population.

The Dzanga-Sangha Dense Forest Special Reserve is not only a mouthful; it is also a project of protection and integrated development for the forest region of the southwestern Central African Republic. Local communities living within the reserve depend on the forest's rich biodiversity (more than 3,600 species of plants and 208 species of mammals, including 15 species of primates) for their own survival. In turn, the success or failure of WWF's conservation efforts in the region depends on the supportive attitude and active participation of the local population. It seems only fair that in a forest where each living organism is dependent on so many others for its survival, the people managing and exploiting the resource should also be interdependent.

The government of the Central African Republic has also acknowledged the necessity for local community participation by instituting a new category of protected land, called the "special reserve with multiple uses," which protects the flora and fauna but allows certain controlled human activities, such as community hunting, big game safari hunting, logging, and cultivation of crops. In the Dzanga-Sangha Dense Forest Special Reserve's 4,579 square kilometers, two core areas of total protection (Dzanga-Ndoki National Park) make up only 1,220 square kilometers, or 26 percent. The remaining 3,359 square kilometers, which surround the park, come under the new "special reserve" category of integrated protection and rural development.

The region's history and current economic situation required a conservation program that would address social issues as well as protect the ecosystem. In the early 1970s, a Yugoslav group arrived in the Central African Republic and exclaimed, "There's wood in them there hills," and, reminiscent of the Yukon gold rush days, people came from all corners of the country to make their fortunes by harvesting timber. The sleepy fishing village of Bayanga, made up of seven small huts, grew almost overnight into a boomtown of more than 4,000 inhabitants. But with a drop in the world market price of wood, combined with an increase in local transportation costs and basic mismanagement of the sawmill, the Yugoslavs closed their doors in 1986, leaving 95 percent of the population out of work and owing several months' back wages. With no work and not enough capital to return home, many former sawmill workers turned to poaching to make ends meet.

Most of the poaching is done with wire snares for duikers (*Cephalophus* sp.). Unfortunately, the snares are indiscriminate killers and often kill or maim females and young and many protected species, such as gorillas (*Gorilla gorilla gorilla*), leopards (*Panthera pardus*), and bongos (*Tragalaphus euryceros*). The wildlife was being

An Inuit fishing in a kayak in the Arctic.
Courtesy Bryan and Cherry Alexander.

Dog sleds are used by the Inuit in the Arctic, and are also used in conjunction with motorized vehicles. Courtesy Bryan and Cherry Alexander.

An Inuit in a kayak in Isabella Bay, Canada, where WWF is working with
local people to create a whale sanctuary. Courtesy WWF-Canada.

Aerial photograph of the impressive polygon tundra in the Lena
Delta Nature Reserve. Courtesy WWF/Peter Prokosch.

Valeri Michaelovich Dormidontov demonstrates the function of a fox trap.
Courtesy WWF/Peter Prokosch.

Valeri Michaelovich Dormidontov (left), inspector in Siberia's Lena Delta Nature Reserve and member of Ewenk ethnic group, and Andrew Lwanow-Smolensky, project leader of the Social Ecological Union, one of the largest environmental organizations in Russia, survey the Lena Delta. Courtesy WWF/Peter Prokosch.

Protea gaguedi. This pink flower in Nyika National Park is one of the bee's favorite flowers. Courtesy WWF/Sandra Mbanefo.

The German government has helped establish beekeeping clubs in Malawi. Here, honey is being harvested by the Tiwonge Bee Keeping Club at Nyika National Park. Courtesy WWF/Rick Weyerhaeuser.

Reef scene in Ambergris Cay in Haiti. Courtesy WWF/Jack S. Grove.

Fishermen's children in the village of Luly in Haiti.
Courtesy WWF/Evelyn Wilcox.

A man weaving a basket in Haiti in Les Arcadins, an archipelago proposed as
the country's first national park. Courtesy Michael Lutskey.

decimated at an alarming rate. If these practices continued, experts felt that within five years a rich, vibrant, thriving forest would become a biological wasteland.

WWF first became interested in the area through support of research on western lowland gorillas. The region around Bayanga was also found to have the largest concentration of forest elephants (*Loxodonta africana cyclotis*) in the country. With the additional strong presence of bongos, dwarf forest buffaloes (*Syncerus caffer nanus*), golden cats (*Profalis aurata*), chimpanzees (*Pan troglodytes*), and colobus monkeys (*Colobus guereza*), WWF researchers recommended to the Central African Republic's government that this Garden of Eden be classified as a national park and reserve. On December 29, 1990, our hopes were realized when the National Assembly adopted laws 90.017 and 90.018 for the creation of Dzanga-Ndoki National Park and the Dzanga-Sangha Dense Forest Special Reserve. With the downfall of the logging company, ecotourism presented the best long-term option for rational development of the region. Ecotourism has the potential to create employment, foster education, and generate the necessary funds to preserve the area's rich natural heritage.

To motivate the population living within the reserve to protect and rationally manage the natural resources for their own benefit, 40 percent of the vision fees paid by each tourist, along with a percentage of safari hunting fees, goes to the local communities. The ACYS was created to coordinate and harmonize the different points of view concerning the management of the community's "conservation dividend." The ACYS has also received outside assistance in the form of a $5,000 grant from the John D. and Catherine T. MacArthur Foundation to support institutional development of private, nonprofit conservation organizations in Africa and Asia.

Opinions on how best to use this money varied. Meetings were held with the local population, and the idea of an association to represent the interests of the community was well accepted. People throughout the Dzanga-Sangha Dense Forest Special Reserve echoed the sentiments of Victor Babon, a local nurse, who stood up during one town meeting and said: "We are capable of managing this money ourselves."

Eventually, residents of the reserve decided to organize themselves into subassociations according to profession or locality to represent equally the smaller, isolated communities. Examples of subassociations are fishermen, livestock raisers, construction workers, gardeners, restaurateurs, bakers, farmers, and the villages of Lidjombo, Yandoumbe, and Babongo. There are now twenty such subassociations, and each is represented by an elected delegate. The delegates meet two times per month to review, compare, and debate requests for financing of small-scale economic alternatives to logging and poaching as well as to represent the local population in helping the WWF project to make decisions relating to resource conservation and utilization.

Through ACYS support, a number of small business enterprises have flourished; there are now four functioning restaurants in Bayanga; the construction workers purchased a brick press and are now making bricks for the construction of WWF houses, offices, and a garage; fresh garden vegetables are now available on a daily basis in Bayanga; independent artisans are now selling ebony carvings, woven baskets, and butterfly art to visitors of the reserve-park; and fresh eggs, chicken, and pork (alternative protein sources to bush meat) are now more abundant in Bayanga. And last but not least, interest in the association has rekindled a closer relationship and understanding between WWF and the local population. WWF staff members are no longer seen as just antipoaching policemen sent in to protect only wildlife. They are now offering economic alternatives as well as educating the local population about conservation and the need to preserve natural resources in a sustainable fashion.

Julien Dobanti, a former poacher who is now working as an antipoaching guard for the WWF project and who has also received funding support from the ACYS to enlarge his vegetable garden, sums things up rather nicely: "I used to poach. I've killed many elephants. I always thought that our animals and trees would be here forever. But I now know that I was wrong. Just look at the northern part of our country. It's now a desert, and where once there were thousands of elephants, there are now only a handful. We cannot repeat the mistakes of the north here in the south."

Unfortunately, all residents of the Dzanga-Sangha Dense Forest Special Reserve do not share Dobanti's newfound awareness. But inroads are being made, and attitudes are beginning to change. Community associations like the ACYS are attempting to make people take a more integrated, systemic view of their environment. Many people in central Africa currently see themselves as separate from, rather than part of, nature. In a continent where each day is a struggle simply to feed and clothe one's family, the "bigger" issues, like overpopulation, deforestation, desertification, global warming, extinction, and pollution of the environment just do not seem as pressing.

Conservation will not succeed simply because it is the right thing to do. But as long as conservation is more beneficial (in other words, more profitable) than the alternatives of poaching and uncontrolled logging, man can coexist with nature. We hold the future in our own hands. Granted, it is a responsibility of monstrous proportions, but do we really have a choice? We are rapidly running out of wildlife, habitats, and, most important, we are running out of time.

The Dzanga-Sangha project came just in the nick of time. Its success depends on its innovative idea to integrate wildlife protection with rural development, to ensure that the local population realizes direct benefits from WWF's conservation effort. The formation of the ACYS, combined with the economic incentives of conservation, has made that original idea a reality of local participation and mutual benefit.

Kan Pwotektè Aniviwonman Haiti

We Can Protect the Environment of Haiti

Nen pran kou je kouri dlo.

(When the nose is hurt, it is the eyes that cry.)[1]

The first time I saw the Les Arcadins region of Haiti was underwater. I knew then that it would make a perfect marine park. I made the 7.2-kilometer trip from shore to the site in the company of U.S. and Haitian scuba divers on the catamaran *Tap tap La Mer,* named after Haiti's *tap taps* (small buses) that weave in and out of traffic in Port-au-Prince, Haiti's capital. As we approached the Les Arcadins Bank, the color of these Caribbean waters became a gorgeous aquamarine blue.

Once in the water, we could clearly see coral formations 6 meters below us. Two very large specimens of the sponge *Niphates digitalis* swayed below us at an unusually shallow depth. Sponges, such as this basket sponge, thrive on the seagrass meadows and coral reef habitats of Les Arcadins due to the sheltered nature and, thus far, healthy environmental conditions at the site. We watched invertebrates (e.g., polychaetes), small crabs (*Stenorynchus seticornis* and *Dromidia antillensis*), and fish (pomacanthids) feeding and seeking refuge among an amazing variety of sponge species, including the basket sponge, the axinellid sponge (*Ectoplasya ferox*), and the chicken leg sponge (*Xestospongia tierneyi*).

The Les Arcadins Bank is situated in La Gonave Bay, about halfway between the mainland and the Haitian-owned island of La Gonave. The bank, approximately 5 kilometers square and ranging in depth from 13 to 19 meters, is marked by three small, uninhabited islands surrounded by extensive seagrass meadows and coral reefs. The platform surrounding this bank is generally deeper than 21 meters. The islands and surrounding coral reefs are rich in biological diversity. So finely balanced ecologically, the area gives life to hundreds of fish and invertebrate species by providing an ideal breeding and nursery area for the diversity of species that sustain the life of the people of Luly, the neighboring fishing community.

The largest island, only 1.6 kilometers long, is surrounded by a white sand beach and rich tidal pools. A lighthouse sits at one end, facing the entrance to La Gonave Bay. Once, the Haitians told us, plentiful hawksbill sea turtle populations shared their feeding grounds among the seagrass meadows with huge quantities of Queen conchs and other mollusk and invertebrate species. They said that in the past, large populations of reef fish also claimed the underwater world of Les Arcadins, but now, although there is still an amazing variety of fish, they are fewer in number, there is no sign of the sea turtle, and the conchs are harvested only in small numbers.

As we made our way that day, skimming along the waves of the bay, we talked about the small fishing villages that dot the island's western coast, interspersed among the resort hotels. We saw *nasses* (fish traps) and an occasional small *canot* (boat), powered only by the wind. It seemed that the Les Arcadins region served a great many fishing communities, such as Montrouis, Saint-Marc, and Gonaïves, but the village that the divers were most familiar with was Luly. As we sailed home that afternoon, we saw what was to become a familiar sight: small white specks on the horizon. The Luly fishing fleet was sailing back home.

The idea of declaring Les Arcadins a national marine park has been the dream of many. Local Haitian divers, tourists, and world-renowned marine conservationists like Jacques Cousteau, who visited Les Arcadins in 1985, have promoted the idea of establishing a protected area here. One dive master, impatient with the lack of progress in creating the park, always announces to his divers as they enter the water that as far as he is concerned, it is a specially protected area and should be treated as such. Nothing should be disturbed.

Until recently, a lack of coastal development, low levels of industrial pollution, and difficult access to the sea protected Haiti's coral reefs from damage. However, in an impoverished country like Haiti, little of the natural resource base is left untouched. Although its 1,500-kilometer coastline, one of the longest in the Caribbean, is still home to some undisturbed reefs, seagrass meadows, and mangrove wetlands, unsustainable fishing and deforestation of the slopes above the sea are beginning to have a devastating effect on Haiti's marine environment. A growing shortage of fertile land is forcing farmers onto steeper slopes near the sea. The resulting deforestation and destructive farming practices are eroding the soil and blanketing nearby reefs and seagrass beds with silt.

Haiti's population is projected to increase from 5.2 million in 1985 to 6.5 million in 2006. When Christopher Columbus landed on the island in 1492, he found more than 300,000 indigenous inhabitants, who called their country Ayiti, meaning "land of high mountains." However, as Europeans started to colonize the island, disease and malnutrition, added to the hardships of forced labor, decimated the native population, and African slaves were imported as a supplementary work force. In 1804, when Haiti was officially established—the first nation of self-liberated slaves in the history of mankind—there were virtually no indigenous people left.[2] Today, Haiti's burgeoning population has felled 90 percent of Haiti's forest cover, and its once-rich waters are being rapidly depleted by artisanal fishermen. The rural poor are harvesting fish before they can spawn, making it impossible for fish populations to recover. Moreover, the illegally used, small-mesh fish traps used to capture juvenile fish (in some cases, all that is left of the fish stocks) are taking large numbers of species like parrot fish and doctor fish, species that help maintain the natural balance of reefs and attract the recreational divers so necessary to the tourist economy.

Despite these serious problems, some government officials, villagers, and businessmen have been working to conserve—in fact, to restore—Haiti's diverse natural heritage. Following a USAID-funded marine park feasibility study of Les Arcadins,[3] WWF, with the support of the Haiti Hotel Association, the scuba diving industry in Haiti, and key individuals, conducted a two-year USAID-funded research and planning effort to establish a marine park at Les Arcadins.[4] The richness of the area and the need to conserve it for future generations were unmistakable. It soon became clear, however, that a park could be effectively established only if the people in the nearby village were involved.

WWF scientists and field teams began working with fishermen's cooperatives, village residents, government agencies, and environmental groups in Haiti to plan a marine park and fish reserve in the Les Arcadins region. In 1990, WWF chose Luly as its project site. WWF rented a house from the village's voodoo priest as a base of operations and opened the doors to the Les Arcadins region's first ecological "visitors' center."

The project was designed and funded, following the concept of the WWF-US Wildlands and Human Needs Program, to combine conservation efforts with development needs of the community and the nation. WWF and its backers, the

USAID Biodiversity Support Program and the United Nations Development Program (UNDP), agreed that if a marine park could be established and then publicized beyond the borders of Haiti, it could bring back some tourism revenues to a country that had a thriving tourism industry as recently as six years ago, provide a model for sustainable fisheries projects in Haiti, and help sustain the local community. The tourism industry had suffered a decline because of the country's unstable economy and government.

Luly, or "Kalili," has a population of about 2,500 people, living mostly in small adobe and tin-roofed houses. Houses are built in groups, or *lakou,* to accommodate extended families. The fishermen say that Kalili has no season and that every day is harvest day. They are not like the farmers, who must wait to plant their crops during the rainy season. In Haiti, the full-time fishermen know that they are professionals, carrying on a long tradition that extends back for centuries. The people of Luly also sell fish traps and nets, sails, and boats. Their livelihoods depend on the continuing productivity of Les Arcadins's seagrass meadows and coral reefs, which supply breeding grounds for more than 200 species of fish, crustaceans, corals, and sponges.

Luly's residents understand that overfishing endangers their livelihood, and local fisheries teams are firmly committed to community welfare. The fishermen of Luly traditionally organize into small teams that go to sea together. Success at bringing in the catch depends greatly on the sense of community and trust within these teams. WWF is expanding on this way of thinking to build community participation and cooperation in planning for the marine park, which will protect the coral reefs and fish stocks offshore from Luly.

Luly's fishermen have traditionally used simple fish traps and gill nets to harvest fish in shallow waters. However, they might be able to relieve pressure on reef fish populations by expanding their fishing grounds into deeper waters, where they could troll for large schooling fish such as yellowfin tuna, wahoos, and deep-sea snappers. WWF and its local partners, the fishermen, are researching whether deeper waters will provide the catches that they need, and they are testing affordable alternatives to expensive deep-sea fishing gear. If the experiment is successful, WWF hopes to share its findings with other villages in the surrounding region.

To build up the fish stocks and help ensure plentiful catches in the future, WWF has also proposed setting aside a fish breeding reserve within the proposed marine park that would be off-limits to fishermen and tourists. Evidence from a similar reserve in the Philippines suggests that some fish stocks can replenish themselves within a year. If the idea of a fish reserve is accepted, training in monitoring and evaluation will be part of Luly's ongoing public awareness and education program.

WWF has received a good response and cooperation from local leaders in setting up the environmental awareness program. Today, it is successfully addressing community concerns about the creation of a marine park and reserve in the traditional fishing zone. Selected Luly representatives, or *animateurs,* are explaining marine conservation issues to other members of the community. Informal meetings are held weekly, and a trip to the neighboring island of Saint Lucia is being planned for local leaders from the region, including a representative from Luly, to learn from other fishermen in the Caribbean how they collaborated on setting up a marine park and reserve.

Over a period of a year and a half in the early 1990s, WWF's Haitian partners launched several other pilot projects to meet the expectations of the villagers and to find out which conservation methods could be the most effective to meet the project's goal of marine park establishment and fisheries conservation in the Les Arcadins region. WWF's Haitian project field coordinator, Dr. Marlene Gay, who has a doctorate degree in education from Columbia University, has designed a field program that creates a greater public awareness for conservation of the natural environment and support for the park.

The results have been varied but rewarding. Existing local groups, ranging from the small fisheries teams to women's and young adults' groups, have begun to organize themselves better and talk about conservation and park development. Local groups that showed an interest have been contacted and supported by WWF's field office in Luly. Self-financed activities and projects, supported by small grants from WWF, are under way, such as a soft drink concession and the making of candles for sale by the women's group. Two agricultural groups are successfully growing vegetables for sale and consumption. These small enterprises foster self-respect and offer a better life for the residents of Luly.

The work continues, with better and better results. In the summer of 1992, WWF's field team turned to the children of Luly and the neighboring communities of Williamson and Saintard. They held a summer camp for fifty children between the ages of six and ten in the village of Luly. The children visited the three small islands of Les Arcadins by boat, composed a song about protecting their environment, and formed the Environmental Protection Club, which WWF hopes may become a national club to enable Haitian children to better protect their natural heritage and form support for the park. The children read from four booklets put together by WWF, designed especially for Haiti and published in Creole, featuring characters called the Queen Conch, the Spiny Lobster, the Sea, and the Environment. They even had a WWF camp T-shirt, in Creole, to wear. And all of this was accomplished in the face of a political coup that displaced the first fairly elected president of Haiti in history and that plunged the country into economic and social chaos.

Yet WWF hopes to work with its local partners to get the Les Arcadins National Marine Park established, possibly in 1993. During this final stage of park preparation, the Luly fishermen and their families will be called on to help draft a management plan for the park and reserve, along with the marine park advisory committee convened by WWF several years ago, which has representatives from the Haiti Hotel Association, the four national environmental groups, Luly fishermen, and government fisheries and tourism departments. In any event, it is certain that Haitians will struggle to keep the idea alive in the midst of coups, embargoes, and a nation coping with hunger, poverty, and the most serious kind of environmental degradation. It is that important to them.

ALISON WILSON

Sacred Forests and the Elders

When you fly in a small plane from Kenya's capital, Nairobi, to the coastal port of Mombasa, it is the intensity of color that strikes you on your approach to the Indian Ocean. For almost half an hour, the vast, brown expanse of Tsavo National Park and the Taru Desert has passed below, thousands of square kilometers of monotonous thorn scrub, the scourge of those early European explorers pushing through to the East African hinterland. But gradually the scene changes from sepia to technicolor. Lush groves of bananas and mangoes and large plantations of coconut palms, cashew, and kapok trees appear. The coastal strip is densely inhabited; among the plantations cluster small, palm-thatched houses, each with a neatly swept compound and perhaps a small field of maize or cassava. Where the land meets the sea, large tourist hotels and neat villas surrounded by palms and casuarinas overlook a dazzling strip of white coral sand. Hues of emerald, jade, and aquamarine mark the ocean's shallows, and out beyond the reef the dark blue depths complete the picture of a tropical paradise.

The East African coast has been settled for thousands of years. The past century has seen an explosion of the human population; the past few decades, an explosion of the tourist industry. There is little sign here of the indigenous forests that once flourished along these shores (although two significant areas remain, in the Arabuko-Sokoke Forest, near Malindi, and in the Shimba Hills National Park, near Kwale). But all along Kenya's coast, tucked away behind the tourist hotels and hidden amidst the plantations and pastures, are small—often very small—forest patches. Tiny they are, most just a few hectares in extent, but their size belies their cultural and biological significance. They are known to the local people as *Kayas,* and with the permission of nearby villagers, we may visit one.

Only a few meters into the forest, a silence descends. The distant roar of waves breaking on the reef is barely audible, a muted whisper. The strong, warm wind of the *kusi,* the southeast monsoon, is stilled. The air inside the forest is humid, the dim light a relief from the glare of the midday sun. Underfoot, a thin layer of dry leaves carpets the sandy soil. Close inspection reveals a steady commerce of small ants and millipedes going about their business of converting the litter into a richer loam. Herpetophobes may want to tread cautiously here, for these coastal forests harbor some of the world's deadliest—and most beautiful—snakes. Mambas (both green and black), puff adders, vine snakes, and boomslangs are among the most to be feared, but they are shy and rarely seen. Scattered around the forest floor, the bleached-white shells of giant African land snails catch the eye, and here and there low outcrops of weathered limestone, the remnants of an ancient coral reef, break through the leaf litter. Around these rocks, gnarled roots of ancient fig trees curve and twist.

It is a mere five minutes' walk to the heart of the forest—and here is a small clearing surrounded by tall trees, which include the endangered *mbamba kofis* and African ebonies much sought after by local wood-carvers and furniture makers; huge, portly baobabs; and enormous figs, from whose branches hang long-whiskered aerial roots. The silence is broken only momentarily by the swish of a hornbill's wings and the rustling of smaller birds, unseen in the undergrowth.

This peaceful clearing is sacred to the local people; it is revered and protected by custom and used for ceremonies and burials. Known as the Sacred Grove, it is guarded by a council of elders, respected old men who alone decree how the surrounding forest can be used: which trees can be cut and why; which herbal and ritual plants can be gathered; how close cultivation can come to the forest's edge; and, most important, who may enter the forest and clearing.[1] The Sacred Grove, with its surrounding *Kaya* forest, is one of about thirty found in Kenya's coastal districts of Kilifi (north of Mombasa) and Kwale (south of Mombasa).[2] These small forest remnants are islands of biodiversity in a sea of agriculture, plantations, and sleek tourist developments.

It is a curious paradox, therefore, that historically the *Kayas* have been preserved not despite human settlement but because of it. Several centuries ago, people fleeing fierce northern tribes settled in the coastal forests, building small fortified villages that they called *Kayas* (homesteads). These people came to be known as the Mijikenda, the "people of the nine villages," who later split into the separate tribal groups found on the coast today: the Digo, Giriama, Rabai, Ribe, Kambe, Jibana, Chonyi, and Kauma peoples. The typical *Kaya* was a clearing in the forest, fortified with a palisade and entered by narrow paths. The Mijikenda cultivated crops and grazed livestock outside the forest but retreated into the village at night, closing the paths with doors, which were often elaborately carved. Each group had its sacred charm (*fingo*) buried in the center of the clearing.

Later, as the threat from the northern raiders diminished, the people left their hidden villages and built homes outside the forest. But the clearings, which had been used for prayers and sacrifices—the Sacred Groves—were still the focus of religion and ceremony, and selected elders lived out their old age in the *Kayas* and were buried in the forest.

But the old men are dying, as old men must do, and now the ancient traditions regarding the *Kayas* are dying too. Few young people mind the old customs; most of them have moved away in search of jobs or land to cultivate.

When the old men go, who will guard the *Kayas?* And why is it so important that these small forest remnants be saved?

East Africa's coastal forests once stretched for hundreds of kilometers from just south of Somalia's border with Kenya down into Tanzania. Botanically, they are called the Zanzibar-Inhambane regional mosaic,[3] a mixture of forest, woodland, and scrub that has prehistoric links to the great rain forests of central and western Africa. Home to more than half of Kenya's rare trees and shrubs, the coastal forests also harbor rare and endemic mammals and birds.[4] Some of these species, such as the delightful golden-rumped elephant shrew, the shy Ader's duiker, Clarke's weaver, and the Sokoke scops owl, are found nowhere else on earth.

Now, however, very little of this lowland forest remains. Some 42,000 hectares in the two southern coastal districts have been designated as forest reserves (a dubious honor and historically no guarantee of protection), but most have succumbed to demands for land and for firewood and building poles by Kenya's rapidly expanding population. Strip mining for limestone, lead, iron ore, and marble has also taken a toll. But perhaps the greatest threat in recent years has been the property boom, as developers eager to cash in on the thriving tourist industry have moved in to convert "useless bush" into ultramodern tourist hotels surrounded by lush landscaped gardens.[5]

Although *Kayas* are small (their combined area is probably around 2,000 hectares) and often isolated, their value in terms of biodiversity is out of proportion to their size. The elders' protection has been a fruitful legacy, for in these tiny forests are found species of trees that have disappeared or are in great danger elsewhere. As significant as their biological value is, though, it is the *Kayas'* cultural and historical value that may ultimately be the key to their survival.

In 1986, botanist Anne Robertson began a preliminary survey of the *Kayas,* funded by IUCN and WWF. Working in conjunction with the National Museums of Kenya and with a Kenyan volunteer, Quentin Luke, Robertson recognized that preservation of the *Kayas* was a conservation project in which the local community was a vital component. Working with the village elders, Robertson listed the known *Kayas* and described their conservation status. A gloomy picture emerged as the extent of threats to the *Kayas* was realized. At her urging, the survey was extended by WWF in 1988, and Luke joined Robertson as a full-time member of the team. Over the next few years, the two carried out extensive botanical surveys of Kenya's coastal forests, promoted conservation of endangered plant species and communities, developed education and training programs, and followed up the proposals of the original *Kaya* survey, which included securing conservation status for the *Kayas* and gazetting them as protected areas.

Safeguarding the *Kayas* became a matter of the utmost urgency. But how to go about it? National park status was considered, but this designation, which affords strict protection to both flora and fauna, would have denied the Mijikenda peoples access to their sacred groves. Another option was to have the *Kayas* declared forest reserves.[6]

The forest departments of African countries are, like most other government institutions, underfunded and overstretched. The idea that the only good forest is a forest that produces timber (the faster growing, the better) is a seemingly incurable colonial hangover. In this, Kenya's Forest Department has been no exception, although attitudes are changing with a new generation of foresters, who recognize the value and significance of indigenous species. Moreover, the Forest Department has also lacked the resources (money, equipment, and trained ecologists) to enforce protection of either trees or fauna in the forest reserves.

Well aware of the Forest Department's shortcomings and fearful that their rights to use the *Kayas* would be denied, the elders met the suggestion that their forests be designated as forest reserves with less than enthusiasm. Despite the old men's active opposition, in 1988 the district councils decided to designate the *Kayas* in Kilifi District as forest reserves.

In Kwale, however, wiser counsel has prevailed. At the urging of Robertson and Luke, and with the support not only of the elders but also of Kenya's Parliament, most of the *Kayas* have been declared national monuments under the Antiques and Monuments Act.[7] They would thus come under the care of the National Museums of Kenya, which has expertise not only in ecology and conservation but also in the preservation of Kenya's cultural heritage. A special unit, the Coastal Forest

Conservation Unit, funded by WWF, has been set up at the museum, with Quentin Luke at the helm. The unit will care for the *Kayas* that have been gazetted.

Help has come for the *Kayas,* and not a moment too soon. But how effective will the national monument status be? Within a few months of being gazetted, part of the Sacred Grove and *Kaya* on Chale Island was taken over by a foreign property developer in a dubious deal with local officials and land speculators.[8] Within weeks, much of the bush had been cleared and a hotel had been hastily erected. The elders and the National Museums of Kenya are fighting for this land allocation to be revoked, and their cause has been taken up by the local press. One of Kenya's leading weekly newspapers, the *Weekly Review,* reported the anguish of elders Hamidi Mwakirenje, Abdalla Ali Mnyenze, and Said Hemed Mwarandami. "The spirits of our ancestors have warned us of calamity should our sacred groves be destroyed," they said. "Already, drought has come to our land, and strange portents such as baboons eating goats and monkeys eating eggs have been witnessed by us. We are appealing to President Moi to help us regain our land."[9]

The Chale Island case will be the acid test of the strength of the *Kayas'* shield. Perhaps heads will roll. At the very least, the *Kayas* have been brought to the nation's attention, and their conservation is now very much supported not only by the public but also by some prominent politicians. It must be some comfort to the old men of the forests that perhaps, after all, their beloved Sacred Groves may survive.

JEFFREY A. MCNEELY, *Secretary-General,*
Fourth World Congress on National Parks and Protected Areas

AFTERWORD

People and Protected Areas: Partners in Prosperity[1]

A small sign nestled among the pines by the side of a road in central Bhutan quotes the Lord Buddha: "The forest makes no demands for its sustenance and extends protection to all beings, offering shade even to the axe man who destroys it."

This quotation encapsulates the relationship between people and nature. Most people—especially those who live closest to nature—well appreciate the values of the forests, savannahs, coral reefs, wildlife, and soils that support human society in a difficult world. But at the same time, people are often tempted to try to wrest more from the environment than can be sustained.

When I was working in the Himalayas back in the early 1970s, I saw this process firsthand. Wood is required for house building and fuel is needed for cooking and heating, but forests are also needed to protect villages from avalanches and landslides. Most mountain peoples have responded to this dilemma by developing cultural means of conserving the forests and preventing individual desires from undermining the interests and well-being of the larger community. Mingma Norbu Sherpa describes in part one of this book how the custom of Nepal's *shingi nawas*, or forest guards, functioned in the past, how the forest guards' function was replaced by a new Forestry Department and unenforceable regulations, and how the Sherpas' traditional system is now being rekindled to replace the ineffective controls imposed by central government.

Variations of this story can be told for many parts of the world. For most of human history, the natural world has been protected from the most disruptive human influences by relatively humble technology; cultural and ecological factors, such as taboos preventing overexploitation; tribal warfare, which kept wide areas as wilderness "buffer zones" between groups; landownership by ancestors or lineages rather than by individuals; and many other community-based resource management systems.

But in the past few generations, a fundamental change has occurred. The world's collection of highly diverse adaptations to local environmental conditions has been replaced by a world culture characterized by very high levels of material consumption. Economic growth based on conversion of fossil fuels to energy, greatly expanded international trade, and improved public health measures have spurred such a rapid expansion of human numbers that new approaches to resource management have been required. These powerful incentives to produce more goods have overwhelmed the conservation measures of local communities, bringing overexploitation and poverty to many rural communities and great wealth to cities and certain individuals.

Overexploitation is to be expected in times of very rapid cultural change, as traditional controls break down and people learn to exploit resources in new ways. Technological innovations, such as plantation agriculture, industrial logging, and tourism, tend to favor overexploitation of biological resources and weakening of traditional approaches to conservation, especially when a technologically superior group moves into a region occupied by groups with simpler technology. Today, technology enables the dominant society to harvest resources from alternative locations as local resources are exhausted. The market-driven economy derives no particular advantage from adopting the traditions of sustainable, conservative use that may have characterized the groups it has overwhelmed, earning most of the cash benefits of the forest but paying few of the long-term environmental costs. These costs remain with the local people, who must live with the consequences of the resource management decisions imposed on them from outside.

Schools, improved medical care, transportation, radio and television, a common language, hydroelectricity, and other influences are often welcomed by rural and indigenous peoples. Such influences have enabled even the most remote areas to become part of the nation both economically and ecologically. What were once locally self-sufficient and sustainable human systems have become part of much larger national and global systems, whose higher productivity is both welcome and undeniable but whose long-term sustainability is far from proven. Further, these influences are also encouraging land use practices that are unsustainable, especially deforestation and use of unsuitable land for agriculture.

The mid–twentieth century period of nation building necessarily involved strengthening of central governments and rapid exploitation of resources to fuel development. But in the late twentieth century, the even more challenging task of building ecologically and economically viable nations will require more sensitive and productive relations with local peoples and local ecosystems. The need now is for reestablishing cultural means of controlling overexploitation of forests, savannahs, land, and wildlife. Based on ecological, political, and economic reality, today's conservation measures must be part of the cultural fabric if they are to make their necessary contribution to human welfare.

The loss of traditional knowledge about resource use is one of the central problems of our times, and it may be that protected areas can play a useful role in helping to revive, renew, and reinterpret these traditional approaches to make them adaptive to modern conditions. This book contains a number of examples of how this challenge is being addressed in various parts of the world.

Emerging from Western history and experience in temperate zones, the belief in an untouched and untouchable wilderness has been one of the foundations of the protected area movement. But this view of nature was based on ignorance of the historical relationship between people and their habitat and of the role people play in maintaining biodiversity in forests and savannahs.

For recent research is finding that virtually all terrestrial habitats have been substantially altered by people. In tropical Asia, for example, studies have shown that the great majority of the mature forests are not virgin forests in the proper sense but merely old forests that have reached a fairly stable equilibrium of ecological succession after some early clearing. Kakadu and Uluru in Australia, Yellowstone burial sites nearly 1,000 years old in the United States, and the Lost City of the Sierra Nevada in northern Colombia are examples cited in this book that demonstrate substantial past human activity in what are now national parks.

In Africa, the great, game-filled savannahs are maintained by the human action of fire. Even in the wetter parts of Africa, forest composition and structure have been greatly influenced, even in apparently remote areas, by past human settlements, collection of forest products, and selection of species of particular interest to people. Thus, so-called pristine forests in most of Africa are, in fact, forests that have previously undergone significant modification.

In North America, humans have influenced the environment from the time they first moved into the continent some 12,000 years ago. Pre-Columbian human settlement modified forest extent and composition, expanded grasslands, and rearranged the local landscape through countless artificial earthworks. Agricultural fields, towns, roads, and trails were common, having local impacts on soil, climate, hydrology, and wildlife. In tropical America, many of the tree species now dominant in the mature vegetation were and still are the same species protected, spared, or planted in the land cleared for crops as part of the practice of shifting cultivation. At the time of the voyage of Christopher Columbus, the great "pristine" forests of Amazonia supported a human population of some 8.6 million people, and archaeologists are now finding that virtually all of Amazonia was under human occupation at some point during the past 6,000 years or so.

In short, the biodiversity our world enjoys today is the result of complex historical interactions among physical, biological, and social forces over time. Virtually all of our planet's forests and grasslands have been affected by the cultural patterns of human use, and the resulting landscape is an ever-changing mosaic of managed and unmanaged patches of habitat, whose diversity is reflected in their size, shape, and arrangement. When society decides that any particular ecological snapshot is worthy of special protection, it obviously must consider the needs and desires of the people who helped mold the landscape and who will need to adapt to its changes.

Partnership between local human communities and protected area management agencies can benefit both protected areas and biodiversity, but this partnership faces formidable challenges. Some protected area staff members may believe that the cooperative approach could ultimately reduce the quality of the protected area and that strong legislation supported by vigorous law enforcement is the best option for long-term conservation. And indeed, experience has shown that local people often are as likely as anyone else to misuse privileges under cooperative management, especially when they have lost resource-use rights or when the structure of privilege is imposed on them from the outside. Local traditions and laws, such as those enforced by the *shingi nawas* in Nepal or the Kogi *Mamas* of Colombia, are usually the most effective in controlling use or access to protected areas. A cooperative approach between people and protected areas is clearly the most appropriate approach for the late twentieth century and beyond.

Protected area managers have needed to change their perceptions during this process of adapting to change. In the early days, management of protected areas was essentially a policing task, and local people were seen as a management problem. Then protected area managers recognized how important science was to their profession, and nature was often seen as the main management challenge. But today, the park guard and the park naturalist are being joined by the park community affairs officer, and earning the support of local people is being seen as a challenging management opportunity.

Despite the many good examples of community involvement cited in this book, far more needs to be done to build support from local communities for protected areas. This will require a combination of incentives and disincentives, economic benefits and law enforcement, education and awareness, employment in the protected area and employment opportunities outside, and enhanced land tenure and control of new immigration (especially if the buffer zones around protected areas are targeted for special development assistance). The key is to find a balance among the competing demands, and this will usually require a site-specific solution.

Governments have lacked the political will to mobilize the resources—human, financial, cultural, and moral—to ensure integration of ecological principles with economic development. Based on the deliberations at the Fourth World Congress on National Parks and Protected Areas and the work described in this book, I propose ten principles that could help demonstrate that integrating conservation with development of local human communities is both relatively painless and likely to lead to enhanced benefits to the community, the nation, and the world.

I. BUILD ON THE FOUNDATIONS OF THE LOCAL CULTURE

Very often, cultural elements are already available for contributing to conservation. Any laws or regulations emanating from central governments should be adapted to take advantage of local predispositions. Cultural diversity parallels ecological diversity, and local traditional adaptations are often the most environmentally sound. Research on traditional means of resource management needs to be carried out as a very high priority, before these cultural elements are washed away with the tide of modernism. Traditional means of resource management also need to be put into forms that would be useful to development planners and to protected area managers; workshops should be held to train resource managers to be sensitive to cultural means of conservation and to collaborate productively with local people.

Where such practices have died out, special efforts may be required to reintroduce them.

2. GIVE RESPONSIBILITY TO LOCAL PEOPLE

Long-term cultural stability in the past has shown that local people are fully able and competent to enforce regulations for the benefit of their community. Local development priorities therefore should be debated in village and district councils, and development projects should be at least partially funded locally in order to build local commitment. In some areas, it would be possible to establish management units under the control of local village councils, and local people should serve on the advisory board of each protected area. A key point is that local responsibility should follow local institutional patterns, and it is usually better to strengthen local institutions than to create new ones. The ultimate goal should be comanagement, which involves commitment and involvement of the local people in all aspects of management. One important way to build confidence is through participatory management, which enables local people to help generate the information on status and trends in resource use that will guide management.

3. CONSIDER RETURNING OWNERSHIP OF AT LEAST SOME PROTECTED AREAS TO INDIGENOUS PEOPLE

In cases in which indigenous cultures have long-established landownership rights in areas of outstanding national or even international importance, consideration should be given to recognizing their ownership of these lands legally and formally, with the government then leasing back the lands for use as national parks that enable local people to have an appropriate voice in how the area is managed. Such lease-back arrangements are proving very successful in Australia, New Zealand, and Canada, meeting the needs of all parties. Where it is not feasible to return ownership to local people, protected area managers can at least recognize traditional rights over specific resources within the protected area, including water, medicinal plants, and sacred sites.

4. HIRE LOCAL PEOPLE

Special efforts should be made to hire local people for work in protected areas in their region. Employment both gives local people a stake in the success of the protected area and enables them to make a unique contribution to the way in which the area is managed. It may be possible to create a new post of "community rangers," selected by local communities and serving as extension officers for the protected area. These community rangers could help protect cultural sites, rehabilitate degraded areas, and manage wildlife.

5. LINK GOVERNMENT DEVELOPMENT PROGRAMS WITH PROTECTED AREAS

Each nation should review its protected area policies and legislation to ensure that human concerns are being appropriately addressed and that conservation is well integrated into other development concerns. National conservation strategies, national biodiversity strategies, and other such instruments can be effective means of coming to grips with the problems of integrating people, conservation, and development. First priority for providing schools, health centers, family planning programs, agricultural development, small hydroelectric facilities, improved communications, and other desired developments should go to the villages closest to protected areas. Care should be taken to ensure that the local villagers know that these benefits are flowing to them because of their proximity to a protected area and that continuation of the benefits depends on their ongoing support. Further, it is unlikely that protected areas will ever be able to conserve biodiversity if they are surrounded by degraded habitats that limit gene flow, alter nutrient and water cycles, and produce regional and global climate change, so local people need to be given incentives to help them manage areas outside protected areas in ways that are consistent with national conservation objectives.

6. GIVE PRIORITY TO SMALL-SCALE LOCAL DEVELOPMENT

Mega-projects, such as major dams, may be attractive to development agencies, but history has shown that they seldom bring widely disbursed and sustainable benefits. It is usually far better to concentrate at the village level, with customized development projects that can enhance productivity of the best soils and provide local sources of energy; such development can be coupled with stronger regulations to reduce human impact on important habitats. If basic changes in the pattern of living of traditional subsistence farming and grazing communities are to be facilitated, attractive and meaningful economic alternatives—such as carefully planned and controlled tourism—must be made available.

7. INVOLVE LOCAL PEOPLE IN PREPARING MANAGEMENT PLANS

Each protected area should have a management plan, and the plan is most likely to be effective if it is developed in close collaboration with the local people. The preparation of management plans need not be a specialized task requiring major outside expertise. Workshops should be held in and around the protected area concerned as a means of enabling local people to contribute their views; such workshops need to be preceded by a patient period of participatory research and problem analysis with a wide range of individuals in the community. Even when strong management action is required, many levels of protection and permissible human use are possible, and the full range of these must be discussed in an open manner. The level of protection should be finely tuned to the agreed management objectives, which should be discussed and agreed on with local people.

8. HAVE THE COURAGE TO ENFORCE RESTRICTIONS

Once it has been agreed on with the local people that certain restrictions (which often may be those that existed when the local culture was still intact) are desirable and necessary, the regulations need to be strictly and equitably enforced. No apologies are needed for any restrictions that may be necessary; people have always had to live with restrictions on their behavior, and letting people destroy a protected forest because "they have always been able to cut trees" is destructive to the community at large. Enforcement should, whenever possible, be administered by local people, and at least a portion of any fines should go back to the village.

9. BUILD CONSERVATION INTO THE EVOLVING NEW NATIONAL CULTURES

As nations are built, literacy becomes widespread, mass media become more effective, and new cultures are formed, conservation needs to become part of every possible section of the national development process and thereby become part of the new national culture rather than just the discrete responsibility of a national parks department. At the same time, schools near protected areas must have a sufficiently flexible curriculum to enable them to incorporate material that is relevant to the local resources. As modern nations become increasingly urbanized, new efforts are required to promote awareness of the importance of cultural diversity and the adaptiveness of local cultures to local environmental conditions. This awareness may well be a prerequisite for mobilizing the resources needed to address the environmental problems of the rural areas with the greatest biodiversity. It will also require development and packaging of sound and convincing arguments to demonstrate that protection of critical natural areas helps support food production outside these areas, through such means as watershed protection, soil formation, microclimate amelioration, conservation of genetic resources, harvesting of minor forest products, and practice of animal husbandry on marginal lands.

10. SUPPORT DIVERSITY AS A VALUE

People have long recognized that diversity is the key to their survival, using a wide range of means to wrest a living from a reluctant environment. Mixed systems, transhumance, terraces, agroforestry, local varieties, hunting and fishing, and the forestry-agriculture-wilderness interface are essential to most cultures. This diversity needs to be maintained as a matter of highest importance. What works in one place will not necessarily work in the next valley, and small countries have different imperatives from large countries. What is required is a series of local adaptations based on local cultural diversity, not a "universal elixir" to solve all conservation problems.

The great naturalist George B. Schaller once pointed out that protected areas are necessary because "some day man may want to rebuild what he has squandered, and from such samples of original habitat he can then not only draw genetic stock but also learn how the ecological pieces have adjusted to create a harmonious system."

Perhaps more important, protected areas must continue to make their significant contributions to regional land use. A mosaic of logged and mature forest, as part of an integrated system of land use ranging from strict protection to systematic exploitation, would appear to be the best available compromise between resource exploitation and conservation of the maximum possible biological and cultural diversity. We must avoid falling into the trap of seeing nature only as a collection of isolated protected areas. Rather, society needs to learn a very important lesson from indigenous peoples: humans are part of nature. This lesson implies that we must address past violations and restore the viability and the functioning of the natural landscapes. If we are successful in rebuilding (and improving) the relationship between people and the rest of nature, we may look back on the twentieth century as a time when national parks and other protected areas were the key to enabling nature's vitality to survive the grossest excesses of a consumer-oriented society, and enabling people to live again as a balanced part of nature.

NOTES

INTRODUCTION

1. David Maybury-Lewis, *Millennium: Tribal Wisdom and the Modern World* (London: Viking Penguin, 1992).
2. Claude Martin, *The Rainforests of West Africa* (Basel, Switzerland: Birkhäuser, 1991).
3. Julian Burger, *Gaia Atlas of First Peoples: The Future for the Indigenous World* (London: Gaia Books, 1990).
4. Ian Portman, *Luxor: A Guide to the Temples and Tombs of Ancient Thebes* (Cairo: The American University in Cairo Press, 1989).
5. Burger, *Gaia Atlas of First Peoples,* p. 20.
6. Elizabeth Kemf, personal communication, 1992.
7. Martin, *Rainforests of West Africa.*
8. Debra Jopson, "Land Feud," *Far East Economic Review* (Hong Kong), February 1993.

Part One

IN SEARCH OF A HOME

1. Leigh Patrick Fermor, *Roumeli: Travels in Northern Greece* (London: John Murray, 1966).
2. David Harmon, "Indicators of the World's Cultural Diversity" (paper presented at the Fourth World Congress on National Parks and Protected Areas, Caracas, Venezuela, February 10–21, 1992).
3. "Indigenous People: A New Partnership International Year 1993" (New York: United Nations, Department of Information, 1992).
4. Alan Thein Durning, "Guardians of the Land: Indigenous Peoples and the Health of the Earth," Worldwatch Paper no. 112 (Washington, DC: Worldwatch Institute, December 1992).
5. Harmon, "Indicators of Cultural Diversity."
6. Durning, "Guardians of the Land."
7. Jeffrey McNeely, "The Contributions of Protected Areas to Sustaining Society" (paper

presented at the Fourth World Congress on National Parks and Protected Areas, Caracas, Venezuela, February 10–21, 1992).

8. Robert Scharff, *Yellowstone and Grand Teton National Parks* (New York: David McKay, 1966), pp. 1–8.

9. Aubrey L. Haines, *Yellowstone National Park: Its Exploration and Establishment* (Washington, DC: U.S. Department of the Interior, National Park Service, 1974), pp. 7, 41.

10. David Foster, in *Applying the Yellowstone Model in America's Backyard: Alaska, Aboriginal Involvement in Parks and Protected Areas,* edited by Jim Birckhead, Terry deLacey, and LauraJane Smith (Canberra, Australia: Panther, 1992), p. 364.

11. Ibid., p. 363.

12. Stephen Amend and Thora Amend, "Human Occupation in the National Parks of South America: A Fundamental Problem," *Parks* (published by IUCN, Gland, Switzerland), January 1992, pp. 4–8.

13. Ibid.

14. Ibid.

15. J. D. Waugh and R. Perez Gil, *Regional Review, North America* (Gland, Switzerland: IUCN, 1992), p. 12.7.

16. John MacKinnon, Kathy MacKinnon, Graham Child, and Jim Thorsell, *Managing Protected Areas in the Tropics* (Gland, Switzerland, and Cambridge, England: IUCN and United Nations Environment Program, 1986), p. 1.

17. UNESCO-UNEP, *Conservation, Science and Society,* vol. 1 (Paris: UNESCO, 1984), p. I.

18. *1990 United Nations List of National Parks and Protected Areas* (Gland, Switzerland, and Cambridge, England: IUCN and United Nations Environment Program), pp. 10–14.

19. Ibid.

20. Jim Thorsell, personal communication.

FISHERMEN OF THE DESERT

1. Elizabeth Kemf, "Dolphins and Fishermen Cooperate to Hunt Food," *WWF News* (Lausanne, Switzerland), no. 53 (May–June 1988).

2. Pierre Campredon, Luc Hoffmann, and Hadya Kane, "Why Natural Resources Conservation Requires the Development of Fishermen's Communities" (paper presented at the Fourth World Congress on National Parks and Protected Areas, Caracas, Venezuela, February 10–21, 1992).

3. Kemf, "Dolphins and Fishermen Cooperate to Hunt Food."

4. A. R. G. Price, A. Jeudy de Grissac, and R. F. G. Ormond, "Coastal Assessment of the Parc National du Banc d'Arguin, Mauritania: Understanding Resources, Exploitation

Patterns and Management Needs," *Marine Conservation and Development Report* (Gland, Switzerland: IUCN, 1992).

5. "Le Parc National du Banc d'Arguin: Milieu vivant" (Banc d'Arguin National Park: A Haven for Life) (Gland, Switzerland: Fondation Internationale du Banc d'Arguin, 1988).

6. Campredon, Hoffman, and Kane, "Natural Resources Conservation."

7. Ibid.

8. Ibid.

VIETNAM'S GUARDIANS OF THE ISLANDS

1. Vo Quy, "Luan Chung Khoa Ky Thuat, Ve Voun Quoc Gia Con Dao" (Hanoi: Hanoi University, Center for Natural Resource Management and Environmental Studies, 1987) (in Vietnamese only).

2. Elizabeth Kemf, pp. 31–33 of a chapter from *Into the Blue,* an anthology of dolphin myths, legends, and biology edited by Virginia McKenna (London: Aquarian Press, 1992).

GIFTS FROM THE NORTH WIND

1. "James Bay and Northern Quebec Agreement," government of Quebec, Canada, 1976.

2. Ibid.

3. Cree Trappers Association, Val d'Or, Quebec, Canada, personal communication.

4. Philip Rhaphals, *New Scientist* (London), February 15, 1992, p. 50.

5. Mercédès Lee, "Brief Political Update of James Bay" (focusing south of the border) (New York: National Audubon Society, July 12, 1992).

6. Rhaphals, *New Scientist,* p. 50.

7. Lee, "Brief Political Update."

GRASS ROOTS IN A HIMALAYAN KINGDOM

1. This chapter is based on a joint paper titled "Indigenous Peoples and Protected Area Management: New Approaches to Conservation in Highland Nepal," presented by Dr. Stan Stevens and Mingma Norbu Sherpa at IUCN's Fourth World Congress on National Parks and Protected Areas, held in Caracas, Venezuela, in 1992.

KUNA YALA

1. This chapter is based on a paper presented by Dr. Guillermo Archibold at the Fourth World Congress on National Parks and Protected Areas, held in Caracas, Venezuela,

in 1992, titled "Pemasky: Espíritu del Pueblo Kuna," and on his chapter in *Toward a Green Central America: Integrating Conservation and Development,* edited by Valerie Barzetti and Yanina Rovinski and published by Kumarian Press in cooperation with the Panos Institute, 1992 (London).

Part Two

BOUNDARIES AND BLOODLINES

1. James Morrison, "Protected Areas and Aboriginal Interests in Canada," background paper prepared for WWF-Canada, Toronto, 1993.
2. Press release, "Indian and Northern Affairs," Ottawa, Canada, November 12, 1992.
3. Morrison, "Protected Areas."

CAMPFIRE IN ZIMBABWE

1. This chapter is based partially on a booklet titled "People, Wildlife, and Natural Resources: The CAMPFIRE Approach to Rural Development in Zimbabwe," edited by Dick Pitman for the Zimbabwe Trust, Harare, Zimbabwe, July 1990.
2. Environmental Consultants Ltd., *People, Wildlife, and Natural Resources—the CAMPFIRE Approach to Rural Development in Zimbabwe* (Harare, Zimbabwe: Conlon, 1990).
3. The Zimbabwe Trust, Wildlife, *Relic of the Past, or Resource of the Future?* (Harare, Zimbabwe: Quote, 1992), p. 48.
4. Center for Applied Social Sciences, World Wide Fund For Nature, and Zimtrust Coordinating Committee, *Wildlife Utilization in Zimbabwe's Communal Lands: Collaborative Programme Activities* (Harare, Zimbabwe: Center for Applied Social Sciences, World Wide Fund For Nature, and Zimtrust Coordinating Committee, June 1989), p. 281.
5. D. J. Jansen, "Sustainable Wildlife Utilization in the Zambezi Valley of Zimbabwe: Economic, Ecological and Political Tradeoffs," Multispecies Animal Production Systems Project Paper no. 10 (Harare, Zimbabwe: World Wide Fund For Nature, 1990).
6. *CAMPFIRE Newsletter* (Harare, Zimbabwe), no. 1 (March 1992).

PARADISE GAINED OR LOST?

1. William J. Smole, "Yanoama Horticulture in the Parima Highlands of Venezuela and Brazil," *Advances in Economic Botany* (published by The New York Botanical Garden) 7 (1989): 115–128.
2. David G. Campbell and H. David Hammond, eds., "Floristic Inventory of Tropical

Countries: The Status of Plant Systematics, Collections, and Vegetation, plus Recommendations for the Future" (New York: The New York Botanical Garden, 1988).

3. N. J. Collar and P. Andrew, "Birds to Watch: The ICBP World Checklist of Threatened Birds," ICBP Technical Publication no. 8 (Cambridge, England: International Council for Bird Preservation, 1988).

BUTTERFLY RANCHING

1. I. Craven and Y. de Fretes, "Arfak Mountains Nature Conservation Area Irian Jaya Management Plan 1988–92," WWF project no. 3770, Implementation of Conservation in Irian Jaya, Indonesia (Gland, Switzerland: WWF International, 1987).

2. Ibid.

3. Ibid.

4. Ibid.

5. Ibid.

6. Ian Craven, "A Management Prescription for the Arfak Mountains Strict Nature Reserve 1991–92," WWF project no. 3770, Implementation of Conservation in Irian Jaya, Indonesia (Gland, Switzerland: WWF International, 1991).

7. Malcolm Stark, "Semi-annual Progress Report," WWF project no. 3770, Implementation of Conservation in Irian Jaya, Indonesia (Gland, Switzerland: WWF International, July–December 1991).

8. Craven and de Fretes, "Arfak Mountains Nature Conservation Area."

9. Ibid.

10. D. Womsiwor, D. Neville, and S. Mandosir, "Pengelolaan Kawasan Penyangga Pada Cagar Alam Pegunungan Arfak, Manokwari, Irian Jaya," dalam *Prosiding Seminar Nasional Pengelolaan Kawasan Panyangga* (Irian Jaya, Indonesia: Kanwil Kehutanan Irian Jaya/WWF, October 1990).

11. Craven and de Fretes, "Arfak Mountains Nature Conservation Area."

12. Ibid.

13. Ibid.

14. Ibid.

15. I. Craven, "An Assessment of Implementation of the Arfak Mountains Strict Nature Reserve," WWF project no. 3770, Implementation of Conservation in Irian Jaya, Indonesia (Gland, Switzerland: WWF International, 1990); I. Craven, M. Purba, P. Djoko Setiono, D. Womsiwor, and S. Thamrin, "Community Involvement in Protected Area Establishment and Management in Irian Jaya" (paper presented at the Fourth World Congress on National Parks and Protected Areas, Caracas, Venezuela, February 10–21, 1992).

16. Ibid.

17. Stark, "Semi-annual Progress Report."

18. Craven and de Fretes, "Arfak Mountains Nature Conservation Area."

19. Convention on the International Trade in Endangered Species of Wild Fauna and Flora.

20. Stark, "Semi-annual Progress Report."

Part Three

NATURE IN THE CROSSFIRE

1. For a more detailed coverage of the subject, the reader may want to refer to the conflict management manual for park managers being developed jointly by IUCN and the Keystone Center.

ALUNA: THE PLACE WHERE THE MOTHER WAS BORN

1. "Estrategia para la conservación de los bosques tropicales de la Sierra Nevada de Santa Marta" (Santa Marta, Colombia: IUCN and Fundación Pro–Sierra Nevada de Santa Marta, April 1991).

2. "Indigenous Concept About Territory for the National Government," unpublished paper by the Committee on Territorial Reorganization and the Indigenous Communities, Sierra Nevada de Santa Marta, April 13, 1992.

3. "Protected Area Data Sheet" (unpublished), World Conservation Monitoring Center (WCMC), Cambridge, England, 1992.

4. Juanita Londono, "Componente: Cuenca media del Río Frío vivienda campesina y construcción alternativa" (proyecto de investigación sobre tecnología de contención, vivienda campesina e impacto en el entorno), unpublished paper by the Fundación Pro La Sierra Nevada Instituto Nacional de Vivienda de Interés Social y Reforma Urbana (INURBE), Santa Marta, Colombia, 1992.

DANCE OF A THOUSAND CRANES

1. Elizabeth Kemf, "Dance of a Thousand Cranes," *New Scientist* (London), October 8, 1988.

2. *The Directory of Asian Wetlands,* a database on the wetlands of twenty-four countries, was developed under the sponsorship of the International Union for Conservation of Nature and Natural Resources (IUCN), the International Council for Bird Preservation (ICBP), and the International Waterfowl and Wetlands Research Bureau (IWRB), with funding from WWF, the World Wide Fund For Nature.

3. Kemf, "Dance of a Thousand Cranes."

4. Jeb Barzen, personal communication, 1991.

5. Jeb Barzen, "Restoration Mixes Science, People and Luck in Vietnam," *ICF Bugle* (Baraboo, Wisconsin), May 1991.

6. Barzen, "Restoration Mixes Science, People and Luck."

7. Le Dien Duc, "Wise Use of Wetlands in Vietnam," unpublished paper (Hanoi: University of Hanoi, Center for Natural Resource Management and Environmental Studies, 1992).

8. George Archibald, "A Bird's-Eye View of Cambodia," *ICF Bugle* (Baraboo, Wisconsin), May 1992.

THE WINDS OF CHANGE

1. Quoted from *Karen: At One with the Forest,* a multivision slide production (Bangkok: Wildlife Fund Thailand, 1992).

2. Ketty Faichampa, "At the Edge of the Forest: Local Communities Around Huay Kha Khaeng Wildlife Sanctuary," unpublished paper, Yale University, School of Forestry and Environmental Studies, 1989.

3. "Protected Area Data Sheet" (unpublished), World Conservation Monitoring Center (WCMC), Cambridge, England, 1992.

4. Elizabeth Kemf, "Dam Controversy Growing in Thailand," *WWF News,* no. 46 (1987).

5. "Protected Area Data Sheet."

6. Faichampa, "At the Edge of the Forest."

7. David Hulse, personal communication with Karen village elder.

CONFLICT IN CAMEROON

1. This chapter is based on a study financed by the Institute of Animal Research (IRZ) in Cameroon. Special thanks to the technicians of the IRZ's Wildlife Program, who helped in collecting the information.

PEOPLE IN BLUE

1. S. Mbanefo, *WWF News,* no. 77 (June 1992).

2. J. Newby, "Parks for People—A Case Study from the Aïr Mountains of Niger," *Oryx* (Oxford, England) 26 (1), 19–28 (1992).

3. H. Lhote, *La Chasse chez les Touaregs* (Paris: Amiot-Dumont, 1951).

4. J. Newby, "Millions of Birds Find Refuge in Niger," *WWF News,* no. 28 (March–April 1984).

5. J. Newby, "The Sahel Lives," *WWF News,* no. 37 (September–October 1985).

TOURISM VERSUS TURTLES

1. D. Margaritoulis, D. Dimopoulos, and E. Kornaraki, "The Loggerhead Sea Turtle *Caretta caretta* on Zakynthos: An Update of Monitoring and Conservation Work" (Gland, Switzerland: WWF International, February 1992).

2. Dimitrios Dimopoulos, personal communication.

3. D. Dimopoulos, "A Short Report on Zakynthos," unpublished report, Sea Turtle Protection Society of Greece, Athens, Greece, 1992.

4. Margaritoulis, Dimopoulos, and Kornaraki, "Loggerhead Sea Turtle."

5. Dimopoulos, "Short Report on Zakynthos."

6. Bellerive Foundation, Hellenic Society for the Study and Protection of the Monk Seal (HSSPMS), and Seal Rehabilitation and Research Center (SRRC), "The Mediterranean Monk Seal: Conservation in Action," Bellerive Foundation project pack (Geneva, Switzerland: Bellerive Foundation, 1992).

7. J. Jacobs and A. Panou, "Project 3871: Monk Seal Conservation in the Eastern Mediterranean," WWF project progress report (Munich: University of Munich, Institute of Zoology, October 1992).

8. Ada Vlachoutsikou and M. Scoullous, "Monk Seal Conservation in the Eastern Mediterranean," WWF project no. 3871, unpublished report, WWF International, Gland, Switzerland, November 1992.

9. Ibid.

10. Bellerive Foundation, HSSPMS, and SRRC, "Mediterranean Monk Seal."

11. Jacobs and Panou, "Project 3871."

12. Margaritoulis, Dimopoulos, and Kornaraki, "Loggerhead Sea Turtle."

Part Four

CREATIVE COMMUNITIES

1. Sally W. Weaver, in *Resident Peoples and National Parks,* edited by P. C. West and S. R. Breslin (Tucson: University of Arizona Press, 1991), p. 317.

2. Ibid.; "Principles of Joint Management Agreements: A Literature Review" (Prince George, British Columbia: Planning and Conservation Services, Northern British Columbia Region, August 1990).

THE GREEN ROOF OF CENTRAL EUROPE

1. Hillary French, "Green Revolutions: Environmental Reconstruction in Eastern Europe and the Soviet Union," Worldwatch Paper no. 99 (Washington, DC: Worldwatch Institute, November 1990).

2. "Ecological Bricks for Our Common House of Europe" is an initiative launched in 1990 by a consortium of Austrian, Hungarian, German, and Czechoslovak NGOs to protect the natural habitats along the former Iron Curtain. As of 1993, some 135 NGOs had declared their support for this initiative. The coordinating office is at WWF-Austria, Ottakringerstrasse 114-116 A, Vienna, Austria.

3. Alexander Zinke, "Europas Wilder Osten," *Panda Magazin* (WWF-Switzerland, Zurich, Switzerland) 24(2) (June 1991).

4. Elizabeth Kemf, "The Bohemians and Their Forests." *WWF News* (May–June 1992).

5. French, "Green Revolutions."

6. Goetz Schuerholz, "Management Plan for Sumava Biosphere Reserve," WWF project no. 4575, unpublished report, WWF International, Gland, Switzerland, July 1991.

SIBERIA'S KEEPERS OF THE TUNDRA

1. M. Davydona and V. Koshevoi, *Nature Reserves in the USSR* (Moscow: Progress, 1989); A. Knystautas, *Naturparadies USSR* (Munchen, Germany: Suddeutscher Verlag, 1987).

2. Y. V. Labutin et al., *Flora and Fauna* (Siberia, USSR: Yakutskian Branch of Academy of Science, Institute of Biology, 1985).

KAN PWOTEKTÈ ANIVIWONMAN HAITI—WE CAN PROTECT THE ENVIRONMENT OF HAITI

1. This common Creole saying is used by Haitians to express the interconnectedness of life.

2. Francisco di Blasi, "What Hope for Haiti?," *People and the Planet* 1 (4) (1992).

3. Evelyn Wilcox, "Feasibility of Establishing a Marine Park at Les Arcadins, Haiti," unpublished report prepared for the United States Agency for International Development, Washington, DC, 1986.

4. Evelyn Wilcox et al., "Action Plan: Les Arcadins National Marine Park, Haiti" (Washington, DC: United States Agency for International Development and World Wildlife Fund, 1989).

SACRED FORESTS AND THE ELDERS

1. S. A. Robertson, "NMK and WWF-I Working with the Elders to Protect the Sacred *Kaya* Forests of Coastal Kenya," unpublished report, WWF International, Gland, Switzerland, 1992.

2. S. A. Robertson, "The Status of *Kaya* Forests," in *Endangered Resources for Development,* vol. 1 (Nairobi, Kenya: National Environment Secretariat, 1984).

3. F. White, "The Vegetation of Africa: A Descriptive Memoir to Accompany the AET-FAT/UNESCO Vegetation Map of Africa" (Paris: UNESCO, 1983).

4. L. Brown, *East African Coasts and Reefs* (Nairobi, Kenya: East African Publishing House, 1974).

5. J. Schoorl and N. Visser, "Towards Sustainable Coastal Tourism: Environmental Impacts of Tourism on the Kenya Coast" (Nairobi, Kenya: Royal Netherlands Embassy, 1991).

6. Robertson, "Working with the Elders."

7. Ibid.

8. *Weekly Review* (Nairobi, Kenya), July 10, 1992.

9. Ibid.

AFTERWORD

1. My thanks to Elizabeth Kemf, David Sheppard, and Allen Putney for their helpful comments.

Categories and Management Objectives of Protected Areas

I. Strict nature reserve/scientific reserve · To protect nature and maintain natural processes in an undisturbed state in order to have ecologically representative examples of the natural environment available for scientific study, environmental monitoring, and education and for the maintenance of genetic resources in a dynamic and evolutionary state.

II. National park · To protect outstanding natural and scenic areas of national or international significance for scientific, educational, and recreational use. These are relatively large natural areas not materially altered by human activity where extractive resource uses are not allowed.

III. Natural monument/natural landmark · To protect and preserve nationally significant natural features because of their special interest or unique characteristics. These are relatively small areas focused on protection of specific features.

IV. Managed nature reserve/wildlife sanctuary · To ensure the natural conditions necessary to protect nationally significant species, groups of species, biotic communities, or physical features of the environment where these may require specific human manipulation for their perpetuation. Controlled harvesting of some resources can be permitted.

V. Protected landscape or seascape · To maintain nationally significant natural landscapes that are characteristic of the harmonious interaction of man and land while providing opportunities for public enjoyment through recreation and tourism within the normal life-style and economic activity of these areas. These are mixed cultural and natural landscapes of high scenic value where traditional land uses are maintained.

VI. Resource reserve · To protect the natural resources of the area for future use and prevent or contain development activities that could affect the resource, pending the establishment of objectives based upon appropriate knowledge and planning. This is a "holding" category, used until a permanent classification can be determined.

VII. Anthropological reserve/natural biotic area · To allow the way of life of societies living in harmony with the environment to continue undisturbed by modern technology. This category is appropriate where resource extraction by indigenous people is conducted in a traditional manner.

VIII. Multiple use management area/managed resource area · To provide for the sustained production of water, timber, wildlife, pasture, and tourism, with the conservation of nature primarily oriented to the support of the economic activities (although specific zones may also be designated within these areas to achieve specific conservation objectives).

Two additional categories encompass protected areas in the foregoing eight categories:

Biosphere reserve · To conserve for present and future use the diversity and integrity of biotic communities of plants and animals within natural ecosystems and to safeguard the genetic diversity of species on which their continuing evolution depends. These are internationally designated sites managed for research, education, and training.

World Heritage site · To protect the natural features for which the area is considered to be of outstanding universal significance. This is a select list of the world's unique natural and cultural sites nominated by countries that are parties to the World Heritage Convention.

EDITOR'S NOTE: This system of categories is currently under revision by the Commission on National Parks and Protected Areas (CNPPA); the revised categories will be published in 1993.

List of Acronyms

ACAP · Annapurna Conservation Area Project
ACYS · Association Communautaire de Yobe-Sangha
AEDP · Aboriginal Employment Development Policy
AKE · Association of Kuna Employees
ANPWS · Australian National Parks and Wildlife Service

CAMPFIRE · Communal Areas Management Plan for Indigenous Resources
CANARI · Caribbean Natural Resources Institute
CASS · Center for Applied Social Sciences
CATIE · Tropical Agronomic Center for Research and Education
CCC · Caribbean Conservation Corporation
CCPY · Committee for the Creation of the Yanomami Park
CNPPA · Commission on National Parks and Protected Areas
CRES · Center for Natural Resource Management and Environmental Studies

DNPWM · Department of National Parks and Wildlife Management
DOGIT · deed of grant in trust

EEC · European Economic Community
ESD · ecologically sustainable development

FIBA · Fondation Internationale du Banc d'Arguin
FUDENA · Fundación Para La Defensa De La Naturaleza

GIS · geographic information system
GTZ · Gessellschaft für Technische Zusammenarbeit

HIMAT · Colombian government agency for water management and land improvement

HSSPMS · Hellenic Society for the Study and Protection of the Monk Seal

HTA · Clyde River Hunters and Trappers Association

IAF · Inter-American Foundation

ICF · International Crane Foundation

IFTA · Insect Farming and Trading Agency

IGC · Inuvialuit Game Council

INDERENA · National Institute of Natural Resources and the Environment

IRC · Inuvialuit Regional Corporation

IRZ · Institute of Animal Research

IUCN · World Conservation Union (International Union for Conservation of Nature)

KSDA · Natural Resources Conservation Office

MASTS · Marine Conservation Strategy for Torres Strait

MGBDP · Malawi-German Beekeeping Development Project

N.T. · Australia's Northern Territory

NGOs · Nongovernmental organizations

NRMAs · Nature reserve management areas

PEMASKY · Management Project for the Forested Areas of Kuna Yala

PHPA · Directorate General of Forest Protection and Nature Conservation

SADA-AMAZONAS · Autonomous Service for the Development of the Federal Amazon Territory

SENA · National Training Service for Apprentices

SES · Foundation for Higher Education

SRRC · Seal Rehabilitation and Research Center

STPS · Sea Turtle Protection Society of Greece

TEAM · The Environmental Awareness Mobilization Project

UNDP · United Nations Development Program

UNEP · United Nations Environment Program

UNESCO · United Nations Educational, Scientific, and Cultural Organization

USAID · United States Agency for International Development

WFT · Wildlife Fund Thailand

WMAs · Wildlife management areas

WWF · World Wide Fund For Nature (in the United States and Canada, World Wildlife Fund)

YAPSEL · Yayasan Pembangunan Sosial Ekonomi dan Lingkungan (Social Economic Development and Environmental Foundation)

BIBLIOGRAPHY

Aleksandrova, V. D. *Vegetation of the Soviet Deserts*. Cambridge, England: Cambridge University Press, 1988.

Amend, Stephen, and Thora Amend. "Human Occupation in the National Parks of South America: A Fundamental Problem." *Parks* (published by IUCN, Gland, Switzerland), January 1992.

————, eds. *Espacios sin habitantes: Parques nacionales de América del Sur*. Gland, Switzerland: IUCN; Caracas, Venezuela: Editorial Nueva Sociedad, 1992.

Archibald, George. "A Bird's Eye View of Cambodia." *ICF Bugle* (Baraboo, Wisconsin), May 1992.

Barzen, Jeb. "Restoration Mixes Science, People and Luck in Vietnam." *ICF Bugle* (Baraboo, Wisconsin), May 1991.

Bellerive Foundation, Hellenic Society for the Study and Protection of the Monk Seal (HSSPMS), and Seal Rehabilitation and Research Center (SRRC). "The Mediterranean Monk Seal: Conservation in Action." Bellerive Foundation project pack. Geneva, Switzerland: Bellerive Foundation, 1992.

Blasi, Francisco di. "What Hope for Haiti?" *People and the Planet* (London) 1 (4) (1992).

Bodley, John H. *Victims of Progress*. Palo Alto, California: Mayfield, 1982.

Brown, L. *East African Coasts and Reefs*. Nairobi, Kenya: East African Publishing House, 1974.

Burger, Julian. *Gaia Atlas of First Peoples: The Future for the Indigenous World*. London: Gaia Books, 1990.

Campbell, David G., and H. David Hammond, eds. "Floristic Inventory of Tropical Countries: The Status of Plant Systematics, Collections, and Vegetation, plus Recommendations for the Future." New York: The New York Botanical Garden, 1988.

Campbell, Joseph. *The Hero with a Thousand Faces*. Princeton, NJ: Princeton University Press, 1949.

————. *The Masks of God: Oriental Mythology*. New York: Viking Penguin, 1962.

Campbell, Joseph, and Bill Moyers. *The Power of Myth.* New York: Doubleday, 1988.

Campredon, Pierre, Luc Hoffmann, and Hadya Kane. "Why Natural Resources Conservation Requires the Development of Fishermen's Communities." Paper presented at the Fourth World Congress on National Parks and Protected Areas, Caracas, Venezuela, February 10–21, 1992.

Center for Applied Social Sciences, World Wide Fund For Nature, and Zimtrust Coordinating Committee. *Wildlife Utilization in Zimbabwe's Communal Lands: Collaborative Programme Activities.* Harare, Zimbabwe: CASS, WWF, and Zimtrust Coordinating Committee, June 1989.

Chernov, Y. U. I. *The Living Tundra.* Cambridge, England: Cambridge University Press, 1985.

Colchester, M. "Venezuela: New Biosphere Reserve for the Upper Orinoco." Information sheet. United Kingdom and Malaysia: World Rainforest Movement, 1991.

Collar, N. J., and P. Andrew. "Birds to Watch: The ICBP World Checklist of Threatened Birds." ICBP Technical Publication no. 8. Cambridge, England: International Council for Bird Preservation, 1988.

Committee on Territorial Reorganization and the Indigenous Communities. "Indigenous Concept about Territory for the National Government." Unpublished paper. Sierra Nevada de Santa Marta, Committee on Territorial Reorganization and the Indigenous Communities, April 13, 1992.

Craven, Ian. "A Management Prescription for the Arfak Mountains Strict Nature Reserve 1991–92." WWF Project no. 3770, Implementation of Conservation in Irian Jaya, Indonesia. Gland, Switzerland: WWF International, 1991.

Craven, Ian, and Y. de Fretes. "Arfak Mountains Nature Conservation Area Irian Jaya Management Plan 1988–92." WWF Project no. 3770, Implementation of Conservation in Irian Jaya, Indonesia. Gland, Switzerland: WWF International, 1987.

Davydona, M., and V. Koshevoi. *Nature Reserves in the USSR.* Moscow: Progress, 1989.

Diamond, Jared. *The Rise and Fall of the Third Chimpanzee* (chaps. 13–16). London: Vintage, 1992.

Dimopoulos, D. "A Short Report on Zakynthos." Unpublished report. Athens, Greece: Sea Turtle Protection Society of Greece, 1992.

Dixon, John A., and Paul B. Sherman. *Economics of Protected Areas: A New Look at Benefits and Costs.* Washington, DC: Island Press, 1990.

Durning, Alan Thein. "Guardians of the Land: Indigenous Peoples and the Health of the Earth." Worldwatch Paper no. 112. Washington, DC: Worldwatch Institute, December 1992.

Eguillor Garcia, M. I. "Yopo, Shamanes y Hekuara—aspectos fenomenologicos del mundo sagrado Yanomami." Puerto Ayacucho, Venezuela: Libreria Editorial Salesiana, 1984.

Environmental Consultants Ltd. *People, Wildlife and Natural Resources—The CAMPFIRE Approach to Rural Development in Zimbabwe*. Harare, Zimbabwe: Conlon, 1990.

Ereira, Alan. *The Heart of the World*. London: Jonathan Cape, 1990.

Faichampa, Ketty. "At the Edge of the Forest: Local Communities Around Huay Kha Khaeng Wildlife Sanctuary." Unpublished paper. New Haven, Connecticut: Yale University, School of Forestry and Environmental Studies, 1989.

Fermor, Leigh Patrick. *Roumeli: Travels in Northern Greece*. London: John Murray, 1966.

Flint, V. E., K. I. Boehme, Y. V. Kostin, and A. A. Kuznetsov. *Birds of the USSR*. Princeton, NJ: Princeton University Press, 1984.

Fondation Internationale du Banc d'Arguin. "Banc d'Arguin National Park: A Haven for Life." Gland, Switzerland: Fondation Internationale du Banc d'Arguin, 1988.

Foster, David. In *Applying the Yellowstone Model in America's Backyard: Alaska, Aboriginal Involvement in Parks and Protected Areas,* edited by Jim Birckhead, Terry deLacey, and LauraJane Smith. Canberra, Australia: Panther, 1992.

French, Hillary. "Green Revolutions: Environmental Reconstruction in Eastern Europe and the Soviet Union." Worldwatch Paper no. 99. Washington, DC: Worldwatch Institute, November 1990.

Garcia Montero, P. "La politica ambiental y el desarrollo sustentable en el territorio Federal Amazonas." Unpublished paper. Caracas, Venezuela: SADA-AMAZONAS, n.d.

Haines, Aubrey L. *Yellowstone National Park: Its Exploration and Establishment*. Washington, DC: U.S. Department of the Interior, National Park Service, 1974.

Harmon, David. "Indicators of the World's Cultural Diversity." Paper presented at the Fourth World Congress on National Parks and Protected Areas, Caracas, Venezuela, February 10–21, 1992.

"Indian and Northern Affairs." Press release. Ottawa, Canada, November 12, 1992.

International Union for Conservation of Nature and Natural Resources. *Protected Areas of the World: A Review of National Systems*. Vols. I–IV. Cambridge, England: IUCN, 1991, 1992.

International Union for Conservation of Nature and Natural Resources and Fundación Pro–Sierra Nevada de Santa Marta. "Estrategia para la conservación de los bosques

tropicales de la Sierra Nevada de Santa Marta." Santa Marta, Colombia: IUCN and
Fundación Pro–Sierra Nevada de Santa Marta, April 1991.

International Union for Conservation of Nature and Natural Resources and United Nations Environment Program. *1990 United Nations List of National Parks and Protected Areas.* Gland, Switzerland, and Cambridge, England: IUCN and UNEP, 1990.

Jacobs, J., and A. Panou. "Project 3871: Monk Seal Conservation in the Eastern Mediterranean." WWF project progress report. Munich: University of Munich, Institute of Zoology, October 1992.

"James Bay and Northern Quebec Agreement." Government of Quebec, Canada, 1976.

Jopson, Debra. "Land Feud." *Far East Economic Review* (Hong Kong), February 1993.

Kemf, Elizabeth. "The Bohemians and Their Forests." *WWF News* (Gland, Switzerland) (May–June 1992).

———. "Dam Controversy Growing in Thailand." *WWF News* (Lausanne, Switzerland), no. 46 (1987).

———. "Dance of a Thousand Cranes." *New Scientist* (London) (October 8, 1988).

———. "Dolphins and Fishermen Cooperate to Hunt Food." *WWF News* (Lausanne, Switzerland), no. 53 (May–June 1988).

———. *Month of Pure Light: The Regreening of Vietnam.* London: The Women's Press, 1990.

———. Pp. 31–33 of a chapter from *Into the Blue,* an anthology of dolphin myths, legends, and biology edited by Virginia McKenna. London: Aquarian Press, 1992.

Knystautas, A. *Naturparadies USSR.* Munchen, Germany: Suddeutscher Verlag, 1987.

Labutin, Y. V., V. I. Perfilieva, I. V. Revin et al. *Flora and Fauna.* Siberia, USSR: Yakutskian Branch of Academy of Science, Institute of Biology, 1985.

Le, Dien Duc. "Wise Use of Wetlands in Vietnam." Unpublished paper. Hanoi: University of Hanoi, Center for Natural Resource Management and Environmental Studies, 1992.

Lee, Mercédès. "Brief Political Update of James Bay" (focusing south of the border). New York: National Audubon Society, July 12, 1992.

Lhote, H. *La Chasse chez les Touaregs.* Paris: Amiot-Dumont, 1951.

MacKinnon, John, Kathy MacKinnon, Graham Child, and Jim Thorsell. *Managing Protected Areas in the Tropics.* Gland, Switzerland, and Cambridge, England: IUCN and United Nations Environment Program, 1986.

McNeely, Jeffrey. "The Contributions of Protected Areas to Sustaining Society." Paper presented at the Fourth World Congress on National Parks and Protected Areas, Caracas, Venezuela, February 10–21, 1992.

Margaritoulis, D., D. Dimopoulos, and E. Kornaraki. "The Loggerhead Sea Turtle *Caretta caretta* on Zakynthos: An Update of Monitoring and Conservation Work." Gland, Switzerland: WWF International, February 1992.

Martin, C. A., and R. Lizzaralde. "Los aborigenes en los parques nacionales de Venezuela: Su pasado y presente." Paper presented at the Fourth World Congress on National Parks and Protected Areas, Caracas, Venezuela, February 10–21, 1992.

Martin, Claude. *The Rainforests of West Africa.* Basel, Switzerland: Birkhäuser, 1991.

Maybury-Lewis, David. *Millennium: Tribal Wisdom and the Modern World.* London: Viking Penguin, 1992.

Morrison, James. "Protected Areas and Aboriginal Interests in Canada." Toronto: WWF-Canada, 1993.

Nash, S. V., and I. Craven. "Saving the People, Saving the Land." *Rotunda* (Fall 1989): 40–45.

Newby, J. "Millions of Birds Find Refuge in Niger." *WWF News* (Lausanne, Switzerland), no. 28 (March–April 1984).

———. "Parks for People—A Case Study from the Aïr Mountains of Niger." *Oryx* (Oxford, England) 26 (1), 19–28.

———. "The Sahel Lives." *WWF News*, no. 37 (September–October 1985).

Petocz, R. G. *Conservation and Development in Irian Jaya.* Leiden, The Netherlands: E. J. Brill, 1989.

Planning and Conservation Services, Prince George, British Columbia. "Principles of Joint Management Agreements: A Literature Review." Prince George, British Columbia: Planning and Conservation Services, Northern British Columbia Region, August 1990.

Portman, Ian. *Luxor: A Guide to the Temples and Tombs of Ancient Thebes.* Cairo: The American University in Cairo Press, 1989.

Price, A. R. G., A. Jeudy de Grissac, and R. F. G. Ormond. "Coastal Assessment of the Parc National du Banc d'Arguin, Mauritania: Understanding Resources, Exploitation Patterns and Management Needs." Marine conservation and development report. Gland, Switzerland: IUCN, 1992.

Rhaphals, Philip. *New Scientist* (London), February 15, 1992.

Robertson, S. A. "NMK and WWF-I Working with the Elders to Protect the Sacred *Kaya* Forests of Coastal Kenya." Unpublished report. Gland, Switzerland: WWF International, 1992.

———. "The Status of *Kaya* Forests." In *Endangered Resources for Development.* Vol. 1. Nairobi, Kenya: National Environment Secretariat, 1984.

Rogacheva, E. V. *The Birds of Central Siberia.* Husum, Germany: Husum Druck- u. Verlags, 1992.

Sawor, T. "A Survey of the Local Knowledge of the Hatam Tribe about the Ecobiology of Arfak Birdwing Butterflies." Gland, Switzerland: WWF International, 1989.

Scharff, Robert. *Yellowstone and Grand Teton National Parks.* New York: David McKay, 1966.

Schoorl, J., and N. Visser. "Towards Sustainable Coastal Tourism: Environmental Impacts of Tourism on the Kenya Coast." Nairobi, Kenya: Royal Netherlands Embassy, 1991.

Schuerholz, Goetz. "Management Plan for Sumava Biosphere Reserve." WWF Project no. 4575. Unpublished report. Gland, Switzerland: WWF International, July 1991.

Scott, Derek, ed. *Directory of Asian Wetlands.* Database on the wetlands of twenty-four countries. Gland, Switzerland, and Cambridge, England: IUCN, 1989.

Smole, William J. "Yanoama Horticulture in the Parima Highlands of Venezuela and Brazil." *Advances in Economic Botany* (The New York Botanical Garden) 7 (1989): 115–128.

Stark, Malcolm. "Semi-annual Progress Report." WWF Project no. 3770, Implementation of Conservation in Irian Jaya, Indonesia. Gland, Switzerland: WWF International, July–December 1991.

Stone, Roger D. "Wildlands and Human Needs: Reports from the Field." Washington, DC: World Wildlife Fund, 1991.

Thorsell, Jim, and Jacqueline Sawyer, eds. *World Heritage Twenty Years Later.* Gland, Switzerland, and Cambridge, England: IUCN, 1992.

United Nations. "Indigenous People: A New Partnership International Year 1993." New York: United Nations, Department of Information, 1992.

United Nations Educational, Scientific, and Cultural Organization and United Nations Environment Program. *Conservation, Science and Society.* Vol. 1. Paris: UNESCO, 1984.

Vlachoutsikou, Ada, and M. Scoullous. "Monk Seal Conservation in the Eastern Mediterranean." WWF Project no. 3871. Unpublished report. Gland, Switzerland: WWF International, November 1992.

Vo, Quy. "Luan Chung Khoa Ky Thuat, Ve Voun Quoc Gia Con Dao." Hanoi: Hanoi

University, Center for Natural Resource Management and Environmental Studies, 1987 (in Vietnamese language only).

————. "On the Wings of Peace." *Natural History*, November 1990.

Vo, Quy, Le Trong Cuc, Hoang Hoe, and Nguyen Mau Tai. "Biodiversity and Protected Areas in Vietnam." Hanoi: University of Hanoi, Center for Natural Resources Management and Environmental Studies, 1991. (Update presented at the Fourth World Congress on National Parks and Protected Areas, Caracas, Venezuela, February 10–21, 1992.)

Waugh, J. D., Gil Perez, and R. Perez. *Regional Review, North America.* Gland, Switzerland: IUCN, 1992.

Weaver, Sally W. In *Resident Peoples and National Parks,* edited by P. C. West and S. R. Breslin, p. 317. Tucson: University of Arizona Press, 1991.

Wells, Michael, Katrina Brandon, and Lee Hannah. *People and Parks: Linking Protected Area Management with Local Communities.* Washington, DC: World Bank, World Wildlife Fund, and U.S. Agency for International Development, 1992.

West, Patric C., and Steven R. Brechin, eds. *Resident People and National Parks: Social Dilemmas and Strategies in International Conservation.* Tucson: University of Arizona Press, 1991.

White, F. "The Vegetation of Africa: A Descriptive Memoir to Accompany the AETFAT/UNESCO Vegetation Map of Africa." Paris: UNESCO , 1983.

Wilcox, Evelyn. "Feasibility of Establishing a Marine Park at Les Arcadins, Haiti." Unpublished report. Washington, DC: U.S. Agency for International Development, 1986.

Wilcox, Evelyn, et al. "Action Plan: Les Arcadins National Marine Park, Haiti." Washington, DC: U.S. Agency for International Development and World Wildlife Fund, 1989.

Womsiwor, D., D. Neville, and S. Mandosir. "Pengelolaan Kawasan Penyangga Pada Cagar Alam Pegunungan Arfak, Manokwari, Irian Jaya." Dalam *Prosiding Seminar Nasional Pengelolaan Kawasan Panyangga.* Irian Jaya, Indonesia: Kanwil Kehutanan Irian Jaya/WWF, October 1990.

World Conservation Monitoring Center. "Protected Area Data Sheet." Unpublished report. Cambridge, England: WCMC, 1992.

The Zimbabwe Trust, Wildlife. *Relic of the Past, or Resource of the Future?* Harare, Zimbabwe: Quote, 1992.

Zinke, Alexander. "Europas Wilder Osten." *Panda Magazin* (published by WWF-Switzerland, Zurich, Switzerland) 24 (2) (June 1991).

CONTRIBUTORS

Bryan Alexander is a free-lance photographer and writer who specializes in indigenous peoples and the Arctic.

Guillermo Archibold is director general of PEMASKY, the Management Project for the Forested Areas of Kuna Yala, in the San Blas District of Panama.

A. S. M. Banda is parks and wildlife officer with the Department of National Parks, Wildlife and Tourism in Mzuzu, Malawi.

Ookaew Prakobvitayakit Beaver, who has a master of science degree in zoology and a doctoral degree in ecology, is a founding member of the staff of the Department of Biology of Chiang Mai University in Thailand. In addition to her numerous activities as lecturer, editor, consultant, and project advisor, she has carried out research on the wildlife of Doi Suthep, Thailand, for nearly thirty years.

Hilary de Boerr is a free-lance journalist with a master of science degree in international relations from the London School of Economics. She worked for six years for the *Financial Times* in London as environmental features writer, deputy editor of the World Stock Markets page, and news subeditor.

Pierre Campredon, IUCN representative in Guinea-Bissau, has a doctoral degree in animal biology. For more than fifteen years, he has been actively involved with Banc d'Arguin National Park in Mauritania.

Julio César Centeno is a professor of forest industry at the University of the Andes in Mérida, Venezuela. He is former director of the Latin American Forestry Institute and has a master of science degree in structural engineering and a doctoral degree in wood science and technology.

John Cordell, who has a doctoral degree in anthropology from Stanford University, is principal research fellow in the Department of Anthropology and Sociology at the University of Queensland in Australia. He is also director of the University of Queensland's Indigenous Resource Management Program, a community sea rights and conservation initiative to assist Cape York aborigines, Torres Strait Islanders, and Papuans of the Trans-Fly. The program is supported by the John D. and Catherine T. MacArthur Foundation.

Ian Craven is the WWF executant for management planning and implementation of Wasur National Park, Irian Jaya, Indonesia. He has worked with WWF's Irian Jaya Program since 1985 on projects involving local community participation in protected area management.

Sheila Davey is a free-lance journalist who writes mainly on environmental and development issues. She has written for the *Guardian* newspaper in the United Kingdom and has worked as a political correspondent for a news agency in Africa and as a television journalist for the BBC and ITV. She is the author of an international report on child pornography.

Sanjoy Deb Roy retired as inspector general of forests (wildlife) with the government of India in 1992. A member of the Indian Forest Service, he was previously chief wildlife warden of Assam and field director of the Manas Tiger Reserve.

Christopher Elliot works for WWF International in Gland, Switzerland, as senior forests officer. He has worked in Latin America and China and at the World Bank and studied at London and Yale universities.

Stephen Elliott, who has a doctoral degree in ecological sciences, is a lecturer on ecology and conservation in the Department of Biology at Chiang Mai University, Thailand. He has carried out several surveys of Doi Suthep National Park and is presently engaged in research concerning dry tropical forest trees.

Joanna Gould is a journalist with the Maruia Society, an environmental organization in New Zealand, and is editor of the society's magazine. She graduated from Aberdeen University in Scotland with a master of science degree with honors in geography before moving to New Zealand in 1985.

Arlin Hackman is director of the Endangered Spaces Campaign at WWF-Canada and is a member of the IUCN Commission on Parks and Protected Areas. He has fifteen years' experience working on parks and protected areas, primarily for nongovernmental conservation organizations, including a coalition that successfully lobbied for 155 new parks in the province of Ontario.

Sir Edmund Hillary, who in 1953 was the first mountaineer to climb Mount Everest, is founder and chairman of the Himalayan Trust and a member of WWF's Advisory Council.

Luc Hoffmann, who has a doctoral degree in zoology, is vice president emeritus of WWF International and a founder of WWF. He is former vice president of IUCN and founder and president of the Fondation Internationale du Banc d'Arguin (FIBA) in Mauritania and of the biological station of the Tour de Valat in France.

David L. Hulse is a project executant for WWF-US in Vietnam. Prior to this, he was Southeast Asia program officer at WWF-US and planning and evaluation officer with the Population and Community Development Association in Thailand. He has a bachelor of arts degree in environmental studies and earth science and a master's degree in public policy with concentration in international development from Harvard University.

Philip Hunsicker is former director of rural development of the Dzanga-Sangha Dense Forest Special Reserve in the Central African Republic.

Peter Jackson is chairman of the Cat Specialist Group of IUCN. He has had a lifelong involvement with India as a journalist and conservationist. He was project manager of WWF's Operation Tiger from its inception in 1973 until 1979.

Diane Jukofsky, who has a bachelor of arts degree in English, has been codirector of the Rainforest Alliance's Conservation Media Center in Costa Rica since 1989. Prior to this, she was vice president for programs at the Scientists' Institute for Public Information in New York, served as press secretary to Congressman Sam Gejdenson in Washington, DC, and worked for an American magazine and for the National Wildlife Federation in Washington, DC.

Hadya Amadou Kane, who has a degree in agronomy, has been director general of Banc d'Arguin National Park in Mauritania since 1985. Prior to this, he was head of the Department of Nature Conservation and head of the National Plant Protection Department and, from 1984 to 1985, was in charge of economic and social affairs.

Elizabeth Kemf, who has a master of arts degree in creative writing, is a journalist, photographer, and poet who has contributed articles to the *International Herald Tribune, Geo, New Scientist,* and London's *Sunday Times Magazine.* She is the author of the book *Month of Pure Light: The Regreening of Vietnam,* on which two television films have been based: National Geographic/Channel Four's *Vietnam: After the Fire* and BBC/Nature's *Vietnam the Country, Not the War,* in which she is a copresenter. She is presently senior conservation editor with WWF International, and she edited the organization's international newspaper, the *WWF News,* from 1981 to 1991.

Annette Lees, a biologist, is associate director of the Maruia Society, an environmental organization in New Zealand, where she directs the society's tropical forest program in the South Pacific. She has had extensive field experience in the identification and establishment of protected areas in the Pacific and has an ongoing interest in nature conservation issues in South America, after two years' work and travel there.

Connie Lewis is associate director of the Keystone Center, a U.S. nongovernmental organization specializing in resolution of local, national, and international public policy conflicts, especially those involving environmental and natural resource issues. She has a bachelor of science degree in biology and a master's degree in natural resource policy from the University of California, Berkeley.

Jeffrey A. McNeely was secretary general of the Fourth World Congress on National Parks and Protected Areas in Venezuela in 1992. He is chief conservation officer at IUCN in Switzerland, where he has served in a variety of posts since 1980. Prior to going to IUCN, he worked for twelve years in Thailand, Indonesia, and Nepal. He has written or edited some fifteen books on various conservation-related topics.

Sius Mandosir is a graduate of the Forestry Department of the University of Cenderawasih in Manokwari, Indonesia. He has worked for WWF-Indonesia since 1989, where he has mainly been in charge of butterfly-ranching activities in Irian Jaya.

Claude Martin, who became director general of WWF International in 1993, studied biology at the University of Zurich in Switzerland. He completed his doctoral degree with an ecological study of the barasingha deer, an endangered species in the monsoon forests of central India. At the request of the Ghanaian government, WWF, and the International Union for Conservation of Nature (IUCN), he managed the first rain forest national park in Ghana, Bia National Park, as park director for a number of years. In addition, he contributed to the establishment of Nini-Suhien National Park and other protected areas in Ghana. Among others, Martin has been active in rain forest projects in Liberia, the Côte d'Ivoire, Cameroon, and Madagascar. After his stay in Ghana, he was director of WWF-Switzerland for ten years. In 1991, he published *The Rainforests of West Africa*, the first book to look at a specific tropical forest zone in a comprehensive way.

Sandra Mbanefo is a Nigerian journalist and photographer who has spent the past two and a half years reporting on WWF's field projects in sub-Saharan Africa. She has worked as an on-line editor and television producer for The European Business Channel in Switzerland and taught workshops on video editing. She has a first degree in education and a master of arts degree in telecommunications.

John Newby, who was born in Lincolnshire, United Kingdom, is the son of a Polish farmer. He graduated from Aberdeen University with a bachelor of science degree with honors in zoology. He first worked as a volunteer with the United Nations (he was the first UN volunteer in the field), then in Chadian national parks with the United Nations and with IUCN and WWF. After two years in Niger for WWF and IUCN, he became director of the Africa and Madagascar Program at WWF International in 1991.

Fidele Ngambesso works as rural development extension agent at the Dzanga-Sangha Dense Forest Special Reserve in the Central African Republic.

Hanson L. Njiforti works for the Center for Environmental Studies and Development in Maroua, Cameroon.

Peter Prokosch, a zoologist and marine biologist, is coordinator of WWF's Arctic Program, based in Oslo. He lived for ten years in northern Germany on the Wadden Sea coast while working as project leader for WWF's Wadden Sea Project.

Vo Quy, who has a doctoral degree in ornithology, is founder and director of Vietnam's Center for Natural Resource Management and Environmental Studies (CRES). He is former dean of biology at the University of Hanoi and is the chief architect of Vietnam's national conservation strategy. He is recipient of a number of international honors, including the WWF Gold Medal and the Global 500 Award from the United Nations Environment Program in 1992. He is the chief presenter in the National Geographic/Channel Four television film *Vietnam: After the Fire* and in BBC/Nature's *Vietnam the Country, Not the War.*

Alcida Rita Ramos, author of several books on indigenous societies in Latin America, is professor of anthropology at the University of Brasilia. Since 1968, she has been actively engaged in the defense of Yanomami land rights and, as founding member of the Committee for the Creation of the Yanomami Park, in activities related to that issue. For the past couple of years, she has worked as interpreter and cultural mediator for medical teams involved in the fight against malaria in the Yanomami area.

Kailash Sankhala, author of *Tiger!* and *Bird Sanctuary Bharatpur,* established and managed tiger reserves and national parks throughout India (Project Tiger in Rajasthan, Thar Desert Biosphere Reserve, and Delhi Zoological Park). He is presently a member of the senate of the University of Rajasthan and chairman of Tiger Trust.

Mingma Norbu Sherpa, who has a diploma in parks and recreation from Lincoln College in New Zealand and a master's degree in natural resources management from Manitoba University, is WWF's country representative in Bhutan and Nepal. He was one of the first Sherpa park wardens in Sagarmatha National Park in Nepal before becoming principal investigator and, subsequently, director of the Annapurna Conservation Area Project (ACAP), also in Nepal.

Terry Slavin is a Canadian journalist who writes on environmental and development issues.

Malcolm Stark has a bachelor of science degree in fisheries and wildlife management and a master of science degree in natural resource productivity and management, both from Canadian universities. After almost eight years in the field in Africa as supervisor of field operations and field director for Mwenge International and PLAN International, he became program coordinator for WWF in Irian Jaya, Indonesia, where he oversaw the implementation of nine conservation and community-integrated projects. Following a period as environmental instructor at Lethbridge College in Canada, he is currently working as a consultant in Ghana.

Ngankam Martin Tchamba is assistant professor in the Center for Environmental Studies at the University Center of Dschang in Cameroon. Prior to this, he was lecturer at the Department of Forestry of the University Center and coordinator of the Center for Environmental Studies and Development in Cameroon.

Seri Thongmak, who has a bachelor of science degree from Chiang Mai University, has worked in Thailand's Department of Agriculture and Community Development and is Wildlife Fund Thailand's chief of conservation and extension in the buffer zone of Huay Kha Khaeng and Thung Yai Naresuan wildlife sanctuaries.

Wahyudi Wardoyo is former head of the Sub-Directorate for National Parks and director general of forest protection and nature conservation with the Department of Forestry in Indonisia.

Evelyn Wilcox joined WWF-US in 1990 as senior marine program officer for Latin America and the Caribbean. In 1992, she became marine coordinator of WWF's coastal and marine interests in the region, responsible for program development at field and policy levels. She directs a new WWF Caribbean Coral Reef Initiative as well as providing oversight to the Les Arcadins Marine Park and Fisheries Project in Haiti.

Alison Wilson graduated from Oxford University with a bachelor of science degree with honors in zoology and has a master's degree from Makerere University in Uganda. She has fifteen years' experience as a biologist and conservationist in East Africa and worked for several years for the State Nongame Program in Idaho. At present, she works as a free-lance conservation consultant in Switzerland.

INDEX

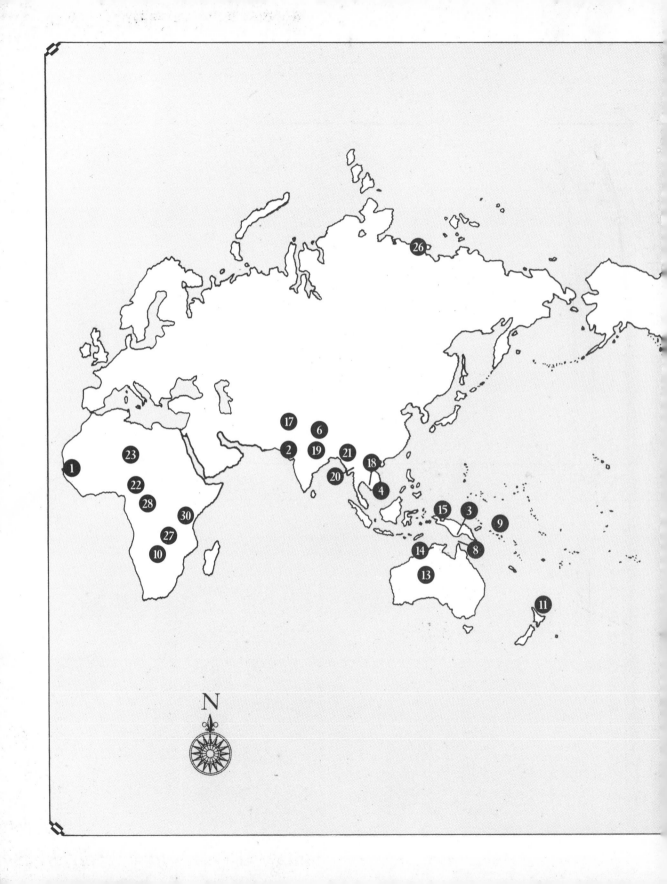